eTUNES

FOUNTAINHEAD PRESS V SERIES

Edited by
Rod C. Taylor

FOUNTAINHEAD
PRESS

Our green initiatives include:

Electronic Products
We deliver products in non-paper form whenever possible. This includes pdf downloadables, flash drives, and CDs.

Electronic Samples
We use Xample, a new electronic sampling system. Instructor samples are sent via a personalized Web page that links to pdf downloads.

FSC Certified Printers
All of our printers are certified by the Forest Service Council, which promotes environmentally and socially responsible management of the world's forests. This program allows consumer groups, individual consumers, and businesses to work together hand-in-hand to promote responsible use of the world's forests as a renewable and sustainable resource.

Recycled Paper
Most of our products are printed on a minimum of 30% post-consumer waste recycled paper.

Support of Green Causes
When we do print, we donate a portion of our revenue to green causes. Listed below are a few of the organizations that have received donations from Fountainhead Press. We welcome your feedback and suggestions for contributions, as we are always searching for worthy initiatives.
Rainforest 2 Reef
Environmental Working Group

Cover Image: © GraphicStock

Design by Susan Moore

Books may be purchased for educational purposes.

For information, please call or write:

1-800-586-0330

Fountainhead Press
Southlake, TX 76092

Web site: www.fountainheadpress.com
E-mail: customerservice@fountainheadpress.com

First Edition

ISBN: 978-1-59871-662-7

Printed in the United States of America

INTRODUCTION TO THE FOUNTAINHEAD PRESS V SERIES

By Brooke Rollins and Lee Bauknight
Series Editors

The *Fountainhead Press V Series* is a new collection of single-topic readers that take a unique look at some of today's most pressing issues. Designed to give writing students a more nuanced introduction to public discourse—on the environment, on food, and on digital life, to name a few of the topics—the books feature writing, research, and invention prompts that can be adapted to nearly any kind of college writing class. Each *V Series* textbook focuses on a single issue and includes multi-genre and multimodal readings and assignments that move the discourse beyond the most familiar patterns of debate—patterns usually fettered by entrenched positions and often obsessed with "winning."

The ultimate goal of the series is to help writing students—who tend to hover on the periphery of public discourse—think, explore, find their voices, and skillfully compose texts in a variety of media and genres. Not only do the books help students think about compelling issues and how they might address them, they also give students the practice they need to develop their research, rhetorical, and writing skills. Together, the readings, prompts, and longer assignments show students how to add their voices to the conversations about these issues in meaningful and productive ways.

With enough readings and composing tasks to sustain an entire quarter or semester, and inexpensive enough to be used in combination with other rhetorics and readers, the *Fountainhead Press V Series* provides instructors with the flexibility to build the writing courses they want and need to teach. An instructor interested in deeply exploring environmental issues, for example, could design a semester- or quarter-long course using *Green*, the first of the *V Series* texts. At the same time, an instructor who wanted to teach discrete units on different issues could use two or more of the *V Series* books. In either case, the texts would give students ample opportunity—and a variety of ways—to engage with the issues at hand.

The *V Series* uses the term "composition" in its broadest sense. Of course, the textbooks provide students plenty of opportunities to write, but they also include assignments that take students beyond the page. Books in the series encourage students to explore other modes of communication by prompting them: to design websites, to produce videos, posters, and presentations; to conduct primary and secondary research; and to develop projects with community partners that might incorporate any number of these skills. Ultimately, we have designed the *Fountainhead Press V Series* to work for teachers and students. With their carefully chosen readings, built-in flexibility, and sound rhetorical grounding, the *V Series* books would be a dynamic and user-friendly addition to any writing class.

ACKNOWLEDGMENTS

As one might expect, a composition reader focused on music simultaneously pulls from resources in writing and music. As such, I have been fortunate to have benefited from the insight of academic colleagues, former students, and fellow musicians and producers. I want to first thank Andrea Lunsford for allowing me the creative space to begin experimenting with the topic of music in a writing classroom while teaching in the Program in Writing and Rhetoric at Stanford University. I also want to thank my students there, as well as those at Tennessee State University, for allowing me to test various versions of this book on them. I much appreciate George Jensen and Kelly Myers for valuable insight into the initial stages of the project and Matt Coen for his wisdom and advice toward the end. A big thanks to Jake Adams for his contributions to this work, both in form of his essay and in sharing his experience as a writing teacher, an accomplished musician, and a music writer, and to Cristina Huerta for her administrative support through the research process.

Throughout the last few years, I have participated in numerous conversations on the topic of the digital age of music with a variety of people in the music business, all of whom have in some way influenced the content and shape of this book. Thanks to Victor Wooten, Steve Lawson, Krista Detor, David Weber, Laurence Juber, Malcolm-Jamal Warner, Artemis Robison, Daniel Levitin, Bob Hemenger, Jim Roberts, Steve Bailey, Chuck Rainey, Jimmy Coppolo, Anthony Wellington, Jessica Meehan, Divinity Roxx, Michael Manring, Darryl Anders, Steve Taylor, Mark Bright, James Waddell, Richard Dodd, and Tommy Sims. And finally, I'm always grateful to my wife Kristen Taylor for her continued support of my involvement in music both as a scholar and as a player, and to my parents, Rick and Ramona Taylor, who encouraged my love of writing and music from an early age.

TABLE OF CONTENTS

INTRODUCTION: "THE DIGITAL AGE OF MUSIC"

By Rod C. Taylor

Few forms of art have enjoyed such widespread appeal as music, and even fewer can boast the longevity and continued vitality over the last hundred years. For example, while scholars and teachers in the western world continue to write about and teach canonical plays, poems, and paintings of the last millennium, the popularity of these modes of expression has waned over the last century in popular culture and among students. Not so with music: its popularity continues to increase, both in terms of consumption and participation. More than likely, each of you reading this introduction has with you some mechanism you can use to listen to or create music, but I doubt many of you have a paintbrush or a book of poetry on your person or in your backpack. The reason has little to do with music being a "better" form of expression. Rather, it has more to do with technological advances over the last fifty years—and even more over the last twenty—that ultimately serve music more than art forms like poetry and painting. It also connects to how the last several decades have influenced the way we think about art.

Perhaps only the Industrial Revolution saw a technological shift as drastic as that of our current age, and such innovation inevitably alters the manner in which people not only live and work but also how they think about themselves, their culture, and the art that surrounds them. In "The Conquest of Ubiquity" (1928), Paul Valery argues that any technologically advanced society "must expect great innovations to transform the entire technique of the arts, thereby affecting artistic invention itself and perhaps even bringing about an amazing change in our very notion of art." Valery's statement held true in the early twentieth century and perhaps proves even more relevant in the twenty-first. In the same way mechanical innovations of the eighteenth and nineteenth centuries led to an epistemological shift in art in the early twentieth century, so to have the technological advancements of the digital age affected the twenty-first.

The argument here—that a direct correlation exists between technological innovation and artistic expression, consumption, and epistemology—applies easily to recorded music, which, along with photography and film, remains one of western culture's more recent art forms. In the postmodern age, epistemological shifts resulting from technological advancements in the digital realm have significantly changed the way music is both created and consumed. For some, this shift has led to positive changes in music—providing new opportunities, new genres, and new creative landscape for musicians. Others, however, see these effects as unequivocally negative, ultimately resulting in a devaluation of authentic musicianship and artistic endeavors. Regardless, most debates on the topic of music these days turn on some effect of the digital revolution.

To aid you in your inquiry into music and the digital age, this collection of essays throws you headfirst into discussions regarding the consequences of the ever expanding technology that affects the world of music. The articles and exercises in *(E)Tunes* provide an appropriate lens through which you can first examine current conversations surrounding music and the digital age and then enter into those conversations yourself, informed and inspired. For example, Jim Roberts's excerpt from *How the Fender Bass Changed the World* shows how technological inventions, as they relate to musical instruments, can spark musical revolutions—some big, some small. His argument regarding the bass guitar (a relatively young instrument by all standards) connects to current debates on the nature of what makes something an instrument, especially as more and more digital "instruments" emerge. Is the computer, the iPhone, or an electronic triggering device an instrument? Some say yes, some say no. Regardless, we continue to witness new genres in music emerge by virtue of these technologies, and dismissing electronic and digital devices as non-instruments has become harder as a result.

Perhaps the most obvious effect of the digital revolution on modern music concerns the manner in which we listen to it—how we purchase, consume, or own songs. While the invention of the Sony Walkman in 1979 may have begun the portable music craze, and the production of CDs proved to be the first successful mass market departure from analog recordings, the Internet and the proliferation of the MP3 from 1998 forward represent the most significant moments for music in the digital age. From record companies to artists to consumers to copyright lawyers, the digitization of music has resulted in the need to rethink the way music is approached in each of these fields. In short, anyone who has anything to do with music has been affected by this shift in medium, whether that affect is realized or not. Those born into the digital world of music might feel like it's no big deal, but for those who had to ride out the transition, that's another story. The evidence of the tension brought about by that adjustment can be seen in various forms in culture, and you'll find several of the essays in this collection that pointedly address that. For example, "Steve Jobs and the iPod 'Burglary Kit,'" by Greg Kot, provides a great starting point for getting your head around the history and importance of this revolutionary medium, as does Eric Harvey's interview with McGill University professor Jonathan Sterne in "Paper Trail: MP3: The Meaning of Format." Additionally, In "Shiny Shiny: A Future History of the CD Revival," Tom Ewing offers a humorous examination of the speed with which music forms are changing.

Just as the MP3 format has changed the ways that fans listen to music, so too has it changed how artists create the music we enjoy—how it is recorded, written, and produced. For example, in "Winners and Losers in Digital Recording," I explore what some highly successful contemporary producers think we have gained and lost in the switch from analog to digital recording, while in "2010: The Year John Cage Broke—Amateur Producers and Unexpected Music," Jesse Walker takes a look at how digital music has brought increased success to amateur artists, a phenomenon that continues to provide new avenues for independent musicians. One such artist is Gregg Gillis, and his contribution to modern music continues to cause tension between artists and record companies. "Mash-Ups & Fair Use: Girl Talk" takes on this controversial artist, who continues to rile record companies with the use of copyright material in his musical creations.

As you might imagine, all of these changes, while revolutionary, continue the symbiotic relationship between record companies and artists. For sure, record companies have taken a beating—both in reputation and sales—since they waged war on Napster in 2000, but music and the music business remain interdependent in that the latter both directs and responds to the digital trends in pop culture and technology. Sometimes the industry responds slowly or even ineffectually, but at other times it initiates the trends. In regards to the sale of music, record companies continue to struggle, as do independent artists, with how to sell their music. That struggle has resulted in various creative and often experimental solutions to the problem. For example, renowned British solo artist and blogger Steve Lawson takes on the notion, put forth by BBC's Ian Youngs in 2010, that rethinking the high price of albums would benefit both artists and record companies. Lawson responds to Youngs's call for a low, flat fee for all music with his blog post, "Music is Worthless," in which he argues that the financial value of music is ultimately connected to fans' gratitude toward the artists and their creations. For this reason, he supports a "pay what you can" model instead.

Unsurprisingly perhaps, artists and fans exists in a ongoing tension with record companies, and from the 1960s forward there have been a few moments when such tension reached a peak and found its way into the public arena. Often these tensions make their way into the public arena through legal battles and academic debate, as with the Napster lawsuit of 2000, but they can also express themselves via the very art form at the heart of the fight. For example, in this collection I have paired two British bands that use their album covers to make political statements, one against the record industry and the other against their own government. The first, XTC's 1978 *Go 2* record cover, contains a straightforward rant (ironically) against the very consumerism that allows for the existence of the bands' success, while Radiohead's 2003 *Hail to the Thief* offers a critique of post-9/11 politics through common cultural signs. Some artists and critics, however, still take a more direct approach in getting their message across to record companies in the post-Napster era, as demonstrated by Adam Frucci's essay, "Record Labels: Change or Die," also included in this collection.

In the same way the MP3 significantly affected the way music is circulated and consumed, so too has the Internet affected the way in which artists share their music, their image, and their videos. The ubiquitousness of YouTube and Twitter, and the power they have to transform (or end) careers, has resulted in a new generation of artists and consumers who treat each as the first place to begin to create, consume, and disseminate music. For example, "The New Rise of a Summer Hit: Tweet It Maybe," by Ben Sisario, and Anthony Cosner's "Gotye's YouTube Orchestra Remix: The Sweetness of the Open Source Pop Star," each examine the role that the Internet and social media have played in changing the way the consumers learn about new music. And while the glory days of MTV and VH1 have long since passed, thanks to the Internet, videos still play a crucial role in generating commercial success in the music business, a reality addressed by Brian Petchers' "The Branding Power of Today's Music Video."

Of course, any book focused on the digital age of music would be remiss to not offer a sample of essays that seek to examine how pop music has adapted to phenomenon of digital music. Despite recent technological advances, in many ways, pop music today still closely resembles what it did twenty years ago. Consider this: artists like Lady Gaga, Nicki Minaj, Justin Bieber, Ke$ha, Miley Cyrus, and Katy Perry are hardly revolutionary in their music or image. For some time now, pop music has defined itself by simple song structures, catchy hooks, and romantic themes. Additionally, over-the-top, offensive spectacle has become commonplace among the most successful pop music artists and products. Still, the digital revolution has done much to increase pop music's exposure, influence, and—some argue—its homogeneity. Such is the case put forth in a recent quantitative study by an analyst at the Spanish National Research Council, an argument that J. Bryan Lowder both summarizes and challenges in his article "Does Pop Music Sound Louder, Dumber, and More the Same? One Study Says So." Regardless of where you come down on that question, there's no denying that someone like Lady Gaga has become a massive pop star, and in "Growing Up Gaga," Vanessa Grigoriadis explores what makes this iconic artist tick, revealing how her artistic motivations are connected to older aesthetic philosophies. Continuing this pattern of asking audiences to consider a more serious approach to a genre often written off as merely commercial, Rossen Ventzislavov, in "The Time Is Now: Acceptance and Conquest in Pop Music," makes a case that the time has come for pop music to take its place alongside other, more traditional aesthetic genres.

The proliferation of digital music over the last two decades has also led to more widespread access to various genres that have hitherto remained largely regional. That in turn, has changed the way we think of music genres. For example, if there has been a distinct area of new ground covered in pop music thanks to digital technology in the last few decades, it's been in country music. Once largely considered a regional genre, the music created in Nashville, Tennessee has greatly expanded its influence on pop culture since the 1990s through artists like Garth Brooks and Shania Twain, but no one epitomizes country music's increased genre hopping in the twenty-first century better than Taylor Swift. Along with Adele, the queen of breakup songs from Music City led album sales in 2012 and doesn't seem to show any signs of slowing down. Such genre bending is widespread and has led to a more complicated identity for the artists (i.e., is Swift country or pop?) and their fan-base (are they country music fans or just Swifties?). Some, like long time country music critic Chet Flippo, feel that country music explosion has made it difficult to locate the center of this genre. In "Nashville Skyline: Searching for the Heart of Country," he ponders the effect of the increased commercialization of a genre that once completely depended on Nashville's local record scene but whose popularity now relies more on large corporations like Wal-Mart and Target, and new digital formats like iTunes, Amazon.com, and Twitter. On that same topic, in "Paisley's Progress," veteran music critic Robert Christgau takes a look at a young male country singer's rise to fame and how his intellectual and artistic journey along the way makes it harder to pigeonhole country music when it comes to politics or background.

In the same way technology has affected the landscape of music creation and consumption, so too has it impacted music science and education. Advancements in neurology have led to a number of noted researchers' taking a vested interest in how our brains work in regards to creativity and musical taste. At the forefront of this field sits Daniel Levitin, a scientist, musician, and educator who seeks to understand how and why we create the music that surrounds us. Included in this work is an excerpt from his international bestselling book *This is Your Brain on Music* (2006)—a work in which he translates and connects recent scientific findings regarding music and taste to a wider public audience. As its title suggest, "My Favorite Things: Why Do We Like the Music We Like" examines why we prefer some songs over others and explores how sound effects our brains (and thus musical taste) from a young age—even from as far back as our mother's womb. While he acknowledges the role our social environment plays in determining what we put in our iPods, he argues for a more complicated—and scientific—explanation. More recently, Gary Marcus, a professor of Psychology and Linguistics, published *Guitar Zero: The New Musicians and the Science of Learning* (2012)—a memoir of his own journey in learning to play a musical instrument, utilizing new techniques learned from studying the brain and language acquisition. In "Learning to Crawl," he challenges the notion that one must possess a "music instinct" to be successful. In fact, he wonders whether such an instinct even exists. Rather, he argues that music and creativity is a learned behavior rather than something hardwired into us at birth.

The field of science, however, is not the only avenue for challenging traditional music education. As music technology changed in the digital age, music education was faced with new realities that traditional curriculum failed to address. Should music education classes embrace electronic and digital instrumentation? Where is the public school curriculum that teaches students how to use their computers as a musical creation platform? Would such a class best be taught in a music class or in a computer science class? Since music education has a long, established existence, the answers to these questions are not easy, but the conversation on how to adapt to digital technology has continued to grow over the last decade, as evinced in a couple of essay included in this book. In "Hip-Hop, Digital Media, and the Changing Face of Music Education," music education professor Matthew D. Thibeault uses the story of rapper Lil Wayne to argue that hip-hop and digital media offer new ways of creating, performing, and understanding music. As a result, Thibeault writes, music education teachers around the world would be best served by attending to the mechanisms at work in hip-hop. Five-time Grammy Award winning musician Victor Lemonte Wooten also argues for a less traditional approach to music education, but he chooses to make his case through fiction rather than an academic essay. In the first chapter from his novel *The Music Lesson: A Spiritual Search for Growth Through Music* (2006), the protagonist (a struggling musician) meets and begins his tutelage under an eccentric music teacher known only as Michael. Michael's methods are far from orthodox, and through this story Wooten offers readers a new way to imagine playing and listening to music.

Each of the topics above manifests themselves in ongoing popular debates regarding music and the digital revolution. Consider Foo Fighters' Dave Grohl's 2012 rant against digital recording at the Grammys, the ever-evolving debate regarding the legality of mashups, or the ongoing fight to legitimize the computer as an instrument. Each represents a potential topic for your own research and writing. While many of the essays here focus on one particular aspect of music, most connect with multiple areas of inquiry and as such provide numerous starting points for further inquiry based on your personal interests. I hope that *(E)Tunes* allows you to quickly immerse yourself in a topic that interests you so that you can speak and write thoughtfully about this fascinating subject. Notice that this collection offers more than just essays *on* music; through the activities that follow the readings, it offers experiences *with* music. After each essay, you will find exercises that can guide you in your inquiry, including some that ask you to create art in your response and others that are multi-media in their focus. Don't be afraid to have fun with it, and feel free to invent your own activities along the way, and, in the process, allow your own creativity to emerge.

Finally, in trying to understand the impact of the digital revolution on music, it helps to revisit cultural critic Raymond Williams's explanation of how various cultural powers exist in relationship to each other. According to Williams, at any given moment in culture, dominant, residual, and emergent forces exist in tension with one another. In other words, a dominant force, trend, or paradigm is always present, but those that it originally fought to replace are still present in a residual fashion, and there are always new ones emerging that will ultimately resist and seek to supplant the one that dominates. When applied to music, these categories allow us to see that while the digital music revolution is presently dominating our culture, analog music—and its accompanying artifacts—function mostly as residual. For example, record players continue to spin The Beatles and Motown hits in homes across America. In fact, recent resistance to the normalizing effects of digital recording on music has led to an increased release of LP records and cassette tapes. Whether this trend is an emerging revolution or simply another retro fad connected to residual modes of listening remains to be seen, but its existence highlights that the analog age is still somewhat present in the twenty-first century. Still, the digital age of music currently dominates the manner in which musicians and their audiences approach their art, and even those resisting it are still reacting to its effects and influence. What is truly emerging as a potential rival to the digital age is up for debate, and I encourage readers to consider what might be around the next corner when it comes to music. The next musical revolution might be driven by technology—or it might be driven by resistance to it. One never knows, but this collection of essays should at least help you get started on the inquiry into finding out.

Invent

The introduction talks about how habits surrounding the consumption of music have drastically changed in the last twenty years. For many students, that time period encompasses most—if not all—of their lives. Think about the ways in which you buy and listen to music. In what ways do you think they are different from your parents' generation? Do you think current methods of acquiring music (notice I didn't say "purchasing") are superior to the older ways? Why or why not? Some people think we have lost something by music going digital. Do you agree? Can you imagine a time where your way of listening to music is outdated? If so, what do you think might change in our future to make that happen?

Compose

Take a moment to try and recall your first experience with music. Jot down everything you can remember about it. Now, compose a paragraph in which you describe the circumstances surrounding the experience (i.e., someone singing to you, hearing a song in a car, listening to a home stereo) and the impact it had on you (i.e., it made you feel happy, sad, energetic). In another paragraph, write down what you can remember about the priority music was given in your household. In other words, was music always being played, or was it seldom heard at home? Reflect on how your early experiences with music might have shaped your current view of music and record those ideas as well.

Divide into groups of three to four people, and, in a "show and tell" fashion, share with each other the details of any and all technological devices on your person or in your backpack that can play music. Discuss what each device can do, how you use it, how often you use it, and when you got it. Discuss whether anyone in the group has ever listened to music via an analog device (i.e., record player or tape deck). If so, what was different about that experience? Finally, plan a short presentation in which you present to the rest of the class the most common attributes of the devices everyone in your group owns (i.e., do they all play videos as well as music? Is each Bluetooth enabled?, etc.).

Using the web, research the invention of digital technology. When was it created and by whom? Why was it invented? Some of the answers might surprise you. Continuing with your research, see what you can find regarding the history of your favorite personal music device. Consider the following questions: When was it invented? By whom? How many versions have there been? How many different models of it are available? As a class, share what information you find. This task will help you as you read the various essays in this book.

Since 1990, Greg Kot has been the music critic at the Chicago Tribune, where he has comprehensively covered popular music. He also co-hosts the nationally syndicated public-radio show "Sound Opinions." His books include I'll Take You There: Mavis Staples, the Staple Singers and the March up Freedom's Highway; Wilco: Learning How to Die; *and* Ripped: How the Wired Generation Revolutionized Music.

excerpt from
RIPPED: HOW THE WIRED GENERATION REVOLUTIONIZED MUSIC—"STEVE JOBS AND THE IPOD 'BURGLARY KIT'"

BY GREG KOT

In 2004, U2 made a deal in Steve Jobs's kitchen in Palo Alto, California. There, singer Bono, manager Paul McGuinness, and Interscope record-company chairman Jimmy Iovine met with the Apple CEO. McGuinness wrote down the details in the back of the diary he carried: for the first time, U2 would allow its music to be used in a television advertisement in return for a royalty on a custom U2 iPod.

The occasion was the release of U2's eleventh studio album, *How to Dismantle an Atomic Bomb*. Instead of releasing the album's first single, "Vertigo," as a video, U2 launched the album with a commercial that showed the band belting out the song interspersed with images of silhouetted iPod-clutching dancers.

The convergence of the world's biggest stadium-rock band and the world's savviest computer company ensured *How to Dismantle an Atomic Bomb* would be a hit: it ended up selling more than 3 million copies in the United States, while "Vertigo" moved 2 million copies (mostly downloads), the Irish quartet's biggest-selling single yet.

At the time, in an interview with this writer for the *Chicago Tribune*, U2 singer Bono acknowledged that associating the band's music with a product was "alarming." But "you've got to deal with the devil."

"The devil here is a bunch of creative minds, more creative than a lot of people in rock bands. The lead singer is Steve Jobs. In the band on lead guitar, [Apple senior vice president] Jony Ive. A beautiful spirit. A man who has helped design the most beautiful art object in music culture since the electric guitar. That's the iPod. . . .

"We looked at the iPod commercial as a rock video. We chose the director. We thought, How are we going to get our single off in the days when rock music is niche? When it's unlikely to get a three-minute punk-rock song on top of the radio? So we piggybacked this phenomenon to get ourselves to a new, younger audience, and we succeeded. And it's exciting. I'm proud of the commercial, I'm proud of the association. We have turned down enormous sums of money to put our songs in a commercial, where we felt, to your point, where it might change the way people appreciated the song. We were offered [and turned down] $23 million for just the music to 'Where the Streets Have No Name.'. . . But we have to start thinking about new ways of getting our songs across, of communicating in this new world, with so many channels, with rock music becoming a niche."

Iovine said the deal represented the best way to expose U2's music, because his label could no longer count on support from commercial radio or MTV. "We're fighting radio, all these ancient things that have stopped putting people like U2 on the air," he said. "We gotta cut through that. TV can cut through that, the Internet can cut through that. You've got to feed that if you want to stay in the game. The iPod commercial didn't hurt with young kids. The iPod is the new electric guitar."

But three years later, the U2 camp was no longer singing Apple's praises. The U2-iPod deal was done back in "the days when iTunes was being talked about as penicillin for the recorded music industry," Paul McGuinness said at his 2008 keynote speech at the MIDEM music conference in Cannes, France.

The penicillin never took. The music industry continued to decline. But as the iPod's status took hold as the ultimate music accessory, the cigarette-sized portal to thousands of songs, Jobs's business thrived.

At the time of the U2 ad, the iPod and the iTunes music store were still in their relative infancy. When the iPod was first introduced in the fall of 2002, it was a cult item, selling 376,000 copies in its first twelve months on the market. Sales crept up to 1.6 million in the first half of 2004. But in the last half of the year, thanks in part to the massive U2 marketing campaign, sales skyrocketed to 6.5 million.

In the last quarter of 2007, Apple reported record revenue of $9.6 billion, 42 percent from iPod sales of 22 million, pushing the six-year total for the portable music players to 141 million.

Meanwhile, the iTunes store, which opened in 2003, reported similar increases. Downloads jumped from 70 million in April 2004 to 300 million a year later. In January 2008, the store marked 4 billion downloads. Three months later, it became the nation's leading music retailer, for the first time surpassing music sales at the world's largest retailer, Wal-Mart Stores Inc.

A number of artists followed U2's lead with iPod commercials, including Bob Dylan, Paul McCartney, Wynton Marsalis, and myriad lesser-knowns. Some of these ads proved effective sales tools not just for the iPod but for the music itself. In the fall of 2007, wispy Canadian singer-songwriter Feist saw sales of her album *The Reminder* jump to twenty thousand a week from six thousand when her video for the song "1234" started airing as an iPod ad. But there was little doubt who was steering the ship.

As Bob Lefsetz, a former record industry executive-turned-commentator, wrote in his Internet-based Lefsetz Letter: "What kind of screwed-up world do we live in where the iPod is cooler than the music it plays?"

In a few short years, Steve Jobs had gone from a tech-head cult figure to the maverick visionary the music industry could no longer ignore. "At first, they kicked us out," he said of major-label CEOs in a 2003 interview with *Rolling Stone*. But as one industry strategy after another failed to stem the tide of Internet file sharing, "we started to gain some credibility with these folks. And they started to say: 'You know, you're right on these things—tell us more.'"

By 2007, Jobs was playing a role in shaping major-label strategy; as the biggest player in selling digital music, he had begun to function much like a fifth CEO among the Big Four labels. In February, he called on his business partners in the music industry to drop all antipiracy software limitations from online music sales.

His prescription was radical medicine by industry standards. Ever since the emergence of Napster, the multinational conglomerates had sought to limit the ways that consumers could copy and share digital music files. Their efforts reached ridiculous proportion in 2005, when Sony BMG imbedded copy-prevention software on CDs of fifty-two releases that unintentionally exposed consumers' computers to debilitating viruses.

The company was pilloried in the media and targeted in several lawsuits, including one filed by the attorney general of Texas. It eventually pulled all the CDs off the market. In 2007, the U.S. Federal Trade Commission commanded Sony BMG to reimburse consumers for damage caused by the "root-kit" software.

Jobs's timing was impeccable. He released his digital-rights manifesto only a few weeks after the trade commission ruling, which capped one of the more embarrassing chapters in the record industry's file-sharing saga. So when Jobs argued that copy-protection efforts by the industry had not worked, and had served only to alienate consumers, he met little public resistance from the labels. He advocated an end to digital rights management systems, which would create a world in which "any [digital] player can play music purchased from any store, and any store can sell music which is playable on all players."

"This is clearly the best alternative for consumers," he wrote, "and Apple would embrace it in a heartbeat."

Two months later at a news conference in London, EMI responded to Jobs's plea by announcing that it would make its digital repertoire available free of digital rights management restrictions. In addition, these digital tracks would be of significantly higher sound quality (256 kilobits per second versus 128 kilobits per second). Jobs appeared alongside the chief executive officer of EMI Music, Eric Nicoli, to answer questions about the new policy.

Jobs was the only executive from the digital domain at EMI's announcement. In addition, he and Nicoli answered questions from the media together, as if they were partners. It was a clear indication that EMI saw Jobs and his iTunes store as its future, the one area of growth in an industry otherwise besieged by bad news.

"We remain optimistic that digital growth will outstrip physical decline" in CD sales, Nicoli said. But it didn't happen soon enough. Nicoli quit five months later as EMI was about to be taken over by the private equity group Terra Firma.

Jobs's publicity coup was couched in corporate double-speak. Tucked inside the announcement was that the price per premium track would increase a dizzying 30 percent at iTunes (to $1.29 from ninety-nine cents).

When asked about the price increase, Jobs responded, "It's not a price increase . . . It's a second product that you get to choose to buy or not."

Technically, he was correct. The iTunes store would now offer consumers two options: copy-protected digital music files of lower sound quality at the old ninety-nine-cents-per-track price, and the new, higher-priced "premium" files, which would be of better sound quality and free of copy-protection software. But even Jobs acknowledged that this latest step merely brought digital files in line with CDs.

What's more, Apple's profit margin on each iTunes sale was enormous. Benn Jordan, an Illinois-based electronic artist who has recorded under ten pseudonyms for a decade, says a contract his independent label signed broke down iTunes revenue for his music this way: 36 percent to the store, 30 percent for the digital distributor, 17 percent to the label, and 17 percent to the artist.

"This should be insulting to artists because iTunes does not promote or manufacture your product," Jordan says. "They simply host bandwidth, which many places will do for much less."

David Byrne, who has recorded for both major and indie labels, says that artists essentially make the same royalty amount from an iTunes sale as they do from a traditional CD sale. "There's no manufacturing or distribution costs" for a download, he says, "but somehow the artist ended up with the exact same amount."

Yet there was little resisting iTunes when it controlled the digital-sales market. Despite the rise of other online music stores, most formidably amazon.com, Apple still represented about 70 percent of digital music business in 2007.

Whereas CD sales had declined to 500 million units in 2007, from 942 million in 2000, digital music sales were booming and overall music purchases hit a record 1.4 billion. Yet most of that growth was attributable to ninety-nine-cent tracks on iTunes, while sales of $15 CDs plunged 15 percent.

Clearly the route to rejuvenating revenue, presumably not just for record labels but for artists, ran through the Internet. Suing consumers had not stemmed the tide of peer-to-peer file sharing, which outdistanced legit downloads twenty to one. Even Steve Jobs acknowledged that only 3 percent of the music on the average iPod was bought from iTunes. Some of the remaining music came from legitimately purchased CDs that had been ripped onto the MP3 players. But the majority of it was, in the industry's eyes, contraband.

McGuinness did not spare his old business partner Jobs in his 2008 MIDEM keynote: "I wish he would bring his remarkable set of skills to bear on the problems of recorded music. He's a technologist, a financial genius, a marketer, and a music lover. He probably doesn't realize it but the collapse of the old financial model for recorded music will also mean the end of the songwriter. We've been used to bands who wrote their own material since the Beatles, but the mechanical royalties that sustain songwriters are drying up. Labels and artists, songwriters and publishers, producers and musicians—everyone's a victim."

The veteran manager's words reflected the grave doubts sweeping through the industry about Jobs and his true motives. No other major quickly followed EMI to offer unrestricted files to iTunes. Universal, U2's label, pointedly announced that it would seek deals with other digital stores to sell its unprotected files. In 2008 it followed through on its threat, joining Warner Bros. and Sony BMG in striking a digital music distribution deal with iTunes's top competitor, Amazon. The labels grumbled that iTunes pricing wasn't flexible enough. They were also vexed by Apple's refusal to license its software so that other music stores could sell music that could be played on the iPod, and so that other digital devices could play songs bought from iTunes. "Hardware makers should share with the content owners whose assets are exploited by the buyers of their machines," McGuinness demanded.

In 2009, Apple finally reached a compromise with the majors and introduced a three-tiered pricing structure for its 10 million-song iTunes store (sixty-nine cents, ninety-nine cents, and $1.29). In exchange, the labels agreed to remove all copy-protection restrictions. It was a positive step in untangling the web of distrust that had settled over the relationship between the music industry and Apple.

But by then the big labels were looking for other business partners to bully, most notably Internet service providers (ISPs).

"I've met a lot of today's heroes of Silicon Valley," McGuinness railed. "Most of them don't really think of themselves as makers of burglary kits. They say: 'You can use this stuff to e-mail your friends and store and share your photos.' But we all know that there's more to it than that, don't we? Kids don't pay $25 a month for broadband just to share their photos, do their homework, and e-mail their pals."

He called on Internet service providers to share their revenue, or else: "We must shame them. Their snouts have been at our trough for too long."

At about the same time, the Songwriters Association of Canada proposed a $5-a-month licensing fee on every wireless and Internet account in the country, in exchange for unlimited access to all recorded music.

The deal aimed to put $1 billion annually in the pockets of artists, publishers, and record labels. The money would be distributed to artists based on how frequently their music is swapped online; the more downloads, the more money the people responsible for the music would accrue.

For sixteen cents a day, the plan proposed to give computer users access to every song that could possibly be made available online. But a lot of questions needed to be answered before the plan could be set in motion, including who would collect and distribute the money—a job that wireless carriers and Internet service providers weren't equipped to do, and would likely fight to avoid.

The proposal also opened the door to government involvement in the music industry, hardly a happy prospect. A few months earlier, the French government stuck its nose into the downloading fray by creating an antipiracy agency charged with shutting down customers' Internet access if they engage in illegal file sharing.

If the Canadian songwriters' plan was deeply flawed, it at least had the advantage of appearing far less punitive than any previous industry proposal dealing with file sharing.

A more refined version of that approach was put on the table at the South by Southwest music conference in Austin, Texas, in March 2008. There, music consultant Jim Griffin proposed that broadband users pay for any music they download through a fee bundled into their monthly Internet access bill. His plan would allow consumers to download, upload, and share music without restriction, and create a pool of money collected from Internet service providers to compensate music copyright holders, but do it without government involvement.

"Government involvement in the arts is abhorrent to me, and I do not favor a tax," Griffin said. Instead he proposed a fee on broadband users. The fee would not apply to users who do not download music. Still, Griffin expected that "seventy to eighty percent of users would pay" to gain access to all the music their hard drives could hold.

"Our industry now functions on a tip jar," he said. "We have to make it roughly involuntary to pay" in the same way that "sports has made it roughly involuntary to pay with cable TV deals."

A week later he was hired by Warner Bros. to put his plan into motion. It envisioned a live-and-let-live world in which peer-to-peer file sharing would coexist with iTunes and other legitimate MP3 music stores. With an estimated 750 million people expected to be hooked into wireless broadband networks in Western Europe and the United States alone in the next decade, the potential revenue from licensing fees on Internet service providers could be substantial.

Yet such a forward-thinking plan might already be too little too late for the industry, said Sandy Pearlman, a McGill University professor and former producer for Blue Oyster Cult and the Clash. A portable database containing all the music ever recorded is imminent, he said. "Once this paradise of infinite storage is entered," he said, "it will represent the end of all intellectual property rights."

Invent

In 2004, referring to Apple's senior vice president, Bono claims that Jony Ive was "a man who has helped design the most beautiful art object in music culture since the electric guitar." That's a big claim. What do you think Bono means by that? Do you think he was right in putting so much importance on the iPod? Why do you think he would seek to put such importance on one man or one device?

Compose

In this essay, Kot outlines the failure of the record industry to solve the problems posed by the MP3 and illegal downloading. With the invention of the iPod, he argues, Steve Jobs solved the problem for them, at least to some extent. Take a moment and brainstorm on paper about other forms of technology that have threatened to make a particular company less relevant or even obsolete (think email vs. the US Postal Service, for example).

Kot begins his essay by recounting the now famous collaboration between U2 and Steve Jobs, which resulted in a significant boost in sales for each. As Kot points out, Bono (the lead singer of U2) claimed that while the band was previously reluctant to allow their music to be used in commercials, they now had begun "thinking about new ways of getting [their] songs across" to the public. To that end, Bono saw the iPod as the answer. You can find the original iPod commercial on YouTube (YouTube search: "U2 iPod commercial"). Reread the first page and a half of the article out loud and then, as a class, watch the video/commercial. In small groups, discuss the following questions, and then report your ideas to the larger group. Why do you think this commercial was so successful at reaching audiences for both the band and Apple? U2 is an older band that made their big splash in the 80s; how might this collaboration help them win a younger audience? Do you think, as some did, that the band was "selling out" to a cheesy marketing campaign? Why or why not?

You can find Steve Jobs's full official announcement of Apple's collaboration with U2 on YouTube as well (YouTube search: Apple Special Music Event—the U2 part comes in around minute 34:00). The announcement includes a speech from U2's frontman, Bono. Watch the video, especially the section that features Bono and U2's guitarist, The Edge. In it, they talk about the new direction of music since the advent of the MP3. They put a lot of hope in the ability of the iPod to "rescue" the record music industry. Did it work? Do you think the iPod still as popular today as it was then? How might you go about finding evidence to support these questions regarding the popularity of a particular technological device like the iPod and its relationship to the record industry? Using the web, and working in pairs, work to discover concrete evidence to support your answers to these questions.

Luiz Augusto Buff de Souza e Silva is a Brazilian lawyer, specializing in Entertainment and Copyright Law, with a second degree in Music Business and Management from Berklee College of Music. Luiz developed his experience in the music industry both as a musician and by working at companies such as Ted Kurland Associates and Soundtrack Group. More recently, Luiz served as VP of Operations in the consulting firm Digital Cowboys.

MASH-UPS & FAIR USE: GIRL TALK

By Luiz Augusto Buff

With the development of digital music in the mid-1990s, the act of sampling became very popular and is now a fundamental element for musical styles like Rap and Hip-hop. The use of samples to construct new songs is considered a derivative work and usually a license is required. Copyright owners have already successfully sued Hip-hop artists that tried to use samples without these licenses.

Another sample-based derivative work is the Mash-Up; a type of composition that blends two or more pre-recorded sounds creating an entirely new musical composition. While Mash-Ups are also considered a derivative work, artists like Gregg Gillis—known as DJ Girl Talk—are trying to push the boundaries of the strictures of the law by trying to include these musical collages under the fair use concept.

Girl Talk's latest album, *All Day*, was released as a free download on November 15th and has more than 350 samples of different sound recordings in approximately seventy minutes of runtime. Obtaining all of the necessary licenses for each sound recording used would have been very costly and extremely time consuming. Gillis, having planned to release the album for free, decided to move forward without licensing a single track—not even the three-minute use of Black Sabbath's "War Pigs"—claiming that his creations fit the guidelines of fair use. However, to determine congruency with the fair use doctrine, it is necessary to understand the origins and basis of the fair use concept.

FAIR USE REVISITED

Following a tendency that had been developed through case law, the 1976 Copyright Act recognized the fair use doctrine as a defense against copyright infringement. The goal of that concept was to permit certain uses of copyrighted works that encouraged the advancement of learning and knowledge and to provide wide access to creative works for the public. It is important to understand that fair use is not an affirmative right, but merely a defense against a copyright infringement. There is a false common belief that it is considered "fair use" to use an unlicensed, copyrighted work as long as one gives credit to the author or copyright owner (the assumption that a use is fair can be risky, and technically speaking, it is considered fair only when a court decides so). The Copyright Act listed certain types of use that are likely to be considered as fair, such as criticism, comment, news reporting, teaching, scholarship and research. This list is just illustrative and there are other types of uses that can be considered fair as well. Also, Section 107 of the Copyright Act lists four main factors to be considered by a court to determine whether or not a particular use is fair:

> The purpose and character of the use, including whether such use is of commercial nature or is for nonprofit educational purposes;
>
> The nature of the copyrighted work;
>
> The amount and substantiality of the portion used in relation to the copyrighted work as a whole;
>
> The effect of the use upon the potential market for, or value of, the copyrighted work.

GIRL TALK

The first factor focuses on the observation of how the work is being used. If the use is related to information and/or education, it is more likely to be considered as fair since there are public benefits in these purposes. In general, the nonprofit character will weigh towards fair use, but the commercial use by itself does not discard the fairness of the use, since most uses are commercial to some extent. The court's main concern is finding out if the user stands to profit from exploitation of the copyrighted material without paying the customary price for the licenses—and Girl Talk does profit from the act. The transformative quality of the use is also analyzed here as a means to distinguish infringement and fair use. A use that is transformative, rather than imitative, has more of a chance to be qualified as fair, for it inserts the piece in a different context and purpose. Girl Talk's sample works are transformative, in that he transforms different pieces of existing sounds recordings into a new work of his own. However, his purposes are strictly commercial and do not involve educational value or critical commentary. In addition, the good faith of the defendant is extremely relevant in court analysis of the first factor.

As the album was distributed on a website called Illegalart.net, the presumption of good faith can be quite a stretch.

When analyzing the nature of the copyrighted work, the court must determine if the work was published or unpublished, or if it is a factual or creative work. As musical works are creative in essence, this factor usually weighs against fair use- even more so when it is an unpublished work, in which case, the original author has the right of first use before a derivative creator. Gregg Gillis' samples come from published original works—a fact that does not harm the first use principle. The third factor refers to the portion of the copyrighted material used. There is no absolute rule to determine how much of a work can be used to be considered fair. Not only is the size and proportion of the work relevant, but also the qualitative dimension of the portion used. The greater the amount used, the less likely a use will be considered fair. Yet in some cases, the use of even a very small part- if considered signature to a song- may characterize the use as an infringement.

Probably the most important of the four factors is the final, stating that it is important to analyze the value and the potential market of a copyrighted work. Any use of a copyrighted work—fair or unfair—it will automatically affect the copyright owner to some extent, as since they are not receiving any licensing incomes. This is tolerated due to the public benefits afforded from the fair use of the work. However, if the new work competes with, or reduces the potential commercial market for the original copyrighted material, then the use will most likely be deemed unfair. Again, a commercial use has a presumed adverse impact on the market for the original copyrighted work and reduces the credibility of fairness. Girl Talk's main argument relies on the last two factors: He alleges that his work is based on various small portions of original works, and the substantiality of it will not substitute or harm the copyright holder's original or potential markets.

CONCLUSION

Girl Talk is aware of the risks that he is taking by not licensing the samples that he uses. There is no way to prevent a lawsuit of copyright infringement by claiming fair use and only a court has the power to determine his particular uses as fair or infringed. The expenses needed to prove fair use in court can be very high, sometimes surpassing the amount needed to obtain the legitimate licenses in the first place. Although Girl Talk has not yet faced a lawsuit for copyright infringement, the major distributors of digital music decided to not offer his albums on their websites. Major labels and publishers are most likely holding their moves against the artist because they are afraid of the negative attention and the potential setting of precedent in favor of the fair use.

Invent

Since music and film went digital in the last part of the twentieth century, copyright laws have been revised multiple times. For many in the record and film industry, sampling or downloading music was tantamount to theft. In fact, many of the RIAA's and MPAA's public service ads equated electronic piracy to stealing a car, a handbag, or movie off the shelf at a DVD store. (YouTube search: Piracy = Stealing). Is there a difference between illegal downloading and stealing a CD from a physical store? If so, what is that difference? Why do you think most young people don't have a problem with illegally downloading or sampling music?

Compose

The author claims that Girl Talk's compositions are "transformative" rather than "imitative," thus making his songs unique works of art. Others, however, have argued that his creations are mere copies of what others have done and should not be considered true art. Take a minute and write down your answers to the following question: What makes something an original work of art?

Collaborate

Girl Talk's music challenges long established views on intellectual property and artistic creation. In small groups, share your view of art and the rights of intellectual property. What do you think should be "protected," and what do you think should be "fair use"? Be careful to explain the logic behind your views on each topic.

Explore

Learn a bit more about mashups. Via YouTube, watch Gregg Gillis demonstrate how quickly he can create a mashup song (YouTube Search: Girl Talk Creates a Mashup). Does the ease and speed with which he can create a song diminish its artistic value? Look up a bio of Gregg Gillis via Google and visit his home page (illegal-art.net). Note his educational background and how he transitioned to becoming a full-time artist. Research the history of sampling (which existed long before the digital age). Explore the differences between sampling in the 60s, 70s 80s, 90s, and now.

Ben Sisario is a media reporter at the New York Times, covering music and the music business. He is the author of Doolittle, a book about the Pixies, and has contributed to Rolling Stone, Spin, New York Press and WFUV, a public radio station in New York City. He has also taught at the Clive Davis Institute of Recorded Music at New York University.

THE NEW RISE OF A SUMMER HIT: TWEET IT MAYBE

BY BEN SISARIO

For decades, the song of the summer would emerge each year following a pattern as predictable as the beach tides.

Pop radio would get it rolling before school let out, and soon the song—inevitably one with a big, playful beat and an irresistible hook—would blare from car stereos everywhere. Then came prom singalongs as the song finally became ubiquitous around the Fourth of July. In 1987, it was Whitney Houston's "I Wanna Dance With Somebody." In 2003, Beyoncé's "Crazy in Love."

But the success of this summer's hit, Carly Rae Jepsen's cheerfully flirty "Call Me Maybe," shows how much the hitmaking machine, as well as the music industry itself, has been upended by social media.

Only a year ago, the charts were dominated by stars who had come out of the old machine of radio and major-label promotion: Katy Perry, Rihanna, Adele, Maroon 5. This year's biggest hits—"Call Me Maybe," Gotye's "Somebody That I Used to Know" and Fun.'s "We Are Young"—started in left field and were helped along by YouTube and Twitter before coming to the mainstream media.

For "Call Me Maybe," which was No. 1 for nine weeks, the longest run of the year, the critical piece was YouTube. After Justin Bieber and friends posted a video of themselves lip-syncing to it in February, hundreds of fan tributes followed. Alongside Ms. Jepsen's own video, which has been watched 212 million times, versions by Katy Perry, the Cookie

Monster ("Share It Maybe") and the United States Olympic swim team turned it into a yearlong audiovisual meme.

A tribute version even brought the song to the attention of President Obama. In an interview with KOB-FM, a New Mexico radio station, he said: "I have to admit, I've never actually heard the original version of the song. I saw this version where they spliced up me from a whole bunch of different speeches that I made. They kind of mashed together an Obama version of it."

Nearly two-thirds of teenagers listen to music on YouTube, more than any other medium, Nielsen said last week. Ms. Jepsen said in a recent interview that "the viral videos are what's been the driving force for this. It was insane to see that the music could spread that far because of the Internet. It's a cool thing. It changes the game completely."

YouTube, Twitter and Facebook are now record labels' textbook tools for starting a marketing campaign, and if the numbers there are big enough, they can be used in pitches to radio and television programmers.

To introduce Cher Lloyd, a 19-year-old singer who was on "The X Factor" in Britain, Epic Records set up a "queen" fan to beat the drum on Twitter, and coached Ms. Lloyd on what to mention online—a TV appearance, for example, or the Twitter handles for radio D.J.'s.

"In this day and age, artist development is about how do you turn 10 Facebook likes into 100, into 1,000," said Scott Seviour, Epic's senior vice president for marketing.

The song catapulted Ms. Jepsen, apple-cheeked and giggly at 26, from obscurity to worldwide fame. Five years ago she placed third on "Canadian Idol," and last fall she released "Call Me Maybe" in Canada to preview her second album. By the Christmas holiday it was a minor hit in Canada, when Mr. Bieber heard it.

"It's supposed to be a fun song," Ms. Jepsen said. "Not to take yourself too seriously, to put you in a good mood."

Mr. Bieber's role in popularizing the song reflects the importance of both social media and old-fashioned celebrity promotion. On Dec. 30, 2011, he told his 15 million Twitter followers that "Call Me Maybe" was "possibly the catchiest song I've ever heard lol." Shortly thereafter, he and Mr. Braun signed Ms. Jepsen to their label in the United States, Schoolboy, which is affiliated with Interscope Records and the Universal Music Group.

To exploit the success of the single, which has sold eight million downloads around the world, Ms. Jepsen delayed the release of her album. Called *Kiss*, it will now be released next month, when she will also hit the road as an opening act for Mr. Bieber.

The song's trajectory also demonstrates the continuing power of radio, which record executives say is still essential to turn any song—no matter how much online buzz it has—into a genuine smash.

In March and April, when "Call Me Maybe" was getting tens of millions of views on YouTube, it still had relatively low radio play—fewer than 5,000 spins a week on Top 40 stations in the United States, according to Nielsen. It hit No. 1 on iTunes on May 27, but took almost a month to reach No. 1 on Billboard's singles chart, which counts sales as well as airplay and streaming services. By then it had about 20,000 spins a week on multiple radio formats.

"There's not a million-seller out there that doesn't have radio play," said Jay Frank, chief executive of the label DigSin. "But its first million generally doesn't come from radio."

"Call Me Maybe" is a watershed case for the use of social media as a marketing tool, but the song's success will be difficult to replicate—even for Ms. Jepsen as she prepares to release her album. No matter how hard a record company might push, popularity online depends on the enthusiasm of individual fans.

The marketers behind Ms. Jepsen have worked to organize it to some degree, through tools like a Tumblr blog collecting fan tribute videos. But Jonathan Simkin, her manager, said that trying to control the energy wasn't the point.

"That's part of the beauty of how this has grown," Mr. Simkin said. "This is just people who the song struck. I don't want to harness it or limit it. I just want to pinch myself and say, 'Thank God the song affects people this way.'"

Ms. Jepsen said she was not worrying about trying to line up another megahit, because that kind of success is never predictable.

"I never know what is a hit and what isn't a hit," she said. "I just write what feels natural and good. At end of the day you just release it and hope for the best."

Invent

It is widely acknowledged that Justin Bieber's Dec. 30, 2011 tweet led to Carly Jepsen's rise to fame. On that day, he tweeted to his fans the following: "Call me maybe by Carly Rae Jepsen is possibly the catchiest song I've ever heard lol." That tweet sent his fans in search of her music, and that led to the song becoming a #1 summer hit. Shortly after that tweet, he also signed Jepsen to his label. To that end, could it be argued that Bieber's endorsement had more to do with Jepsen's success than social media? To what degree do you think social media can propel an artist to fame on its own (i.e., without big name endorsements)? Sisario notes that "Call Me Maybe" is a watershed case for the use of social media as a marketing tool, but he also goes on to say this phenomenon will be difficult to replicate. Do you agree? Why or why not?

Compose

Sisario claims that "YouTube, Twitter, and Facebook are now record labels' textbook tools for starting a marketing campaign." To that end, he suggests that these media have essentially been co-opted by big corporations. Create a list of possible reasons these forms of media still offer independent artists a chance to make it big without the help of corporations. Then, write a paragraph in which you make a case for whether social media serves independent musicians or record companies better.

Collaborate

Take a moment and read Adam Frucci's short essay, "Record Labels: Change or Die." In light of Sisario's essay, as a group, discuss whether you think record companies have indeed changed enough to survive. In what ways have they accommodated the new forms of media of the digital age, and in what ways have they not? Discuss the ways in which you think they could still improve. Be prepared to share your ideas with the class.

Explore

As many of the essays in this book indicate, the Internet has become the new medium for the consumption and dissemination of music. Carly Rae Jepsen's #1 hit is just one example. Research other examples where musicians have been catapulted to fame via social media. Be sure to explore the context for their success, not just the specific event that led to it.

J. Bryan Lowder is on the culture staff at Slate magazine, where he covers movies, art music, food, books, Bravo TV shows, and other cultural media. He is the assistant editor of Outward, Slate magazine's LGBTQ section, and the editorial assistant for Culture.

DOES POP MUSIC SOUND LOUDER, DUMBER, AND MORE THE SAME?

BY J. BRYAN LOWDER

Washington—According to a new study from researchers at the Spanish National Research Council, the familiar complaint that contemporary popular music has grown loud, predictable and simpler than ever may be exactly right. While we often cast a skeptical eye toward quantitative studies of music like this one, a closer examination of the paper reveals that even for skeptics the analysis may have a point—even if the portrait it paints is incomplete.

Here's how the study worked. The analysts ran 464,411 recordings from all genres of popular music from the period of 1955–2010 (called the "Million Song Dataset") through a complex set of algorithms to analyze three metrics: harmonic complexity, timbral diversity and loudness. The results indicated that, on the whole, popular music over the past half-century has become blander and louder than it used to be.

To understand these findings, it's worth briefly delving into the terms in question. Most people are familiar with the idea that popular songs are constructed chiefly of a melody (usually the lead vocal line or tune) and supporting harmonies called chords (rhythm is the other chief component, but more on that later). The study found that, since the '50s, there has been a decrease not only in the diversity of chords in a given song, but also in the number of novel transitions, or musical pathways, between them. In other words, while it's true that pop songs have always been far more limited in their harmonic vocabularies than, say, a classical symphony, past decades saw more inventive ways of linking their harmonies together than we hear now. It's the difference between Carly Rae

Jepsen's "Call Me Maybe" (2012), which contains four simple chords presented one after another almost as blocks, and Alex North's "Unchained Melody" (1955), which, though also relatively harmonically simple (it employs about six or seven chords, depending on the version), transitions smoothly from chord to chord due to more subtle orchestration.

The research group also discovered that "timbres"—or the distinct "textures" produced by different instruments playing the same note—have gotten more homogenous over time. To be clear, this is not to say that musicians are using fewer or different instruments now than before; rather, since 1955, pop has tended to use a smaller and more homogenous palette of "tone colors" at a given time.

The final finding—that music recordings have grown louder and louder over time—will come as no surprise to those who've been following the so-called "Loudness Wars, " but this seems to represent the first data-driven proof of the phenomenon. As producers compete for the attention of radio listeners to make their artist's recordings a hit, they've been gradually ratcheting up the inherent volume of the tracks at the cost of sound quality and dynamic richness. (You can hear what this sounds like on YouTube.)

So all this study's conclusions seem plausible, but does it really mean that our pop is dumber than before? To answer that, it's important to also ask what the researchers didn't study. For instance, though "Call Me Maybe" is made from a rather blunt and familiar set of four chords, the infectiousness of the song, at least for this listener, is located in both the playful rhythmic friction between the vocals and instruments—rhythm, crucially, was not taken into account in this study—as well as the cappuccino-cozy, almost country quality of Jepsen's voice. (Note how it glides and sometimes endearingly stumbles over her love-drunk lyrics.)

Indeed, so much musical interest in this hip-pop and dance-pop moment of recent years derives from the pervasive four-on-the-floor dance beat—and, crucially, well-crafted rhythmic dissensions from it. ("Unchained Melody," while a gorgeous song, isn't known for its beat.) As tempting as it may be to try to decode the "musical discourse," as these researchers called it, there are certain aspects of music—ineffable and otherwise—that will always elude your dataset.

Invent

The title of this essay seems designed to provoke fans of pop music. How would you describe pop music? What artists do you think currently fall in this category? If you listen to pop music, what about it do you find appealing? What do you think of someone suggesting that pop music is dumb? The title also suggests that songs that are loud and similar are bad. Do you agree? Why or why not?

Compose

Pop music is first and foremost defined by its attempt to appeal to mass audiences, specifically one that is mostly young in age. As such, what was described as "pop music" in the 1960s noticeably sounds different than that from the early twenty-first century. Its style and message generally gives us a window into what the young people of any given moment find appealing. Imagine that you are an anthropologist given the task of learning more about youth culture in the early twenty-first century. All you have to study, however, is a list of the current top 20 songs on the pop charts. Using the Billboard Top 100 as a reference, jot down some notes (feel free to listen to the songs and look up lyrics), and then write a 1–2 page report to your superiors in which you attempt to describe what a young person must be like in today's world.

Collaborate

In 2011, the Australian comedy singing group Axis of Awesome produced a video in which they sing through a host of popular songs, all while playing the same four chords (a I-V-VI-IV chord pattern, for those of you who play music). As a class, watch the video via YouTube (YouTube search: Axis of Awesome: 4 Chords Official Music Video). In small groups, first discuss your thoughts on the fact that so many hit songs have the exact same chord patterns. Do these examples validate the Spanish National Research Council's finding? Does drawing your attention to the similarities and repetition affect the way you think of the songs or the artists who sing them? Next, using the music on your phones or computers, see if can identify other pop songs that fit this pattern, paying particular attention to those that have come out since the video was made in 2011.

Explore

J. Bryan Lowder based his essay on a Spanish National Research Council's report titled, "Measuring the Evolution of Contemporary Western Popular Music." Google that title and take a quick glance through the report, just enough to get a sense of the depth and kind of research involved in the study. Now, take some time to look at other responses to the study (Lowder's is just one of many), and see if you can get a broad sense of how people in the music world responded to the study. Attend carefully to the biography of the person responding to the study, as his or her background could alert you to any potential bias. You might also want to explore the "loudness wars" that Lowder refers to in the fifth paragraph. You can see and hear an example of what he's talking about via YouTube (YouTube Search: The Loudness War by Matt Mayfield).

Vanessa Grigoriadis is a contributing editor to Vanity Fair, Rolling Stone, *and* New York Magazine. *She's the recipient of a* National Magazine Award *for profile writing and lives in New York with her husband and daughter, Olympia.*

GROWING UP GAGA

By Vanessa Grigoriadis

One year ago this month, Lady Gaga arrived for an interview in the dark, oak-paneled lobby of the Roosevelt Hotel, a massive Spanish-style place in the tourist district of Hollywood that was supposed to make the area chic but has largely failed. "Just Dance," the lead single off her first album, *The Fame,* had reached No. 1 in Australia, Sweden, and Canada in early 2008, but in March 2009, she was still an up-and-coming artist in America: a few thousand MySpace plays, a generic website, and a short tour as the opening act for New Kids on the Block. Gaga had a video, though. "My colleagues at radio in those three countries agreed to support her if I made a video," says Martin Kierszenbaum, the president of A&R at her label, Interscope. The "Just Dance" video, shot a few miles from the Roosevelt, features Gaga shimmying with a disco ball in her hands while her friends drape themselves on a couch nearby—though most of those people were extras, not real friends. She didn't know many people on the West Coast. "I don't like Los Angeles," she told me. "The people are awful and terribly shallow, and everybody wants to be famous but nobody wants to play the game. I'm from New York. I will kill to get what I need."

Before the meeting, I assumed that someone with a stage name like "Lady" (her given name is Stefani Joanne Germanotta) was going to be a bit standoffish—that's the strategy employed by most nervous young musicians on the occasion of their first real interview, in any case. But I never thought she was going to actually *be* Lady Gaga. These days, very few artists play the media like Bob Dylan, or stay in character as Devo's Mark Mothersbaugh did in his early career. In the age of VH1's *Behind the Music,* tabloid culture, and reality television, musicians are aware that they should show themselves to journalists in as much mundane detail as they can muster. "But Lady Gaga is my name," she said, amazed that I would have thought otherwise. "If you know me, and you call me Stefani, you don't really know me at all."

Gaga eased into a brown leather couch with as much grace as possible given her outfit, a stiff white jumpsuit with a jacket cut from a Martin Margiela pattern, the enormous shoulder pads stuffed underneath the fabric extending toward her ears. At five-two and 100 pounds, with her hair styled into a mod blonde bob, she looked flush from a strict diet of starvation: "Pop stars should not eat," she pronounced. She was young, skinny, and blonde, but she had a prominent Italian nose, the kind of nose that rarely survives on a starlet. (This was during Gaga's "hair-bow" phase—that would be pre-hair-hat and pre-hair-telephone—and when I asked about the bow's whereabouts, she rested her head on a pillow of her hands and said, "She's sleeping.") In the hallway near her table, families of tourists took pictures of one another with cameras, unaware of her presence, and she recoiled dramatically at every flash. "Oh, cameras," she said, shielding her eyes. "I cannot bear the cameras."

As we began the conversation, Gaga spoke carefully in a very odd accent—some combination of Madonna as Madge and a robot, an affect enhanced by the fact that she refused to remove her lightly tinted sunglasses over the course of two hours. "What I've discovered," said robo-Gaga, with a photo-ready tilt of her head, "is that in art, as in music, there's a lot of truth—and then there's a lie. The artist is essentially creating his work to make this lie a truth, but he slides it in amongst all the others. The tiny little lie is the moment I live for, my moment. It's the moment that the audience falls in love."

Gaga was very taken with her new "bubble dress" at this point, and we talked about its unreality, the beauty of the imaginary. Everyone wanted that dress, but it wasn't a dress at all—it was a bunch of plastic balls. "On my tour," she declared, "I'm going to be in my bubble dress on a piano made of bubbles, singing about love and art and the future. I should like to make one person believe in that moment, and it would be worth every salt of a No. 1 record." She dropped the accent for a moment now—the real girl, unartificed, was right underneath—and leaned in. "I can have hit records all day, but who fucking cares?" she explained. "A year from now, I could go away, and people might say, 'Gosh, what ever happened to that girl who never wore pants?' But how wonderfully memorable 30 years from now, when they say, 'Do you remember Gaga and her bubbles?' Because, for a minute, everybody in that room will forget every sad, painful thing in their lives, and they'll just live in my bubble world."

One year later, the transformation is complete: With six No. 1 hits in the last year, Lady Gaga is the biggest pop star in the world. By definition, a pop star is manufactured— rock stars weren't, at least not until well into the seventies, and that may be part of why rock became pop—and in some ways she has benefited from a very traditional star-making model, one of the last purviews of corporate music labels. But success can have a thousand authors. Several different people have claimed credit for discovering Gaga, 24, shaping her, naming her, making her who she is: Rob Fusari, who co-wrote and produced her early songs, sued her two weeks ago for $30 million, claiming among other grievances that he had a contract for 15 percent of her merchandising. And Gaga, of course, takes the credit herself. "I went through a great deal of creative and artistic revelation, learning, and marination to become who I am," she explains. "Tiny little lie? I wanted to become the artist I am today, and it took years."

All of them are partly right. But in another sense, she was an accident, a phenomenon that happened in New York in the first decade of a new century.

And what a happening. At a time when you wouldn't recognize the faces of the people who make most of the music we listen to (who are those guys in Vampire Weekend, again?), Gaga is visually iconic; in an age of Twitter, the remoteness she has cultivated since her first moment in the spotlight has made her an even bigger star. She completely turns the page on the last decade's era of bimbodom, taking back the limelight from women who made their careers by admitting that they had nothing to say, like Paris Hilton and Jessica Simpson. She also closes a strange era in female pop stardom, with rising talents unable to push through to superstardom (Katy Perry, Rihanna), *American Idol* contestants (Kelly Clarkson), older stars (Gwen, Fergie), tween stars (Miley and posse), and hugely popular musicians who aren't pop in their hearts, like Taylor Swift (country crossover) and Beyoncé (urban crossover). She's riveting in any language, with lyrics that compose their own Esperanto—she's effortlessly global.

Gaga's presence also introduces the formerly unthinkable idea that Madonna, another voracious Italian girl, may really, truly, finally be on her way out. Her new look is an appropriation of Madonna's circa "The Girlie Show" and "Blonde Ambition" (the darkened brows, the platinum-blonde hair, the red lips), and her music-video director, Jonas Åkerlund, is a major latter-day collaborator of Madonna's. But the two are very different: Madonna hasn't had a sense of humor about herself since the nineties, where Gaga is all fun and play. At her core, she's a young art-school student, full of optimism and kindness, childlike wonder at the bubble world. Though she may not be bisexual herself—of the many friends of hers interviewed for this article, not one of them recalls her ever having a girlfriend or being sexually interested in any woman offstage—her politics are inclusive, and she wants to promote images of as many sexual combinations as are possible on this Earth. Gaga says she's a girl who likes boys who look like girls, but she's also a girl who likes to look like a boy herself—or, rather, a drag queen, a boy pretending to be a girl. There's little that gives her more pleasure than the persistent rumor that she is a hermaphrodite, an Internet rumor based on scrutinizing a grainy video. That's not Madonna. Madonna wouldn't pretend she has a penis.

But that's the genius of Gaga: her willingness to be a mutant, a cartoon. She's got an awesome sense of humor, beaming tiny surreal moments across the world for our pleasure every day—like the gigantic bow made of hair she popped on her head last year. "One day, I said to my creative team, 'Gaultier did bows, let's do it in a new way,'" she says. "We were going back and forth with ideas, and then I said"—snaps finger—"hair-bow." She giggles. "We all fucking died, we *died*. It never cost a penny, and it looked so brilliant. It's just one of those things. I'm very arrogant about it." Her videos are global epiphenomena, like the Tarantino-flavored "Telephone," with its lesbian prison themes and Beyoncé guest appearance. "Gaga doesn't care so much about the technical part, but she's involved in every creative aspect," says Åkerlund. "We just allow ourselves to be very stupid with each other, and then you get ideas like sunglasses made of cigarettes."

Gaga also throws in our face something we've known all along but numbly decided to ignore: American celebrities have become very, very boring. (The fact that she has done this at the same time that much of the actual music she makes herself is somewhat boring is another feat.) One of her essential points is that celebrity should be the province of weirdos, like Grace Jones circa Jean-Paul Goude and her pet idol, eighties opera–meets–New Wave cult figure Klaus Nomi, who died of AIDS at 39. To Gaga, our video-game-playing, social-networking, cell-phone-obsessed culture has made all of us smaller, more normal, less interesting—and, except for odd lightning strikes like the *Jersey Shore* cast and Conan O'Brien's anointment of one Twitter fan—famous to no one, after all. "Kudos on MySpace? What is that?" she says, spitting out the words. "That's not emblematic about what I'm talking about. I'm talking about creating a genuine, memorable space for yourself in the world."

The story of Gaga is a story of being young in New York City. Stefani Germanotta grew up in a duplex on the Upper West Side, on one of the eclectic blocks between Columbus and Amsterdam in the West Seventies that are a mix of prewar brownstones, tenements, and modern condos. Her father ran a company that installed Wi-Fi in hotels, and her mother worked for a time as a V.P. at Verizon. They sent Gaga and her younger sister, Natali, 18, to Sacred Heart, a small Catholic girls' school up the street from the Guggenheim. "Sacred Heart may have been prestigious, but there were lots of different kinds of girls," says Gaga. "Some had extreme wealth, others were on welfare and scholarship, and some were in the middle, which was my family. All our money went into education and the house." Her classmates say that her family was tight-knit. "When John Kerry was running for president, Stefani supported him and her father didn't, so she joked about that," says Daniela Abatelli, Sacred Heart '05. Gaga was one of the only students with a job after school, as a waitress at a diner on the Upper West Side. With her early paychecks, she bought a Gucci purse. "I was so excited because all the girls at Sacred Heart always had their fancy purses, and I always had whatever," she says. "My mom and dad were not buying me a $600 purse."

Because her parents told her that they had sacrificed for her education, Gaga took school seriously from a young age. One of her favorite childhood memories is playing a piano concert at Sacred Heart at 8. "There was a line of twenty girls sitting in a row in our pretty dresses, and we each got up to play," she says happily. "I did a really good job. I was quite good." At 11, she began attending a full day of acting classes on Saturdays. "I remember the first time that I drank out of an imaginary coffee cup," she says, closing her eyes. "That's the very first thing they teach you. I can feel the rain, too, when it's not raining." Her lids pop open. "I don't know if this is too much for your magazine, but I can actually mentally give myself an orgasm." She hisses a little, like one of the deviant vampires in *True Blood.* "You know, sense memory is quite powerful."

By eighth grade, she had also realized that acting was a way to meet boys and began auditioning for plays with Sacred Heart's brother school, Regis High School, on 84th Street, near Park Avenue. She always landed the lead: Adelaide in *Guys and Dolls,* Philia in *A Funny Thing Happened on the Way to the Forum.* Jealous older girls stuck in the chorus began calling her "the Germ." "They always talked behind her back, like, 'Gross, she's the Germ! She's dirty!'" says a classmate. Gaga has often mentioned that she was an outcast in high school, but other than adolescent shenanigans like these, her friends from this Pudding-like crowd do not share this recollection. "She was always popular," says Julia Lindenthal, Marymount '04. "I don't remember her experiencing any social problems or awkwardness."

At the time, she had a certain incipient Gaganess: She could be a little overdramatic, spoiled, brassy, but she was also a nice girl (not to say a good girl), recalled by many as kind and generous—a theater chick who was starting to express her own feelings through songwriting. A fan of Pink Floyd and the Beatles, she started a classic-rock cover band and began entering open-mike nights at the Songwriters Hall of Fame on the Upper West Side. She even cut a demo of her love ballads, and her parents gave out copies as favors at her large Sweet 16 party, at the Columbus Club. "Everyone was playing her demo, like, 'Whoa, she's going to be a star,'" says Justin Rodriguez, Regis '03. "She was by far the most talented person in high school, but she'd do so many random acts of kindness, like saying, 'Your singing has gotten so much better, you're working hard and I've noticed.' She wasn't a diva at all."

Like many private-school girls, by 15, Gaga had a fake Delaware I.D. purchased on Macdougal Street. She also started dating a 26-year-old Greek waiter from the restaurant. "That's part of why I needed a job after school, too," she says. "My dad wouldn't give me money to go out on the weekends because he knew I was going downtown and being bad." Soon, she had her first tattoo: a G clef on her lower back. ("Before I made my first big music video, I decided to turn that tattoo into a huge side piece," she says. "I just couldn't face the world with a tramp stamp.") She was still a good girl at school, even if she got in trouble with the teachers once in a while: not for short kilts but inappropriate shirts. "I was fifteen to twenty pounds heavier than I am now," says Gaga. "I would wear shirts that were low-cut, and the teachers would tell me I couldn't wear them, and I'd point to another girl who was wearing the same thing. 'Well, it looks different on her.' It wasn't fair." She shimmies her shoulders a bit. "At that time, my breasts were much bigger, and firm, and delicious." (Another high-school nickname: Big Boobs McGee.)

After the World Trade Center was attacked, Gaga cried for days and wore black, in mourning. "As she came down the aisle to get Communion at the special Mass for 9/11, her steps were in this serious cadence," says a friend. "She used to wear a lot of makeup, but she didn't have any on. I remember thinking, *Wow, she is so over-the-top*." Gaga also had an odd habit of refusing to let cast members in plays call her by her real name backstage. "If you tried to say 'Hey, Stefani' to her, she'd put on the voice of her character, and say, 'No, I'm Ginger!'" says a friend. "It was so bizarre, because we were kids."

After high school, Gaga moved to an NYU dorm on 11th Street and enrolled in Tisch, but quickly felt that she was further along creatively than some of her classmates. "Once you learn how to think about art, you can teach yourself," she says. By the second semester of her sophomore year, she told her parents that she wasn't going back to school—she was going to be a rock star. Her father reportedly agreed to pay her rent for a year on the condition that she reenroll if she was unsuccessful. "I left my entire family, got the cheapest apartment I could find, and ate shit until somebody would listen," she says.

Gaga moved into an apartment on the Lower East Side, with a futon for a couch and a Yoko Ono record hung over her bed. In high school, she had blonde highlights and let her curls run wild, but now she dyed her hair black and began to straighten it. She started the Stefani Germanotta Band with some friends from NYU, recording an EP of her Fiona Apple–type ballads at a studio underneath a liquor store in New Jersey. "Stefani had a following of about fifteen to twenty people at each show," says the guitarist, Calvin Pia. Says her manager at the time, Frankie Fredericks, "We'd kick it, jam, get drunk. She said she wanted to have a record deal by the time she was 21."

It was a lofty goal. What was missing, almost entirely, was any idea of how to get there. Like Madonna, she had a powerful sexual charisma. But whereas Madonna had seemed to calculate every step, every coupling, every stylistic turn in her quest for stardom, Gaga's story is partly one of youthful drift, waiting for lightning to strike, for the brilliant accident to happen. Gaga, though, had something Madonna didn't have: a truly great voice.

Gaga's year off from school was set to end in March 2006—her father had set a cutoff date of her birthday. A week before, the Stefani Germanotta Band performed at the Cutting Room on the same bill as Wendy Starland, a young singer-songwriter in the mold of Peter Gabriel. Starland had been working on tracks with Rob Fusari, a 38-year-old producer in Parsippany, New Jersey, who was known for his success with R&B hits for Destiny's Child and Will Smith. He mentioned to Starland that he was interested in locating a female singer to front a band like the Strokes—she didn't have to be good-looking, or even a great singer, but she had to have something about her you couldn't take your eyes off. "Stefani's confidence filled the room," says Starland. "Her presence is enormous. And fearless. I listened for the pitch, the tone, and timbre of her voice. Was she able to have a huge dynamic range? Was she able to get soft and then belt? And I felt that she was able to do all that while giving out this very powerful energy."

Gaga erupted in giggles when Starland ran up to her after the performance and told her, "I'm about to change your life." They rushed outside the club together, and Starland called Fusari on her cell phone. "Rob said, 'Why are you waking me up?' I said I found the girl. 'What? It's really one in a million. What's her name?' Stefani Germanotta. 'Um, you gotta be kidding me. What does she look like?' Don't worry about that. 'Does she have any good songs?' No. 'How is her band?' Awful." Starland laughs. "I wasn't pitching a product. I was pitching the girl."

When Fusari first met Gaga, he didn't see the private-school thing and thought she looked like "a Guidette, totally *Jersey Shore*." Then she jumped on his piano. "She didn't have that kind of undersinging character voice of Julian Casablancas, so I dropped the Strokes thing right away," says Fusari. "I thought she was a female John Lennon, to be totally honest. She was the oddest talent." Gaga began taking the bus from Port Authority to meet him at his New Jersey studio at 10 a.m., writing grungy songs with Zeppelin or Nirvana riffs on the piano and singing her quirky Jefferson Airplane lyrics over them. "I'm a hippie at heart, and Rob and I got tattoos one day," she says. "I wanted a tattoo of a peace sign, in memory of John and Yoko. I love that they traveled the world and said 'Give peace a chance,' and when asked to elaborate, they replied, 'No, just give peace a chance.' They thought the simplicity of that phrasing would change the world. It's so beautiful."

The two of them worked on rock songs for four months, but the reaction among their colleagues was negative; they also tried the singer-songwriter route, like Michelle Branch or Avril Lavigne, but those didn't gel either. "With those kinds of records, people are looking at the source of that music, who it's coming from," says Starland. "Those artists are usually classically beautiful, very steady, and more tranquil, in a way." Stefani agreed that her name was not going to fly: Fusari liked to sing Queen's "Radio Ga Ga" when she arrived at the studio, and she says that she came up with Lady Gaga off that joke. (Success indeed has many authors: Fusari says that he made it up inadvertently in a text message; Starland says it was the product of brainstorming.)

Then, one day, Fusari read an article in the *New York Times* about folk-pop artist Nelly Furtado, whose career had stalled since her 2000 hit "I'm Like a Bird": Timbaland, the hot producer of the moment, had remade her as a slinky dance artist. "We weren't going to get past A&R with a female rock record, and dance is so much easier," says Fusari. Gaga freaked out—you don't believe in me, she told him—but, from that day onward, they started working with a drum machine. They also began an affair, which made their artistic collaboration tumultuous. When Fusari didn't like her hooks, she would get teary-eyed and rant about feeling worthless. But he was rough on her, too. Gaga wasn't into fashion at this point: She liked leggings and sweatshirts, maybe with a shoulder out. "A couple times, she came to the studio in sweatpants, and I said, 'Really, Stef?'" says Fusari. "'What if I had Clive Davis in here today? I should call the session right now. Prince doesn't pick up ice cream at the 7-Eleven looking like Chris Rock. You're an artist now. You can't turn this on and off.'"

The problem was that she didn't know how to turn it on: Though she wanted to be a star, she didn't have a clear idea of what a star was, or where the main currents in pop culture were flowing. It was at this point that she began her serious study. Gaga picked up a biography of Prince, started shopping at American Apparel, and became entranced by aughties New Age bible *The Secret,* according to friends. As a Catholic-school girl, she interpreted Fusari's remarks as a signal to cut her skirts shorter and make them tighter, until one day they totally disappeared: All that was left were undies, sometimes with tights underneath.

Starland was still part of the picture: She lived near Gaga's parents' house, and Gaga would come over, crunching Doritos on the couch while watching *Sex and the City.* But when she tried to formalize her role in Gaga's life with a lawyer, she ran aground. "I got a call from my lawyer, who said that Stefani was going to give me a very generous Christmas gift," she says. One evening, she went over to the Germanottas' duplex, where Gaga's family, including her sister and grandmother, were celebrating, alongside a new little dog that Gaga liked to put booties on for fun. In the living room, Gaga presented her with an enormous Chanel box, revealing a black quilted purse with a gold chain. This might be a *Mean Girls* moment, where Gaga sticks it to an early collaborator, but in her naïve way, Gaga thought she was giving Starland something of great worth: the kind of purse she wanted so badly when she was young.

Bursting with confidence, Gaga was ready to be transformed. The dance-music scene that she'd fallen into turned out to be a perfect fit for her highly sexualized Catholic-school energy—she was a performer, rather than purely a singer. But the business into which she was launching herself was more difficult than ever. There are only four major labels these days; EMI is teetering on the edge, and if it misses its debt payments in June, Citigroup will own a record label. By 2006, labels were asking artists for a "360 deal": Instead of financing an artist's recording and then owning the masters, they wanted to share in the rights that traditionally belonged to the artist, like merchandise, live revenue, and endorsement fees. They were wary of any artist without a proven Internet following—the bet was on MySpace stars like Paramore or Panic at the Disco!—and there was Gaga, trying to go through the front door.

But she had a good track. "Beautiful, Dirty, Rich," a song about her friends from NYU asking their dads for money, drew prospective managers to a showcase downtown— everyone had to see her live because otherwise they didn't get it. She was also invited to Island Def Jam, near Times Square. L.A. Reid walked into the room while she was playing piano and started drumming to the beat on a table. "L.A. told me I was a star," says Gaga. She signed a deal with Island Def Jam for $850,000, according to a member of her camp, but after she produced the tracks, the line went dead. Three dinners were scheduled with Reid, but he canceled on each. Finally, Gaga got a call from her A&R rep at Island Def Jam: He had played a track in a meeting, and after a couple minutes Reid made a slitting motion across his throat. (Island Def Jam did not respond to requests for comment.) She was off the label.

Gaga was devastated. "She couldn't even talk when she told me because she was crying so hard," says Fusari. Unlike most struggling musicians, she chose to decline part of her advance so that she could walk with her masters (two of her six hits are on this original record). This was the first moment Gaga had experienced real hardship—the first moment in her life she really thought she might fail. "I went back to my apartment on the Lower East Side, and I was so depressed," she says. "That's when I started the real devotion to my music and art."

In contrast to Madonna, who gravitated to the forward edge of downtown and took herself with the utmost seriousness, Gaga, following her own instinct, headed toward a scene that was inclusive and fun but not particularly hip. In 2007, hipsters were listening to creative folk-rock bands out of Brooklyn like Grizzly Bear and Animal Collective; Gaga went for hard rock and downtown art trash. She fell desperately in love with Luc Carl, a 29-year-old drummer and manager of the rock bar St. Jerome's on Rivington Street. That's where she met Lady Starlight, an L.E.S. fixture in her thirties—M.A.C makeup artist, D.J., performance artist—who still plays shows for $60 but has a vast knowledge of rock music and style history. Starlight had gone through many incarnations, from mod meets *Cabaret* to Angela Bowie to leather-studded member of Judas Priest, which is what she was rocking at that moment.

"Starlight and I bonded instantly over her love of heavy metal and my love of boys that listen to heavy metal," says Gaga. "In those days, I'd wake up at noon in my apartment with my boyfriend and his loud Nikki Sixx hair, jeans on the floor, his stinky sneakers. He'd have his T-shirt on, no boxers. Then he would go do the books at St. Jerome's. I'd spin vinyl of David Bowie and New York Dolls in my kitchen, then write music with Lady Starlight. Eventually, I'd hear a honk outside my window: his old green Camino with a black hood. I'd run down the stairs yelling, 'Baby, baby, rev the engine,' and we'd drive over the Brooklyn Bridge, dress up, meet friends, play more music." She leans forward. "The Lower East Side has an arrogance, a stench. We walk and talk and live and breathe who we are with such an incredible stench that eventually the stench becomes a reality. Our vanity is a positive thing. It's made me the woman I am today."

Gaga started performing her songs with Starlight at small venues, and go-go dancing under a red lightbulb at Pianos—she'd wear a bikini and Luc Carl's fingerless black gloves, too big for her small hands. Dancing, diet pills, and one real meal a day was the way she finally lost weight, according to a friend. "I was naked on a bar with money hanging out of my tits and ass," she says. (Gaga has been very open about having taken cocaine during this period, but none of her friends from this time recalls any drug use; they say that she told them she only used cocaine when she was alone.) She and Starlight began opening for the glam-rockers Semi Precious Weapons; they looked like hair-metal groupies, running around the stage spraying Aqua Net on fire. "Gaga and I used to go shopping together, too," says Justin Tranter, lead singer of SPW. "Any sex store where 99 percent of the store was made up of DVDs and sex toys and 1 percent was actual clothing was our favorite place to shop. Her mom came to my loft once to pick up one Lucite pump that she left at the show the night before."

Gaga was enjoying herself, and, as usual, she spread her positive energy around. "She tried to make everyone feel good," says Brendan Sullivan, a.k.a. DJ VH1, who worked with her on some early shows. "I'd go to her apartment with my unpublished novel, and she would tell me that I was the most brilliant writer of my generation, the poet laureate of the Lower East Side. No one else was doing that for me." She wasn't talking much to Fusari—the romance was over—but he caught a show with Starlight and was appalled. "It was *Rocky Horror* meets eighties band, and I didn't get it at all," he says. "I told Stefani that I could get her another D.J., but she was like, 'I'm good.'"

But Fusari inserted himself back into the picture, in the spring of 2007, when he heard that his friend Vincent Herbert, a "hustler with a capital *H*," had landed a deal with Interscope to sign new artists. Within a couple days, Herbert had them on a plane to Los Angeles to meet Jimmy Iovine, the head of Interscope. Gaga came to the meeting in short shorts, go-go boots, and a cutoff T-shirt, but Iovine didn't show up; they flew back to New York, then were summoned back two weeks later. Iovine, an executive from Brooklyn who made his name on gangster rap with Dr. Dre and later rode the wave of nineties soft metal, is known for his good ears, and after listening to a few tracks in his office, he stood up and said, "Let's try this."

Gaga was worried that the label didn't think she was pretty enough to be a performer— she was recording tracks with RedOne, a Moroccan-Swedish producer, but they set her up as a songwriter for the Pussycat Dolls and Britney Spears (Spears was running around Los Angeles with a shaved head, so this wasn't a plum assignment). Herbert even spent his own money to send her to Lollapalooza over the summer, and he started to think that her look was wrong—someone in the audience shouted out "Amy Winehouse," and that made him nervous. "I told her that she needed to dye her hair blonde, and she did it right away," says Herbert. "God bless that girl, she really does listen."

On vacation in the Cayman Islands with Luc Carl, Gaga picked a fight, and he told her that he wasn't sure she was going to make it. "One day, you're not going to go into a deli without hearing me," she spat back. Back in New York, she sat down at a table at Beauty Bar with Sullivan, despondent. "I'm getting a nose job," she said. "I'm going to get a new nose, and I'm moving to L.A., and I'm going to be huge." He pleaded with her to be reasonable; like a true city kid, Gaga doesn't even know how to drive. "Whatever," she said. "I have the money. I just want to start fresh."

Sullivan told her about Warhol's *Before and After I* painting of two noses, before and after rhinoplasty, with a word that looks like RAPED at the top. She went up to the Met one afternoon and stood in front of it. She bought books about Warhol, which helped her make sense of her journey while providing a new vocabulary to talk about her creations. "Andy's books became her bible," says Darian Darling, a friend. "She would highlight them with a pen."

For Warhol, stardom was its own art form, empty imagistic vividness one of the most important forces. The person behind the mask could be as seemingly sweet and ordinary as Stefani Germanotta—and still be huge. Before Warhol, however unusual, she'd been in the general category of rock chick. He freed her to invent herself, like so many before her, expand herself, make herself a spectacle. While writing a club song called "Just Dance" with RedOne, Gaga tried to broaden her surface, remaking her style as a blonde space-age queen, a fabulous chick from the Factory era. The music was global-dance-party music—faster beats, synth sounds, with an ethos that made sense to her hippie heart. "Gaga and I believe that the world needs this music, that it is a way to unite," says RedOne. It wasn't the kind of music America was listening to at the moment, but she could be broken overseas and America might follow.

Suddenly, the clouds parted. One of Interscope's big artists, Akon, an R&B singer from Senegal with a massive global following, heard the track and lost his mind about it. Iovine pushed the button. She started working seriously with a choreographer: "I heard that this was the new Madonna, so I was like, 'Okay, let's hit it, pumpkin,'" says Laurieann Gibson. She recorded at the home studio of Kierszenbaum, the company's A&R head, as well. "I liked that she was talking about Prince's arrangements, styling, and presentation," he says. "Interest in Prince ebbs and flows, and two years ago, it was very, very maverick. Artists were saying 'Here's my record and album cover,' not talking about putting screens on the stage." She began wearing her crazy disco outfits everywhere. "She was never out of uniform, if you will," says Kierszenbaum. She also took a personal plunge: The day that she shot the video for "Just Dance" was the same day that she finally left Carl. Her heart may have been broken, but this was her new life. (Friends say that she has not been in love since, and the ritualistic killing of male lovers in her last three videos is related to this breakup.)

The newly liberated Gaga didn't feel like she needed to express her sexuality in a typically feminine way, either, and she became obsessed with androgyny, with the look of Liza Minnelli. She loved the free expression of drag queens—she wanted to wear the same clothes as those guys, cover herself with glitter, wear a wig. Though she wasn't from gay club culture, management began sending her to small clubs around the country. She even performed at a party at the Madison nightclub in the West Twenties hosted by Kenny Kenny, for $150. "When I went backstage to say hello, she said, 'Don't look at me! I don't have my makeup on yet.'" He laughs. "I was like, 'Uh, okay.' I've seen Amanda Lepore without her makeup."

Now, Gaga thought of herself not only as a superstar—she channeled Andy himself. She adopted his round black glasses and his wigs and spouted his wisdom. "It's as if I've been shouting at everyone, and now I'm whispering and everybody's leaning in to hear me," she says. "I've had to shout for so long because I was only given five minutes, but now I've got fifteen. Andy said you only needed fifteen minutes." She even started her own Factory, or the "Haus of Gaga," as she likes to call her entourage. There's Åkerlund; Gibson; her manager, Troy Carter; and the core team of stylist Nicola Formichetti and her primary collaborator Matt Williams, an art-school graduate whom she calls "Dada" (they have dated on and off during the past couple years). In May 2009, after she released "Paparazzi," a seven-minute video—thrown off the top of her mansion by her boyfriend, she's reborn as the robot from Fritz Lang's *Metropolis*—she became the haute-fashion world's pet. "Gaga had some archival pieces from Thierry Mugler, but after 'Paparazzi,' everything changed," says a former member of the Haus. "It happened in the blink of an eye. Suddenly, every fashion designer in the world was e-mailing her images."

Like Warhol at the Factory, when Gaga likes someone, he works; when she's done with him creatively, the door is closed. When Fusari sued her for $30 million in mid-March, over recording and merchandise fees, she immediately responded through her lawyers, saying that he acted as an unlicensed employment agent in his introduction to Herbert. "I developed an artist to grow with that artist," says Fusari, his voice pained. She's changed her cell number, and most of her old friends can't reach her anymore. "You know, she used to send texts out in New York inviting everyone on the Lower East Side to her shows, and not too many people would come," says Sullivan. "And after the vocal coach, dieting, exercising, and all the rest, now everyone wants to go. She has gotten annoyed by that: 'Why didn't they come before?'" He pauses. "You know, once she blew up, and everyone wanted a piece of her, we stopped calling her Gaga. We started calling her Stef again."

This summer, Gaga will come to the United States with her arena tour, one of the only pop stars who can fill a venue that large today. She spent a lot to get here—her tour has been losing about $3 million, according to music-industry sources, because she refuses to compromise on any aspect of the stage show. "I spent my entire publishing advance on my first tour," she told me. "I've had grand pianos that are more expensive than, like, a year's worth of rent." But profits are on their way soon. "Gaga's camp knows the exact date this summer that she will turn it around and get way into the black," says a source. With her 360 deal, Lady Gaga doesn't own as much of Lady Gaga as one would think. Essentially, this is a joint venture among Iovine, Universal Music CEO Doug Morris, and Sony/

ATV publishing head Marty Bandier. It's a good formula for the business: Hot looks and hot singles are the new monster albums.

These days, Gaga doesn't talk about Warhol much anymore—she's fully inhabiting the role she created. "She wants to be crazy, to make statements, make art, channel the past, experiment with performance art, try everything," says David LaChapelle, a collaborator and friend. "In Paris, she took four hours out of four days to visit museums. That's just not done by a pop star at the beginning of a career—not when you're in the bubble, when it's all about you." She's still overly dramatic—talking about monsters, or archly trying to presage her fall by covering herself in blood and hanging from a noose at the VMAs. "I feel that if I can show my demise artistically to the public, I can somehow cure my own legend," she explained recently. She turns down most interview requests, uninterested in combating misperceptions about her work. "Andy said that the critics were right," she says, with a shrug.

It's an unlikely rise, and an unlikely name, and a totally unreal image. But what's reality? "I believe that everyone can do what I'm doing," says Gaga, spreading her arms wide. "Everyone can access the parts of themselves that are great. I'm just a girl from New York City who decided to do this, after all. Rule the world! What's life worth living if you don't rule it?"

Invent

From the very beginning of this essay, Grigoriadis draws attention to the artificial nature of pop music and its stars. Do you think that there are "authentic" pop stars? Why do you think spectacle must necessarily be a part of a pop star's ascension to pop fame (think Miley Cyrus)? This article focuses on a female pop star. Do male pop stars have the same pressure to conform to these kinds of standards? What differences exist between what female and male pop stars must do in order to reach the top?

Compose

This article connects to another in the book, *The Time is Now: Acceptance and Conquest in Pop Music*. In it, author Rossen Ventzislavov uses Lady Gaga as an example when speaking to the role that the "forging of a pop personae" plays a part in the "co-optation of the public's imagination." In short, he argues that pop stars introduce themselves to the public in very strategic ways, often blurring the lines between fact and fiction when it comes to their personae. Grigoriadis notes Gaga's skill at doing just that at key moments in her career (her ambiguous sexuality, for example). Work to identify the moments in "Growing Up Gaga" where we can see her constructing her pop personae, then compose a paragraph or two where you offer a narrative summary of how Stefani Germanotta created "Lady Gaga."

Manufacture your own pop star! "By definition, a pop star is manufactured," Grigoriadis writes, and through "Growing Up Gaga," she offers us a backstage pass, so to speak, to the manufacturing of one of today's most successful and radical pop stars. Now it's your turn to create one. Using this essay as a guide, come up with a list of qualities that pop stars must have if they hope to achieve Lady Gaga-style fame. Remember, music is just part of it (and often not even the most important part). What kind of personality does your pop star need? What will he or she wear? How will he or she behave? These are just a few examples of the types of questions your group might explore in manufacturing a pop star. After deciding on the elements of your pop star, create a presentation where you introduce him/her to the world. Feel free to get creative in how you do so. For example, you could create a Facebook page, Twitter account, or a MySpace page where your star's music can be played. Have fun with it, but remember to attend carefully to the attributes that will make your creation a star.

Almost any writer on current pop music icons will quickly point out that the notion of a pop star is nothing new. Grigoriadis is no exception, and throughout her article she specifically gestures toward antecedents to Lady Gaga. David Bowie, Devo's Mark Mothersbaugh, Madonna, Grace Jones, New York Dolls, Liza Minnelli, and Andy Warhol are, in some fashion, all presented as precursors and influential figures for the personae Lady Gaga adopts. Pick one or two of these pop culture figures and research their history, working to construct a story about the manner in which they grew into the cultural icon for which they are now recognized.

Daniel J. Levitin is a James McGill Professor of Psychology, Music, and Computer Science at McGill University and Dean of Arts and Humanities at the Minerva Schools at KGI. He is the author of two international best-sellers: This Is Your Brain On Music: The Science of a Human Obsession *and* The World in Six Songs: How the Musical Brain Created Human Nature. *He is currently one of the best-selling scientist writers of the last ten years. Prior to entering academia, Levitin was a record producer and engineer with artists such as Blue Öyster Cult, Santana, and Stevie Wonder.*

excerpt from
THIS IS YOUR BRAIN ON MUSIC—"MY FAVORITE THINGS: WHY DO WE LIKE THE MUSIC WE LIKE"

By Daniel J. Levitin

You wake from a deep sleep and open your eyes. It's dark. The distant regular beating at the periphery of your hearing is still there. You rub your eyes with your hands, but you can't make out any shapes or forms. Time passes, but how long? Half an hour? One hour? Then you hear a different but recognizable sound—an amorphous, moving, wiggly sound with fast beating, a pounding that you can feel in your feet. The sounds start and stop without definition. Gradually building up and dying down, they weave together with no clear beginnings or endings. These familiar sounds are comforting, you've heard them before. As you listen, you have a vague notion of what will come next, and it does, even as the sounds remain remote and muddled, as though you're listening underwater.

Inside the womb, surrounded by amniotic fluid, the fetus hears sounds. It hears the heartbeat of its mother, at times speeding up, at other times slowing down. And the fetus hears music, as was recently discovered by Alexandra Lamont of Keele University in the UK. She found that, a year after they are born, children recognize and prefer music they were exposed to in the womb. The auditory system of the fetus is fully functional about twenty weeks after conception. In Lamont's experiment, mothers played a single piece of music to their babies repeatedly during the final three months of gestation. Of course, the babies were also hearing—through the waterlike filtering of the amniotic fluid in the womb—all of the sounds of their mothers' daily life, including other music, conversations, and environmental noises. But one particular piece was singled out for each baby to hear on a regular basis. The singled-out pieces included classical (Mozart, Vivaldi), Top 40 (Five, Backstreet Boys), reggae (UB40, Ken Boothe) and world beat (Spirits of Nature). After birth, the mothers were not allowed to play the experimental song to their infants. Then, one year later, Lamont played babies the music that they had heard in the womb, along with another piece of music chosen to be matched for style and tempo. For example, a baby who had heard UB40's reggae track "Many Rivers to Cross" heard that piece again, a year later, along with "Stop Loving You" by the reggae artist Freddie McGregor. Lamont then determined which one the babies preferred.

How do you know which of two stimuli a preverbal infant prefers? Most infant researchers use a technique known as the conditioned head-turning procedure, developed by Robert Fantz in the 1960s, and refined by John Columbo, Anne Fernald, the late Peter Jusczyk, and their colleagues. Two loudspeakers are set up in the laboratory and the infant is placed (usually on his mother's lap) between the speakers. When the infant looks at one speaker, it starts to play music or some other sound, and when he looks at the other speaker, it starts to play different music or a different sound. The infant quickly learns that he can control what is playing by where he is looking; he learns, that is, that the conditions of the experiment are under his control. The experimenters make sure that they counterbalance (randomize) the location that the different stimuli come from; that is, half the time the stimulus under study comes from one speaker and half the time it comes from the other. When Lamont did this with the infants in her study, she found that they tended to look longer at the speaker that was playing music they had heard in the womb than at the speaker playing the novel music, confirming that they preferred the music to which they had the prenatal exposure. A control group of one-year-olds who had not heard any of the music before showed no preference, confirming that there was nothing about the music itself that caused these results. Lamont also found that, all things being equal, the young infant prefers fast, upbeat music to slow music.

These findings contradict the long-standing notion of childhood amnesia—that we can't have any veridical memories before around the age of five. Many people claim to have memories from early childhood around age two and three, but it is difficult to know whether these are true memories of the original event, or rather, memory of someone telling us about the event later. The young child's brain is still undeveloped, functional specialization of the brain isn't complete, and neural pathways are still in the process of being made. The child's mind is trying to assimilate as much information as possible in as short a time as possible; there are typically large gaps in the child's understanding, awareness, or memory for events because he hasn't yet learned how to distinguish important events from unimportant ones, or to encode experience systematically. Thus, the young child is a prime candidate for suggestion, and could unwittingly encode, as his own, stories that were told to him about himself. It appears that for music even prenatal experience is encoded in memory, and can be accessed in the absence of language or explicit awareness of the memory.

A study made the newspapers and morning talk shows several years ago, claiming that listening to Mozart for ten minutes a day made you smarter ("the Mozart Effect"). Specifically, music listening, it was claimed, can improve your performance on spatial-reasoning tasks given immediately after the listening session (which some journalists thought implied mathematical ability as well). U.S. congressmen were passing resolutions, the governor of Georgia appropriated funds to buy a Mozart CD for every newborn baby Georgian. Most scientists found ourselves in an uncomfortable position. Although we do believe intuitively that music can enhance other cognitive skills, and although we would all like to see more governmental funding for school music programs, the actual study that claimed this contained many scientific flaws. The study was claiming some of the right things but for the wrong reasons. Personally, I found all the hubbub a bit offensive because the implication was that music should not be studied in and of itself, or for its own right, but only if it could help people to do better on other, "more important" things. Think how absurd this would sound if we turned it inside out. If I claimed that studying mathematics helped musical ability, would policy makers start pumping money into math for that reason? Music has often been the poor stepchild of public schools, the first program to get cut when there are funding problems, and people frequently try to justify it in terms of its collateral benefits, rather than letting music exist for its own rewards.

The problem with the "music makes you smarter" study turned out to be straightforward: The experimental controls were inadequate, and the tiny difference in spatial ability between the two groups, according to research by Bill Thompson, Glenn Schellenberg, and others, all turned on the choice of a control task. Compared to sitting in a room and doing nothing, music listening looked pretty good. But if subjects in the control task were given the slightest mental stimulation—hearing a book on tape, reading, etc.—there was no advantage for music listening. Another problem with the study was that there was no plausible mechanism proposed by which this might work—how could music listening increase spatial performance?

Glenn Schellenberg has pointed out the importance of distinguishing short-term from long-term effects of music. The Mozart Effect referred to immediate benefits, but other research *has* revealed long-term effects of musical activity. Music listening enhances or changes certain neural circuits, including the density of dendritic connections in the primary auditory cortex. The Harvard neuroscientist Gottfried Schlaug has shown that the front portion of the corpus callosum—the mass of fibers connecting the two cerebral hemispheres—is significantly larger in musicians than nonmusicians, and particularly for musicians who began their training early. This reinforces the notion that musical operations become bilateral with increased training, as musicians coordinate and recruit neural structures in both the left and right hemisphere.

Several studies have found microstructural changes in the cerebellum after the acquisition of motor skills, such as are acquired by musicians, including an increased number and density of synapses. Schlaug found that musicians tended to have larger cerebellums than nonmusicians, and an increased concentration of gray matter; gray matter is that part of the brain that contains the cell bodies, axons, and dendrites, and is understood to be responsible for information processing, as opposed to white matter, which is responsible for information transmission.

Whether these structural changes in the brain translate to enhanced abilities in nonmusical domains has not been proven, but music listening and music therapy have been shown to help people overcome a broad range of psychological and physical problems. But, to return to a more fruitful line of inquiry regarding musical taste ... Lamont's results are important because they show that the prenatal and newborn brain are able to store memories and retrieve them over long periods of time. More practically, the results indicate that the environment—even when mediated by amniotic fluid and by the womb—can affect a child's development and preferences. So the seeds of musical preference are sown in the womb, but there must be more to the story than that, or children would simply gravitate toward the music their mothers like, or that plays in Lamaze classes. What we can say is that musical preferences are influenced, but not determined, by what we hear in the womb. There also is an extended period of acculturation, during which the infant takes in the music of the culture she is born into. There were reports a few years ago that prior to becoming used to the music of a foreign (to us) culture, all infants prefer Western music to other musics, regardless of their culture or race. These findings were not corroborated, but rather, it was found that infants do show a preference for consonance over dissonance. Appreciating dissonance comes later in life, and people differ in how much dissonance they can tolerate.

There is probably a neural basis for this. Consonant intervals and dissonant intervals are processed via separate mechanisms in the auditory cortex. Recent results from studying the electrophysiological responses of humans and monkeys to sensory dissonance (that is, chords that sound dissonant by virtue of their frequency ratios, not due to any harmonic or musical context) show that neurons in the primary auditory cortex—the first level of cortical processing for sound—synchronize their firing rates during dissonant chords, but not during consonant chords. Why that would create a preference for consonance is not yet clear.

We do know a bit about the infant's auditory world. Although infant ears are fully functioning four months before birth, the developing brain requires months or years to reach full auditory processing capacity. Infants recognize transpositions of pitch and of time (tempo changes), indicating they are capable of relational processing, something that even the most advanced computers still can't do very well. Jenny Saffran of the University of Wisconsin and Laurel Trainor of McMaster University have gathered evidence that infants can also attend to absolute-pitch cues if the task requires it, suggesting a cognitive flexibility previously unknown: Infants can employ different modes of processing—

presumably mediated by different neural circuits—depending on what will best help them to solve the problem at hand.

Trehub, Dowling, and others have shown that contour is the most salient musical feature for infants, who can detect contour similarities and differences even across thirty seconds of retention. Recall that *contour* refers to the pattern of musical pitch in a melody—the sequence of ups and downs that the melody takes—regardless of the size of the interval. Someone attending to contour exclusively would encode only that the melody goes up, for example, but not by how much. Infants' sensitivity to musical contour parallels their sensitivity to linguistic contours—which separate questions from exclamations, for example, and which are part of what linguists call prosody. Fernald and Trehub have documented the ways in which parents speak differently to infants than to older children and adults, and this holds across cultures. The resulting manner of speaking uses a slower tempo, an extended pitch range, and a higher overall pitch level.

Mothers (and to a lesser extent, fathers) do this quite naturally without any explicit instruction to do so, using an exaggerated intonation that the researchers call infant-directed speech or motherese. We believe that motherese helps to call the babies' attention to the mother's voice, and helps to distinguish words within the sentence. Instead of saying, as we would to an adult, "This is a ball," motherese would entail something like, "Seeeeee?" (with the pitch of the eee's going up to the end of the sentence). "See the BAAAAAALLLLLL?" (with the pitch covering an extended range and going up again at the end of the word *ball*). In such utterances, the contour is a signal that the mother is asking a question or making a statement, and by exaggerating the differences between up and down contours, the mother calls attention to them. In effect, the mother is creating a prototype for a question and a prototype for a declaration, and ensuring that the prototypes are easily distinguishable. When a mother gives an exclamatory scold, quite naturally—and again without explicit training—she is likely to create a third type of prototypical utterance, one that is short and clipped, without much pitch variation: "No!" (pause) "No! Bad!" (pause) "I said no!" Babies seem to come hardwired with an ability to detect and track contour, preferentially, over specific pitch intervals.

Trehub also showed that infants are more able to encode consonant intervals such as perfect fourth and fifth than dissonant ones, like the tritone. Trehub found that the unequal steps of our scale make it easier to process intervals even early in infancy. She and her colleagues played nine-month-olds the regular seven-note major scale and two scales she invented. For one of these invented scales, she divided the octave into eleven equal-space steps and then selected seven tones that made one- and two-step patterns, and for the other she divided the octave into seven equal steps. The infants' task was to detect a mistuned tone. Adults performed well with the major scale, but poorly with both of the artificial, never-before-heard scales. In contrast, the infants did equally well on both unequally tuned scales and on the equally tuned ones. From prior work, it is believed that nine-month-olds have not yet incorporated a mental schema for the major scale, so this suggests a general processing advantage for unequal steps, something our major scale has.

In other words, our brains and the musical scales we use seem to have coevolved. It is no accident that we have the funny, asymmetric arrangement of notes in the major scale: It is easier to learn melodies with this arrangement, which is a result of the physics of sound production (via the overtone series we visited earlier); the set of tones we use in our major scale are very close in pitch to the tones that constitute the overtone series. Very early in childhood, most children start to spontaneously vocalize, and these early vocalizations can sound a lot like singing. Babies explore the range of their voices, and begin to explore phonetic production, in response to the sounds they are bringing in from the world around them. The more music they hear, the more likely they are to include pitch and rhythmic variations in their spontaneous vocalizations.

Young children start to show a preference for the music of their culture by age two, around the same time they begin to develop specialized speech processing. At first, children tend to like simple songs, where *simple* means music that has clearly defined themes (as opposed to, say, four-part counterpoint) and chord progressions that resolve in direct and easily predictable ways. As they mature, children start to tire of easily predictable music and search for music that holds more challenge. According to Mike Posner, the frontal lobes and the anterior cingulate—a structure just behind the frontal lobes that directs attention—are not fully formed in children, leading to an inability to pay attention to several things at once; children show difficulty attending to one stimulus when distracters are present. This accounts for why children under the age of eight or so have so much difficulty singing "rounds" like "Row, Row, Row Your Boat." Their attentional system—specifically the network that connects the cingulate gyrus (the larger structure within which the anterior cingulate sits) and the orbitofrontal regions of the brain—cannot adequately filter out unwanted or distracting stimuli. Children who have not yet reached the developmental stage of being able to exclude irrelevant auditory information face a world of great sonic complexity with all sounds coming in as a sensory barrage. They may try to follow the part of the song that their group is supposed to be singing, only to be distracted and tripped up by the competing parts in the round. Posner has shown that certain exercises adapted from attention and concentration games used by NASA can help accelerate the development of the child's attentional ability.

The developmental trajectory, in children, of first preferring simple and then more complex songs is a generalization, of course; not all children like music in the first place, and some children develop a taste for music that is off the beaten path, oftentimes through pure serendipity. I became fascinated with big band and swing music when I was eight, around the time my grandfather gave me his collection of 78 rpm records from the World War II era. I was initially attracted by novelty songs, such as "The Syncopated Clock," "Would You Like to Swing on a Star," "The Teddy Bear's Picnic," and "Bibbidy Bobbidy Boo"—

songs that were made for children. But sufficient exposure to the relatively exotic chord patterns and voicings of Frank de Vol's and Leroy Anderson's orchestras became part of my mental wiring, and I soon found myself listening to all kinds of jazz; the children's jazz opened the neural doors to make jazz in general palatable and understandable.

Researchers point to the teen years as the turning point for musical preferences. It is around the age of ten or eleven that most children take on music as a real interest, even those children who didn't express such an interest in music earlier. As adults, the music we tend to be nostalgic for, the music that feels like it is "our" music, corresponds to the music we heard during these years. One of the first signs of Alzheimer's disease (a disease characterized by changes in nerve cells and neurotransmitter levels, as well as destruction of synapses) in older adults is memory loss. As the disease progresses, memory loss becomes more profound. Yet many of these old-timers can still remember how to sing the songs they heard when they were fourteen. Why fourteen? Part of the reason we remember songs from our teenage years is because those years were times of self-discovery, and as a consequence, they were emotionally charged; in general, we tend to remember things that have an emotional component because our amygdala and neurotransmitters act in concert to "tag" the memories as something important. Part of the reason also has to do with neural maturation and pruning; it is around fourteen that the wiring of our musical brains is approaching adultlike levels of completion.

There doesn't seem to be a cutoff point for acquiring new tastes in music, but most people have formed their tastes by the age of eighteen or twenty. Why this is so is not clear, but several studies have found it to be the case. Part of the reason may be that in general, people tend to become less open to new experiences as they age. During our teenage years, we begin to discover that there exists a world of different ideas, different cultures, different people. We experiment with the idea that we don't have to limit our life's course, our personalities, or our decisions to what we were taught by our parents, or to the way we were brought up. We also seek out different kinds of music. In Western culture in particular, the choice of music has important social consequences. We listen to the music that our friends listen to. Particularly when we are young, and in search of our identity, we form bonds or social groups with people whom we want to be like, or whom we believe we have something in common with. As a way of externalizing the bond, we dress alike, share activities, and listen to the same music. Our group listens to this kind of music, those people listen to that kind of music. This ties into the evolutionary idea of music as a vehicle for social bonding and societal cohesion. Music and musical preferences become a mark of personal and group identity and of distinction.

To some degree, we might say that personality characteristics are associated with, or predictive of, the kind of music that people like. But to a large degree, it is determined by more or less chance factors: where you went to school, who you hung out with, what music they happened to be listening to. When I lived in northern California as a kid,

Creedence Clearwater Revival was huge—they were from just down the road. When I moved to southern California, CCR's brand of quasi-cowboy, country-hick music didn't fit in well with the surfer/Hollywood culture that embraced the Beach Boys and more theatrical performance artists like David Bowie.

Also, our brains are developing and forming new connections at an explosive rate throughout adolescence, but this slows down substantially after our teenage years, the formative phase when our neural circuits become structured out of our experiences. This process applies to the music we hear; new music becomes assimilated within the framework of the music we were listening to during this critical period. We know that there are critical periods for acquiring new skills, such as language. If a child doesn't learn language by the age of six or so (whether a first or a second language), the child will never learn to speak with the effortlessness that characterizes most native speakers of a language. Music and mathematics have an extended window, but not an unlimited one: If a student hasn't had music lessons or mathematical training prior to about age twenty, he can still learn these subjects, but only with great difficulty, and it's likely that he will never "speak" math or music like someone who learned them early. This is because of the biological course for synaptic growth. The brain's synapses are programmed to grow for a number of years, making new connections. After that time, there is a shift toward pruning, to get rid of unneeded connections.

Neuroplasticity is the ability of the brain to reorganize itself. Although in the last five years there have been some impressive demonstrations of brain reorganization that used to be thought impossible, the amount of reorganization that can occur in most adults is vastly less than can occur in children and adolescents.

Of course, there are individual differences. Just as some people can heal broken bones or skin cuts faster than others, so, too, can some people forge new connections more easily than others. Generally, between the ages of eight and fourteen, pruning starts to occur in the frontal lobes, the seat of higher thought and reasoning, planning, and impulse control. Myelination starts to ramp up during this time. Myelin is a fatty substance that coats the axons, speeding up synaptic transmission. (This is why as children get older, generally, problem solving becomes more rapid and they are able to solve more complex problems.) Myelination of the whole brain is generally completed by age twenty. Multiple sclerosis is one of several degenerative diseases that can affect the myelin sheath surrounding the neurons.

The balance between simplicity and complexity in music also informs our preferences. Scientific studies of like and dislike across a variety of aesthetic domains—painting, poetry, dance, and music—have shown that an orderly relationship exists between the complexity of an artistic work and how much we like it. Of course, complexity is an entirely subjective concept. In order for the notion to make any sense, we have to allow for the idea that what seems impenetrably complex to Stanley might fall right in the "sweet spot" of preference for Oliver. Similarly, what one person finds insipid and hideously simple, another person might find difficult to understand, based on differences in background, experience, understanding, and cognitive schemas.

In a sense, schemas are everything. They frame our understanding; they're the system into which we place the elements and interpretations of an aesthetic object. Schemas inform our cognitive models and expectations. With one schema, Mahler's Fifth is perfectly interpretable, even upon hearing it for the first time: It is a symphony, it follows symphonic form with four movements; it contains a main theme and subthemes, and repetitions of the theme; the themes are manifested through orchestral instruments, as opposed to African talking drums or fuzz bass. Those familiar with Mahler's Fourth will recognize that the Fifth opens with a variation on that same theme, and even at the same pitch. Those well acquainted with Mahler's work will recognize that the composer includes quotations from three of his own songs. Musically educated listeners will be aware that most symphonies from Haydn to Brahms and Bruckner typically begin and end in the same key. Mahler flouts this convention with his Fifth, moving from C-sharp minor to A minor and finally ending in D major. If you had not learned to hold in your mind a sense of key as the symphony develops, or if you did not have a sense of the normal trajectory of a symphony, this would be meaningless; but for the seasoned listener, this flouting of convention brings a rewarding surprise, a violation of expectations, especially when such key changes are done skillfully so as not to be jarring. Lacking a proper symphonic schema, or if the listener holds another schema, perhaps that of an aficionado of Indian ragas, Mahler's Fifth is nonsensical or perhaps rambling, one musical idea melding amorphously into the next, with no boundaries, no beginnings or endings that appear as part of a coherent whole. The schema frames our perception, our cognitive processing, and ultimately our experience.

When a musical piece is too simple we tend not to like it, finding it trivial. When it is too complex, we tend not to like it, finding it unpredictable—we don't perceive it to be grounded in anything familiar. Music, or any art form for that matter, has to strike the right balance between simplicity and complexity in order for us to like it. Simplicity and complexity relate to familiarity, and *familiarity* is just another word for a schema.

It is important in science, of course, to define our terms. What is "too simple" or "too complex"? An operational definition is that we find a piece too simple when we find it trivially predictable, similar to something we have experienced before, and without the slightest challenge. By analogy, consider the game tic-tac-toe. Young children find it endlessly fascinating, because it has many features that contribute to interest at their level of cognitive ability: It has clearly defined rules that any child can easily articulate; it has an element of surprise in that the player never knows for sure exactly what her opponent will do next; the game is dynamic, in that one's own next move is influenced by what one's opponent did; when the game will end, who will win, or whether it will be a draw is undetermined, yet there is an outer limit of nine moves. That indeterminacy leads to tension and expectations, and the tension is finally released when the game is over.

As the child develops increasing cognitive sophistication, she eventually learns strategies—the person who moves second cannot win against a competent player; the best the second player can hope for is a draw. When the sequence of moves and the end point of the game become predictable, tic-tac-toe loses its appeal. Of course, adults can still enjoy playing the game with children, but we enjoy seeing the pleasure on the child's face and we enjoy the process—spread out over several years—of the child learning to unlock the mysteries of the game as her brain develops.

To many adults, Raffi and Barney the Dinosaur are the musical equivalents of tic-tac-toe. When music is too predictable, the outcome too certain, and the "move" from one note or chord to the next contains no element of surprise, we find the music unchallenging and simplistic. As the music is playing (particularly if you're engaged with focused attention), your brain is thinking ahead to what the different possibilities for the next note are, where the music is going, its trajectory, its intended direction, and its ultimate end point. The composer has to lull us into a state of trust and security; we have to allow him to take us on a harmonic journey; he has to give us enough little rewards—completions of expectations—that we feel a sense of order and a sense of place.

Say you're hitchhiking from Davis, California, to San Francisco. You want the person who picks you up to take the normal route, Highway 80. You might be willing to tolerate a few shortcuts, especially if the driver is friendly, believable, and is up-front about what he's doing. ("I'm just going to cut over here on Zamora Road to avoid some construction on the freeway.") But if the driver takes you out on back roads with no explanation, and you reach a point where you no longer see any landmarks, your sense of safety is sure to be violated. Of course, different people, with different personality types, react differently to such unanticipated journeys, musical or vehicular. Some react with sheer panic ("That Stravinsky is going to kill me!") and some react with a sense of adventure at the thrill of discovery ("Coltrane is doing something weird here, but what the hell, it won't hurt me to stick around awhile longer, I can take care of my harmonic self and find my way back to musical reality if I have to").

To continue the analogy with games, some games have such a complicated set of rules that the average person doesn't have the patience to learn them. The possibilities for what can happen on any given turn are too numerous or too unpredictable (to the novice) to contemplate. But an inability to predict what will happen next is not always a sign that a game holds eventual interest if only one sticks with it long enough. A game may have a completely unpredictable course no matter how much practice you have with it—many board games simply involve rolling the dice and waiting to see what happens to you. Chutes and Ladders and Candy Land are like this. Children enjoy the sense of surprise, but adults can find the game tedious because, although no one can predict exactly what will happen (the game is a function of the random throw of the dice), the outcome has no structure whatsoever, and moreover, there is no amount of skill on the part of the player that can influence the course of the game.

Music that involves too many chord changes, or unfamiliar structure, can lead many listeners straight to the nearest exit, or to the "skip" button on their music players. Some games, such as Go, Axiom, or Zendo are sufficiently complicated or opaque to the novice that many people give up before getting very far: The structure presents a steep learning curve, and the novice can't be sure that the time invested will be worth it. Many of us have the same experience with unfamiliar music, or unfamiliar musical forms. People may tell you that Schönberg is brilliant, or that Tricky is the next Prince, but if you can't figure out what is going on in the first minute or so of one of their pieces, you may find yourself wondering if the payoff will justify the effort you spend trying to sort it all out. We tell ourselves that if we only listen to it enough times, we may begin to understand it and to like it as much as our friends do. Yet, we recall other times in our lives when we invested hours of prime listening time in an artist and never arrived at the point where we "got it." Trying to appreciate new music can be like contemplating a new friendship in that it takes time, and sometimes there is nothing you can do to speed it up. At a neural level, we need to be able to find a few landmarks in order to invoke a cognitive schema. If we hear a piece of radically new music enough times, some of that piece will eventually become encoded in our brains and we will develop landmarks. If the composer is skillful, those parts of the piece that become our landmarks will be the very ones that the composer intended they should be; his knowledge of composition and human perception and memory will have allowed him to create certain "hooks" in the music that will eventually stand out in our minds.

Structural processing is one source of difficulty in appreciating a new piece of music. Not understanding symphonic form, or the sonata form, or the AABA structure of a jazz standard, is the music-listening equivalent of driving on a highway with no road signs: You never know where you are or when you'll arrive at your destination (or even at an interim spot that is not your destination, but one that provides an orienting landmark). For example, many people just don't "get" jazz; they say that it sounds like an unstructured, crazy, and formless improvisation, a musical competition to squeeze as many notes as possible into as small a space as possible. There are more than a half-dozen subgenres of what people collectively call "jazz": Dixieland, boogie-woogie, big band, swing, bebop, "straight-ahead," acid-jazz, fusion, metaphysical, and so on. "Straight-ahead," or "classic jazz," as it is sometimes called, is more or less the standard form of jazz, analogous to the sonata or the symphony in classical music, or what a typical song by the Beatles or Billy Joel or the Temptations is to rock music.

In classic jazz, the artist begins by playing the main theme of the song; often a well-known one from Broadway, or one that has already been a hit for someone else; such songs are called "standards," and they include "As Time Goes By," "My Funny Valentine," and "All of Me." The artist runs through the complete form of the song once—typically two verses and the chorus (otherwise known as a "refrain"), followed by another verse. The chorus is part of a song that repeats regularly throughout; the verses are what change. We call this form AABA, where the letter *A* represents the verse and the letter *B* represents the chorus. AABA means we play verse-verse-chorus-verse. Many other variations are possible, of course. Some songs have a C section, called the bridge.

The term *chorus* is used to mean not just the second section of the song, but also one run through the entire form. In other words, running through the AABA portion of a song once is called "playing one chorus." When I play jazz, if someone says, "Play the chorus," or, "Let's go over the chorus" (using the word *the*), we all assume he means a section of the song. If, instead someone says, "Let's run through one chorus," or, "Let's do a couple of choruses," we know he means the entire form.

"Blue Moon" (Frank Sinatra, Billie Holiday) is an example of a song with AABA form. A jazz artist may play around with the rhythm or feel of the song, and may embellish the melody. After playing through the form of the song once, what jazz musicians refer to as "the head," the different members of the ensemble take turns improvising new music over the chord progression and form of the original song. Each musician plays through one or more choruses and then the next musician takes over at the beginning of the head. During the improvisations, some artists stick close to the original melody, some add ever distant and exotic harmonic departures. When everyone has had a chance to improvise, the band returns to the head, playing it more or less straight, and then they're done. The improvisations can go on for many minutes—it is not uncommon for a jazz rendition of a two- or three-minute song to stretch out to ten to fifteen minutes. There is also a typical order to how the musicians take turns: The horns go first, followed by the piano and/or guitar, followed by the bass player. Sometimes the drummer also improvises, and he would typically follow the bass. Sometimes the musicians also share part of a chorus—each musician playing four or eight measures, and then handing off the solo to another musician, a sort of musical relay race.

To the newbie, the whole thing may seem chaotic. Yet, simply knowing that the improvisation takes place over the original chords and form of the song can make a big difference in orienting the neophyte to where in the song the players are. I often advise new listeners to jazz to simply hum the main tune in their mind once the improvisation begins—this is what the improvisers themselves are often doing—and that enriches the experience considerably.

Each musical genre has its own set of rules and its own form. The more we listen, the more those rules become instantiated in memory. Unfamiliarity with the structure can lead to frustration or a simple lack of appreciation. Knowing a genre or style is to effectively have a category built around it, and to be able to categorize new songs as being either members or nonmembers of that category—or in some cases, as "partial" or "fuzzy" members of the category, members subject to certain exceptions.

The orderly relationship between complexity and liking is referred to as the inverted-U function because of the way a graph would be drawn that relates these two factors. Imagine a graph in which the x-axis is how complex a piece of music is (to you) and the y-axis is how much you like it. At the bottom left of this graph, close to the origin, there would be a point for music that is very simple and your reaction being that you don't like it. As the music increases in complexity, your liking increases as well. The two variables follow each other for quite a while on the graph—increased complexity yields increased liking, until you cross some personal threshold and go from disliking the piece intensely to actually liking it quite a bit. But at some point as we increase complexity, the music becomes too complex, and your liking for it begins to decrease. Now more complexity in the music leads to less and less liking, until you cross another threshold and you no longer like the music at all. Too complex and you absolutely hate the music. The shape of such a graph would make an inverted U or an inverted V.

The inverted-U hypothesis is not meant to imply that the only reason you might like or dislike a piece of music is because of its simplicity or complexity. Rather, it is intended to account for this variable. The elements of music can themselves form a barrier to appreciation of a new piece of music. Obviously, if music is too loud or too soft, this can be problematic. But even the dynamic range of a piece—the disparity between the loudest and softest parts—can cause some people to reject it. This can be especially true for people who use music to regulate their mood in a specific way. Someone who wants music to calm her down, or someone else who wants music to pep him up for a workout, is probably not going to want to hear a musical piece that runs the loudness gamut all the way from very soft to very loud, or emotionally from sad to exhilarating (as does Mahler's Fifth, for example). The dynamic range as well as the emotional range is simply too wide, and may create a barrier to entry.

Pitch can also play into preference. Some people can't stand the thumping low beats of modern hip-hop, others can't stand what they describe as the high-pitched whininess of violins. Part of this may be a matter of physiology; literally, different ears may transmit different parts of the frequency spectrum, causing some sounds to appear pleasant and others aversive. There may also exist psychological associations, both positive and negative, to various instruments.

Rhythm and rhythmic patterns influence our ability to appreciate a given musical genre or piece. Many musicians are drawn to Latin music because of the complexity of the rhythms. To an outsider, it all just sounds "Latin," but to someone who can make out the nuances of when a certain beat is strong relative to other beats, Latin music is a whole world of interesting complexity: bossa nova, samba, rhumba, beguine, mambo, merengue, tango—each is a completely distinct and identifiable style of music. Some people genuinely enjoy Latin music and Latin rhythms without being able to tell them apart, of course, but others find the rhythms too complicated and unpredictable, and this is a turnoff to them. I've found that if I teach one or two Latin rhythms to listeners, they come to appreciate them; it is all a question of grounding and having a schema. For other listeners, rhythms that are too simple are the deal-breaker for a style of music. The typical complaint of my parents' generation about rock and roll, apart from how loud it seemed to them, was that it all had the same beat.

Timbre is another barrier for many people and its influence is almost certainly increasing, as I argued in Chapter 1. The first time I heard John Lennon or Donald Fagen sing, I thought the voices unimaginably strange. I didn't want to like them. Something kept me going back to listen, though—perhaps it was the strangeness—and they wound up being two of my favorite voices; voices that now have gone beyond familiar and approach what I can only call intimate; I feel as though these voices have become incorporated into who I am. And at a neural level, they have. Having listened to thousands of hours of both these singers, and tens of thousands of playings of their songs, my brain has developed circuitry that can pick out their voices from among thousands of others, even when they sing something I've never heard them sing before. My brain has encoded every vocal nuance and every timbral flourish, so that if I hear an alternate version of one of their songs—as we do on the *John Lennon Collection* of demo versions of his albums—I can immediately recognize the ways in which this performance deviates from the one I have stored in the neural pathways of my long-term memory.

As with other sorts of preferences, our musical preferences are also influenced by what we've experienced before, and whether the outcome of that experience was positive or negative. If you had a negative experience once with pumpkin—say, for example, it made you sick to your stomach—you are likely to be wary of future excursions into pumpkin gustation. If you've had only a few, but largely positive, encounters with broccoli, you might be willing to try a new broccoli recipe, perhaps broccoli soup, even if you've never had it before. The one positive experience begets others.

The types of sounds, rhythms, and musical textures we find pleasing are generally extensions of previous positive experiences we've had with music in our lives. This is because hearing a song that you like is a lot like having any other pleasant sensory experience—eating chocolate, fresh-picked raspberries, smelling coffee in the morning, seeing a work of art or the peaceful face of someone you love who is sleeping. We take pleasure in the sensory experience, and find comfort in its familiarity and the safety that familiarity brings. I can look at a ripe raspberry, smell it, and anticipate that it will taste good and that the experience will be safe—I won't get sick. If I've never seen a loganberry before, there are enough points in common with the raspberry that I can take the chance in eating it and anticipate that it will be safe.

Safety plays a role for a lot of us in choosing music. To a certain extent, we surrender to music when we listen to it—we allow ourselves to trust the composers and musicians with a part of our hearts and our spirits; we let the music take us somewhere outside of ourselves. Many of us feel that great music connects us to something larger than our own existence, to other people, or to God. Even when music doesn't transport us to an emotional place that is transcendent, music can change our mood. We might be understandably reluctant, then, to let down our guard, to drop our emotional defenses, for just anyone. We will do so if the musicians and composer make us feel safe. We want to know that our vulnerability is not going to be exploited. This is part of the reason why so many people can't listen to Wagner. Due to his pernicious anti-Semitism, the sheer vulgarity of his mind (as Oliver Sacks describes it), and his music's association with the Nazi regime, some people don't feel safe listening to his music. Wagner has always disturbed me profoundly, and not just his music, but also the *idea* of listening to it. I feel reluctant to give into the seduction of music created by so disturbed a mind and so dangerous (or impenetrably hard) a heart as his, for fear that I might develop some of the same ugly thoughts. When I listen to the music of a great composer I feel that I am, in some sense, becoming one with him, or letting a part of him inside me. I also find this disturbing with popular music, because surely some of the purveyors of pop are crude, sexist, racist, or all three.

This sense of vulnerability and surrender is no more prevalent than with rock and popular music in the past forty years. This accounts for the fandom that surrounds popular musicians—the Grateful Dead, the Dave Matthews Band, Phish, Neil Young, Joni Mitchell, the Beatles, R.E.M., Ani DiFranco. We allow them to control our emotions and even our politics—to lift us up, to bring us down, to comfort us, to inspire us. We let them into our living rooms and bedrooms when no one else is around. We let them into our ears, directly, through earbuds and headphones, when we're not communicating with anybody else in the world.

It is unusual to let oneself become so vulnerable with a total stranger. Most of us have some kind of protection that prevents us from blurting out every thought and feeling that comes across our minds. When someone asks us, "How're ya doin'?" we say, "Fine," even if we're depressed about a fight we just had at home, or suffering a minor physical ailment. My grandfather used to say that the definition of a bore is someone who when you ask him "How are you?" actually tells you. Even with close friends, there are some things we simply keep hidden—digestive and bowel-related problems, for example, or feelings of self-doubt. One of the reasons that we're willing to make ourselves vulnerable to our favorite musicians is that they often make themselves vulnerable to us (or they convey vulnerability through their art—the distinction between whether they are actually vulnerable or merely representing it artistically is not important for now).

The power of art is that it can connect us to one another, and to larger truths about what it means to be alive and what it means to be human. When Neil Young sings

Old man look at my life, I'm a lot like you were....

Live alone in a paradise that makes me think of two.

we feel for the man who wrote the song. I may not live in a paradise, but I can empathize with a man who may have some material success but no one to share it with, a man who feels he has "gained the world but lost his soul," as George Harrison once sang, quoting at once the gospel according to Mark and Mahatma Gandhi.

Or when Bruce Springsteen sings "Back in Your Arms" about losing love, we resonate to a similar theme, by a poet with a similar "everyman" persona to Neil Young's. And when we consider how much Springsteen has—the adoration of millions of people worldwide, and millions of dollars—it becomes all the more tragic that he cannot have the one woman he wants.

We hear vulnerability in unlikely places and it brings us closer to the artist. David Byrne (of the Talking Heads) is generally known for his abstract, arty lyrics, with a touch of the cerebral. In his solo performance of "Lilies of the Valley," he sings about being alone and scared. Part of our appreciation for this lyric is enhanced by knowing something about the artist, or at least the artist's persona, as an eccentric intellectual, who rarely revealed something as raw and transparent as being afraid.

Connections to the artist or what the artist stands for can thus be part of our musical preferences. Johnny Cash cultivated an outlaw image, and also showed his compassion for prison inmates by performing many concerts in prisons. Prisoners may like Johnny Cash's music—or grow to like it—because of what the artist stands for, quite apart from any strictly musical considerations. But fans will only go so far to follow their heroes, as Dylan learned at the Newport Folk Festival. Johnny Cash could sing about wanting to leave prison without alienating his audience, but if he had said that he liked visiting prisons because it helped him appreciate his own freedom, he would no doubt have crossed a line from compassion to gloating, and his inmate audience would have understandably turned on him.

Preferences begin with exposure and each of us has our own "adventuresomeness" quotient for how far out of our musical safety zone we are willing to go at any given time. Some of us are more open to experimentation than others in all aspects of our lives, including music; and at various times in our life we may seek or avoid experimentation. Generally, the times when we find ourselves bored are those when we seek new experiences. As Internet radio and personal music players are becoming more popular, I think that we will be seeing personalized music stations in the next few years, in which everyone can have his or her own personal radio station, controlled by computer algorithms that play us a mixture of music we already know and like and a mixture of music we don't know but we are likely to enjoy. I think it will be important that whatever form this technology takes, listeners should have an "adventuresomeness" knob they can turn that will control the mix of old and new, or the mix of how far out the new music is from what they usually listen to. This is something that is highly variable from person to person, and even, within one person, from one time of day to the next.

Our music listening creates schemas for musical genres and forms, even when we are only listening passively, and not attempting to analyze the music. By an early age, we know what the legal moves are in the music of our culture. For many, our future likes and dislikes will be a consequence of the types of cognitive schemas we formed for music through childhood listening. This isn't meant to imply that the music we listen to as children will necessarily determine our musical tastes for the rest of our lives; many people are exposed to or study music of different cultures and styles and become acculturated to them, learning their schemas as well. The point is that our early exposure is often our most profound, and becomes the foundation for further musical understanding.

Musical preferences also have a large social component based on our knowledge of the singer or musician, on our knowledge of what our family and friends like, and knowledge of what the music stands for. Historically, and particularly evolutionarily, music has been involved with social activities. This may explain why the most common form of musical expression, from the Psalms of David to Tin Pan Alley to contemporary music, is the love song, and why for most of us, love songs seem to be among our favorite things.

Invent

Levitin begins his essay by demonstrating how our musical tastes are influenced while still in our mothers' wombs. Later on, he points out that the kind of music we like is most likely the result of "chance factors," like the school we went to, the friends we made, and where we lived. How might this information affect the way we view our own musical choices later in life? Does this line of thinking match your musical tastes? What do you think you can learn from reflecting on the origins of your musical tastes?

Compose

Levitin notes that "researchers point to the teen years as the turning point for musical preferences," arguing that around the age of 10 or 11 we begin to take a real interest in music. Think back to that time in your life. Can you remember developing a greater appreciation for music at that age? Write down what you remember about that time period in your life, specifically as it relates to your musical experiences and preferences. What (or who) do you think influenced your musical choices the most? Do you still like those songs/artists? After journaling a bit about that period of your life, make a top ten list of the songs you remember liking the most when you were 10 or 11.

Collaborate

As a class, review the section of the essay where Levitin uses jazz to explain how the familiar and unfamiliar affect our preferences in music. Using classic jazz as an example, he walks readers through the process of developing a "new schema." Break down the process into steps and, as a class, choose a jazz standard to put through the process he describes, working to create within your minds a new schema for this genre. For example, listen to a recording of Billie Holiday singing "All of Me" (YouTube search: Billie Holiday-All of Me) and Louis Armstrong's version as well (YouTube search: Louis Armstrong-All of Me). Now, listen to a purely instrumental version, such as the version performed by Count Basie, Gerald Marks, and Seymour Simons (Spotify: Count Basie-All of Me).

Discuss the experience as a class. Does the process work in the way Levitin suggests? Do you find yourself enjoying the song more by the third time? How much of the music was your mind able to recognize by the time you listened to the purely instrumental version? Of course, you could do this exercise with any number of jazz standards, so feel free to try it again with another tune ("Autumn Leaves" is another good choice).

Explore

In this book, you will notice another essay that concerns the mind and music: "Learning to Crawl," by Gary Marcus. While in his essay Levitin seeks to explain the science behind our listening preferences, Marcus attempts to explain the science behind learning a musical instrument. In using scientific research as their basis for evidence, at times both men delve into similar areas of cognitive science, neuroscience, psychology, etc. Read Marcus's essay, and then explore the differences in how each author makes his case, attending carefully to the rhetorical moves each makes, where they agree and disagree, their uses of evidence, analogies, personal anecdotes, and any other devices you feel warrant examination. Once you have noted the differences, explore what those differences mean in terms of persuading their readers (each is writing for a popular press audience). Do you feel one is more persuasive than the other? Why or why not? Use the knowledge gained here to begin your own exploration into science and music.

Adam Frucci is the founder and editor of Splitsider, a website about comedy in all of its forms. Previously, he was an Associate Editor at Gizmodo and the Deputy Editor of Dvice. He's also a longtime performer at the UCB Theatre in New York City, where he performs improv comedy weekly.

RECORD LABELS: CHANGE OR DIE

BY ADAM FRUCCI

It's a lousy time to be a record label. Profits are tanking, bands are angry—OK Go just ditched EMI—and YouTube and BitTorrent changed the game. Still, some labels are transforming themselves to help musicians in the digital age.

"Change or Die" may sound like hyperbole, or an idle threat, but for the music business, the two alternatives have never been more real. EMI may very well go extinct *in the coming months*, and all of the major labels are fighting losing battles. But all is not lost.

The traditional role of a record label, in the broadest sense, is to bankroll a band until they start making lots of money, at which point the label gets to keep most of it. They own the master recordings a band makes, and by taking on this ownership they put all of their resources behind selling said recordings.

This setup makes sense when bands lacked the wherewithal to produce and record their own albums and when manufacturing and distributing physical copies of albums and marketing said albums costs hundreds of thousands of dollars. It also makes sense when a popular album will sell millions of copies at $15 a pop.

But that's definitely not the case now. Record stores are dying at an alarming rate, and fewer and fewer people are buying CDs every day. It's safe to say that the current generation of teenagers has never perused record stores as a normal activity; it's all downhill from here for physical music sales. And FM radio isn't doing too hot either. In short, everything that the music industry has known to be true for the last few decades is quickly turning to dust. Big labels can still bank on country, R&B and pop acts, but the bottom has already fallen out on alternative groups and other internet-friendly genres. And that's just the beginning.

THE OLD, DEAD WAY OF DOING BUSINESS

The way bands operate has changed so much in the last decade that what a label can provide and what bands require of a label has changed drastically, faster than labels have been able to adapt.

Manufacturing and distribution used to be the cornerstone of a label's business; every major label owned its own plants to make the albums and also dealt with shipping the albums worldwide. Today, only Sony still owns plants that manufacture CDs, with the other three big labels outsourcing manufacturing to them. But they all still have reps who have to go out to record stores and make sure that their albums are getting proper shelf space. They have to deal with defects and returns. There are lots of resources required to deal with the manufacture and distribution of a physical product, but that physical product is quickly headed towards irrelevancy.

The biggest music stores are now virtual, so there's no need for someone to go gladhand every Sam Goody manager so they give you endcap space for *Use Your Illusion II*. The iTunes Music Store sells 25% of the music sold in America as of last August, and that number is definitely going up, not down.

According to the IFPI, physical sales of music dropped 15.4% globally between 2007 and 2008. But in that same year, digital sales rose 24.1%. And Nielsen SoundScan numbers show that the number of units sold between 2006 and 2009 rose from 1 billion per year to 1.7 billion per year, with a unit referring to either an album or a song sold. It's a significant increase, but when someone buying three songs counts the same as someone buying three CDs, you can see why the labels are losing money despite the positive-sounding stat.

But for unsigned bands, companies such as TuneCore and CD Baby act as middlemen between them and digital storefronts like iTunes for very small amounts of money; getting your album up on major stores such as iTunes, Amazon and eMusic will set you back about $47 through TuneCore. And you retain all ownership of your music and keep all royalties, unlike working with a record label.

And TuneCore's internal numbers show that online sales are growing even faster for independent acts than those already well established. TuneCore CEO Jeff Price told me that between 2007 and 2009, TuneCore artists have gone from earning $7-8 million a year to $31 million, with $60 million in earnings projected for 2010. That's insane growth, to be sure, but it's got a long way to go before it represents a sizable proportion of global music sales. To put things in perspective, the IFPI recorded $4.9 billion in sales for 2008.

Furthermore, these days it's easier than ever for musicians to record music without an expensive studio. Software such as Reason, Pro Tools and Logic can be bought for $300 or less, and run on a mid-range laptop. Cheap mics and gear can be found all over eBay and Craigslist. Tie everything together with a $200 to $500 mic preamp analog-to-digital/digital-to-analog box, and you have a mini-studio in your bedroom.

And music blogs have turned the way artists are discovered on its head. It used to be that high-paid A&R executives would scour clubs to find underground bands to sign, acting as the filter between the millions of mediocre bands and the discriminating public. Today, obsessive music fans scour clubs and the web for free, discovering new acts and writing about them on blogs. Labels then discover bands from these blogs. The A&R system is no longer as relevant.

Marketing and promotion, another cornerstone service that labels provide, has also been transformed by the web. You no longer need radio play and ads in Rolling Stone to get your band noticed. When a band makes a music video, there's less of a need for a major label with contacts at MTV to push it through official channels to get it noticed. These days, you can just throw it up on YouTube and get it noticed by some music—or gadget—blogs. The fact that it's a simple click or two from video appreciation to buying actual music is worth more than any paper ad in any dying magazine.

As Voyno from the musicians-as-entrepreneurs blog *New Rockstar Philosophy* told me, it's very possible for a band to use the Internet to replace much of what a label provides:

> There are artists on YouTube who use creative on-the-cheap strategies to garner millions of views that direct traffic to their main site, iTunes pages, Facebook page and bandcamp.com profile. They then build an e-mail/text subscription from their new fans, which allows them to offer new merchandise, tickets for shows and other related info directly to fans. The web traffic analytics from all their sites can help them plan successful tours, target Facebook ads, and make better decisions on how to move forward.

These changes have shaken the foundation of the industry, and the biggest labels have borne the brunt of the losses that these changes wrought.

TOUGH TIMES FOR MAJOR LABELS

EMI is *bleeding* money. Earlier this month, it reported a whopping $2.4 *billion* loss, which, when added to its prior debts, puts it $4.5 billion in debt to CitiGroup. It owes Citi $160 million this month, and it's facing a restructuring plan that'll require an additional investment from its parent company.

EMI is owned by Terra Firma Capital Partners, a British private equity firm that also owns waste management companies, gas stations, residential home builders and movie theaters. To them, the art EMI is releasing is about as important as the trash that Waste Recycling Group collects. If it doesn't make them money, it isn't worth keeping around, 80 years of history or not.

Billboard's Senior Editorial Analyst Glenn Peoples told me that it's not for lack of trying that EMI finds itself in this position. "Labels have cut as many costs as they possibly can, they've taken fewer risks, they've signed fewer artists and tried to make safer bets," he says. "They're doing what they can, but the revenue might not be there to support the way they do business. So it's very possible that the recorded music division of EMI will be sold off and will go elsewhere. An acquisition by Warner Music Group is a possibility, and that would take it down to three majors in recorded music, and that'd be pretty drastic and a lot of concentration between three companies."

An EMI Music spokesperson told me, "EMI Music is doing well. We've reported revenue growth, despite a declining market, and strong operating profit and margin improvement, both in the last financial year and in the current year." But if they can't convince Terra Firma that they have a way out of the quagmire they're in, the possibility of the number of major labels to dropping to three is very real.

And if that happens, what of those remaining three? Universal Music Group is owned by French media conglomerate Vivendi, a company with stakes in the Universal and Canal movie studios and the video game publisher Activision Blizzard amongst other holdings. Sony Music Entertainment is obviously a division of Sony, and we all know Sony has had problems of its own lately. Warner Music Group is the only major without a parent company to answer to, as it spun off from Time Warner in 2004, and its revenue dropped about $3.5 billion last year.

THE UPSIDE OF SIGNING ON THE DOTTED LINE

But all is not lost, and the death of the record label at a business is not a foregone conclusion. Labels from EMI down to the smallest indie labels are racing to change the way they do business. And they still have quite a bit to offer.

Ra Ra Riot is a band from Syracuse, NY who's currently prepping their second album from indie label Barsuk Records. Barsuk is a true indie based out of Seattle, featuring bands such as Death Cab for Cutie, Mates of State, Nada Surf and They Might Be Giants in addition to Ra Ra Riot.

I talked to Josh Roth, Ra Ra Riot's manager, about the reasons bands still have for signing with a label. One big positive that signing to a label provides a band, he told me, is giving them legitimacy. "I think right now with the internet, there are just so many bands out there that it's easy to go unnoticed," he told me. "There's still is a certain charm to having a label saying 'We like this band and we're going to sign them and you should take a listen.' With the amount of bands that are out there, it's hard to filter what is actually good now."

Furthermore, as outlets such as radio and MTV have become less relevant, new venues for being heard and getting paid have opened up. "Commercials are becoming much more relevant," Ra Ra Riot guitarist Milo Bonacci told me.

"That's how a lot of bands get paid or get their music out there. That's how a lot of people hear a song for the first time. I feel like commercials are taking the place of commercial radio." And to get on a commercial, it sure helps to be signed to a label with a nice licensing department.

Of course, there are different types of record labels. A major label, such as EMI, has a lot more money to throw around and can make more promises, but contracts with majors can end up with artists further in the hole due to these deep pockets. As Bonacci told me, "There's more risk. There's more fuel to propel you forward up front, but that's no guarantee." That same fuel could blow up in your face. We've seen how bands who don't hit it big can end up "owing" their major label hundreds of thousands of dollars, after all.

Indie labels (true indie labels, not boutiques under the umbrella of a major) have less resources and therefore will give bands less to recoup. Indies also will often offer the artist a chance to interact with top brass, something that is almost never done at a major. Indies are presumably owned by passionate music fans rather than gigantic multinational holding companies, which is important when a band needs to know that a label is 100% behind them, according to RRR's Bonacci.

And signing to an indie instantly connects you to that labels fans, Bonacci says. "Nobody really cares about Sony records or Universal. You don't seek out stuff that's being released on Universal as a fan. Independent labels, be it Domino or SubPop or whatever, *those* labels have fans."

Indie labels seem to have a better chance of adapting and surviving in tumultuous times. Since for the most part they're private companies with few employees, they're able to make drastic changes in their business models much more quickly than major labels. But that doesn't mean they'll all survive; famed indie label Touch and Go closed down last year, and in addition to repping bands such as TV on the Radio, Ted Leo and the Pharmacists, and Blonde Redhead, they also handled distribution for other venerable indies such as Drag City, Kill Rock Stars, Jade Tree and Merge. It was a huge blow to the indie label scene.

GETTING A CUT OF EVERYTHING

The way labels are moving to stay alive is by becoming involved in the places that bands still make money, such as touring and merchandising. Traditionally, labels only made money off records sold, while any profits made from t-shirts or posters sold on the road went to the band. After all, if the label just owns the master recordings, it can only make money off the sale of said recordings, not any ancillary profits that come from things like touring.

But now some labels are pushing what are called 360 deals, which involve them in virtually everything an artist does. One of the most famous 360 deals was EMI's 2002 deal with Robbie Williams, which was worth a whopping £80 million, giving EMI a piece of basically everything that Williams touched. That didn't go so well, with Williams threatening to withhold albums from the label and trying to get out of his contract. But last week, according to UK trade paper Music Week, Williams' manager Tim Clark publicly came out in support of the embattled label, saying, "My own view is Citigroup would be mad at this stage not to keep EMI on as a going concern. It just would be bonkers."

In any case, 360 deals and general diversification are what big labels such as EMI are looking to move into, according to Billboard's Glenn Peoples. "They're definitely diversifying and they're actually getting into agencies, artist management, concert promotion. There's really no area that the four majors are not pursuing right now."

These deals make the most sense for huge acts with lots of opportunities for branding and licensing. You've seen it in action here on Giz, in fact, with Dr. Dre's Beats headphones and Lady Gaga's new Creative Director "job" at Polaroid. Both those acts are signed to Interscope, a sub-label of Universal that's clearly pushing artists towards these new revenue streams. But many smaller acts are still reluctant to give a label a slice of the entire pie with such a wide-reaching deal.

The fact of the matter is that bands do still need someone working for them, 360 deal or not. For some bands, just having a small team of a dedicated manager, publicist and lawyer who can handle the nitty-gritty of online sales, tour organization, merchandising and marketing will be enough for them. But many can still benefit from the huge networks that labels have with their contacts in every facet of the industry. Sure, you can print your own t-shirts, but a label with contacts with clothing manufacturers, stores and distributors can make that process a lot easier. And just how much of this work do you want to do yourself?

360 deals don't make sense for all bands; Ra Ra Riot manager Roth isn't sold on them. "A lot of labels are also now branching into management because the manager is involved with everything going on with a band. Labels will try to be like a full-service company to a band, but I don't think it'll be very popular." He worries that bands will be setting themselves up to be taken advantage of even more by labels if they give up merchandising and touring profits to them. Having an independent team working for a band and playing middleman between them in the label makes sure there's someone deeply involved in "business stuff" that still has their best interests at heart.

And it makes sense that a manager would be wary of labels moving into their territory, but there's still a distinction between label and manager with these deals. "For example, a new artist signed to a multi-rights deal may use the major label's merchandise company and e-commerce division in addition to its publishing and recorded music companies," Peoples says. "In the past, a manager could pick and choose which merch, e-commerce, publishing and record companies it wanted to work with. Now they're more likely to be under the same umbrella."

Sometimes, a band's management team can replace what a label does entirely. Just yesterday, OK Go announced it was splitting with EMI, whom they didn't have the greatest relationship with, to strike out on their own with a new company called Paracadute. Paracadute is basically OK Go's own team to handle management, promotion and distribution of their records. "The things that a major has to offer above and beyond anybody else are the things that OK Go really didn't need so much," Peoples says. "And that's radio promotion and access to brick and mortar retail. If you're going to create nearly all of your consumer awareness through cheaply made YouTube videos, you don't need this big promotional and distribution system behind you."

But not all bands can do what OK Go has done. The digital world looks a lot more accessible when only viewed through the lens of rock acts. "If you're an R&B act, if you're a straight up pop, a country act, you're going to need radio and you're going to need brick and mortar retail, and that's not going to change anytime soon. Things are changing definitely for alternative rock, rock and indie, but some genres sell a lot better in digital than other genres."

But clearly, the money that's to be made in music is no longer just in album sales. And bands seem to be presented with a choice: they can either allow labels to become more involved in everything that they do, and give up money that used to go exclusively to them in the process, or strike out on their own. Either way, they'll entering a landscape where getting their song on *Gossip Girl* for 40 seconds is more important than any amount of FM radio play, where getting a music video posted to Stereogum is more important than getting it on MTV and where you make more money touring behind an album than selling that same album.

And in order to prove to artists that signing with a label is a better idea than going out on your own, they'll need to make big changes; bigger than they've made so far. "It might be how an addict ends up turning his life around," Peoples says. "He's gotta hit rock bottom. And I dunno if the record industry has hit rock bottom yet, but maybe that's what'll need to happen for there to be really big change."

But at the end of the day, the saving grace of record labels might be a lot more basic than who gets what percentage of merchandise or who deals with distribution. The big question is this: do bands really want to try to make it completely on their own? As Bonacci says, "I don't necessarily want to have all that nitty-gritty stuff to worry about. I'd rather just worry about making music. I don't want to worry about numbers or distribution or marketing or publicity or anything like that. That sounds like a desk job. I used to have a desk job, that's why I'm playing music. Now look at me. I sleep on couches."

Invent Frucci opens his essay with the claim, "It's a lousy time to be a record label." This essay was written in March, 2010. Does this opening statement still resonate with readers? What do you think about record companies today (or do you even think about them at all)? Have the years since this article appeared changed in any way that would bring new meaning to Frucci's stance on record labels?

Compose For the last few decades, the music-listening public has had a complicated and sometimes tense relationship with record companies. Some of that tension goes back even further, but much of it can be traced back to the late 80s and early 90s when the cost of albums sharply increased even though the cost of making albums had sharply dropped. Take a moment and freewrite about your view of record companies, exploring what you know of them, what you think their role should be in music, and why you think people seem to hate them so much.

Collaborate This essay is filled with bold assertions regarding record labels and their future (the title alone provides just one example). Bold claims are interesting, but, in an academic environment, we must make sure that the evidence reasonably supports such claims. Many of Frucci's claims are tied to very specific categories of evidence: facts, reasoning, and examples. For instance, he uses facts (via statistics) to demonstrate the changes in music sales over the last few years, practical reasoning to make a number of predictions regarding the future of music, and a number of real-world examples to support his assertions throughout the essay. In small groups, work together to identify the moments in the text where he provides evidence and then place it under one of the following three categories: facts, reasoning, and examples. After you've completed that task, present your findings to the class, and discuss those areas where you disagree as to the category any particular piece of evidence should fall.

Explore Take a moment to identify and explore some of the predictions that Frucci posits in this essay. See how many came true. Look up statistics and other data to support your findings.

Brian Petchers is a NYC based music video director and video content producer for Forbes. Additionally, he writes about topics and trends in the video and branded content industry. His music videos have appeared on MTV, BET and a wide range of digital platforms. His director website is www.brianpetchers.com and his platform on Forbes is www.forbes.com/sites/brianpetchers.

THE BRANDING POWER OF TODAY'S MUSIC VIDEO

BY BRIAN PETCHERS

When music videos were initially introduced on MTV, for the first time, artists had a real opportunity to put themselves out there for the public to judge them and to perhaps garner a following. Going beyond just the music as heard on the radio, videos enabled artists to convey a more comprehensive message, portray an image and create a brand for themselves. Videos became so powerful they could make or break a single or even a fledgling artist's career. Somewhere down the line, around the time when MTV stopped playing videos, there was a lull in the widespread influence of the video as a key element of artists' ability to effectively brand and gain of a following.

They were unable to be sought out, let alone viewed at one's convenience. In the last six years or so, however, the improvements in web-video technology and its proliferation has allowed the music video to reassert itself as the most powerful artist branding tool, regardless of whether it is played on national television or not.

While the music video has reemerged on television, this is no longer the most powerful venue available as it was in the days of MTV. While a video on 106 and Park, the nation's most viewed music video airing program, which is on BET, can at very best, reach perhaps one million people in one day, a tweet from a major artist can reach ten times that in a matter of minutes. Accordingly, as a music video platform the web has become dominant. This is largely due to two main-advantages (which is inherent in all web content) that it has versus television: *Accessible* and *Shareable*.

ACCESSIBLE

Fans can search out their favorite artists and videos and watch them over and over again, whenever they are in the mood. This embeds the look and sound of the artists into the minds of the fans. Watching videos before bed, on the way to and from work and, even during work, keeps these images relevant in the mind of the viewer; due to consistency rather than only once per day viewing. The accessibility of videos gives artists an opportunity to brand themselves or change their image, knowing it will be seen over and over again, thereby far more quickly accomplishing their marketing objective. Accessibility leads to repetition, which helps develop a strong brand.

The unlimited access of the Internet magnifies everything that goes into an artist's image. Artists need to be extremely mindful of their look and feel down to every last piece of clothing. For up-and-coming artist, this access gives their fans an outlet to constantly keep up with their progress. For already established artists it gives them the opportunity to evolve their image and do it in a way that does not require extensive additional forms of marketing.

For example, Wiz Khalifa has taken his homegrown marijuana-loving rap fan-base and expanded that greatly across all demographics. This was in large part achieved by performing with the internationally known band Maroon 5 in their video "Payphone."

The video for "Payphone" is an epic movie-like music video, something that for Wiz had not yet been a part of his portfolio. The song became a global hit and exposed Wiz to an entirely new fan base. Had no video been shot for this song or if it was not so widely and

easily accessible on the web, it would not in any way have had the impact it did. This giant budget video, tied with the pop/rock song brands, helped springboard Wiz to being much more of a global artist.

Lately Wiz has made all the right moves, further augmenting his brand and popularity but this

Photo by Brian Petchers

video and song certainly standout in his progression. Wiz would not have been able to garner fans and evolve his image had no video for the song existed. At the same time Wiz keeps his older fans happy with constant guerilla-filmmaking style video content.

The "Payphone" video, released 4 months ago, has had more than 60 million views. That is 60 million people seeing Wiz as a pop act rather than just a hip-hop artist. And, for a catchy song like this, people are going to keep coming back to the same video to hear the song and see Wiz and his brand in this capacity. Wiz maintains his success because he can have a foot in both worlds, guerrilla style rap videos and big budget, more widely seen pop videos. Wiz's image outside of web video compliments what his fans see on the Internet.

I was at his show a few weeks ago and it is drastically different than his show just over a year when he first released *Rolling Paper*. Wiz embodies the image of more of a rock-star than a rapper in his live shows (playing with a band, his overall look, and performance) and this is reasserted online and as his track record shows, with accessibility that was almost unfathomable a mere decade ago.

The accessible nature of the web compliments an artist like Wiz who constantly is putting out video content. Wiz is an ideal example of an artist who took advantage of the web and its all access nature, and flooded his fans with content, which has lead to the success of his brand.

SHAREABLE

For an upcoming artist, the shareable nature of the Internet video is what they rely upon to get noticed. The widespread usage of social media has propelled the influence of the music video to new heights. I can now take a video and show it to my friends within minutes of first seeing it. This ability gives the artist an incredible amount of control and power over their brand that did not exist just ten years ago. This is not only the case with fledgling performers but also even the biggest stars.

Justin Bieber's latest video "As Long As You Love Me" was geared to introduce his evolving brand into the adult world. It is a mini-movie where the father of the girl he is pursuing beats him up. Bieber performs with bruises all over his face. This image is something completely new for the teen icon, and almost jarring to see as he gets punched repeatedly in the face.

Bieber is at the point in his career where he needs to make the jump to the adult audiences and this video is intended to be a vessel to accomplish that quickly. The shareable nature of the web and social media had millions of people seeing the "new" Bieber within days. Comments spread like wildfire and, almost instantly, Bieber had evolved and expanded his previously teeny bobber image into something more adult-like.

In addition to getting beaten up this video also portrays him with a girl in various romantic settings, where his previous videos were far more innocent. These shots tie into the overarching theme of transforming Bieber from a teenager into man. The imagery of this video and the fact it was shared globally, branded him in an organic yet still almost immediate way.

The branding power of the web may still be well undervalued as less money is spent now on music videos than in prior times. As time goes on I suspect labels will continue to see its power and utilize the potential as was done with both the Wiz and Bieber videos. Branding on the web is a double-edged sword, however, since if it is not done in the right way, it can hurt an artist's career just as fast as it can help it.

In his essay, Petchers argues that "the improvements in web-video technology and its proliferation has allowed the music video to reassert itself as the most powerful artist branding tool." Do you agree? What about Facebook, Twitter, or other social media outlets? Are videos more powerful for branding than these forms of meda? Videos can be posted easily via Facebook and Twitter, but what about pictures and comments any given artist makes via these same media? Do you think these are also powerful branding tools? What other tools are involved in establishing an artist's brand? Petcher ends his essay with a comment regarding the idea that branding via web videos is "a double edged sword," implying that a web video these days can as quickly ruin an artist's career as launch it. He doesn't speak further to this suggestion, however. Can you think of artists whose careers have tanked as a result of their videos?

Did video kill the radio star? Let's find out. Make a list of artists whom you've first discovered through their videos rather than radio. Next, make a list of artists you already knew but grew to like more (or perhaps less) after being exposed to their videos. Jot down the qualities of the video that affected your view of these artists. Share the list with a partner and see if the same qualities appear on both lists.

As a class or in small groups, use your available technology to watch each of the videos mentioned in Petchers's essay, attending carefully to the "brand" each video seeks to present. The first time, just watch the video, getting a general sense of what each artist is trying to convey. On the second viewing, however, feel free to pause the video and take notes on what you see. Notice the details in each and how they work—or don't work—to support the artist's message and image. Which video proves most successful and why?

Explore

Petchers's essay begins with a reference to MTV, which launched in 1981. Much has been written about the MTV era. Explore the history of the creation of MTV, investigating what led to its initial success and critical acclaim, as well as what led to its eventual decline in popularity. You might also research those artists whose careers were launched by MTV. Make sure to watch the first music video ever shown on MTV: "Video Killed the Radio Star" by the Buggles; you're sure to find it entertaining one way or the other.

Currently the editor and publisher of Cornell Alumni magazine, Jim Roberts is the founding editor of Bass Player magazine and former group publisher in charge of Bass Player, Guitar Player, Keyboard, and other music titles. Inspired by the playing of Jack Bruce in Cream, Jim Roberts shelved his plans to go to law school and became a professional bass player in 1971. He is the author of two books: How the Fender Bass Changed the World (2001) and American Basses (2003). When not writing, editing, or publishing, he plays bass as much as he can.

excerpt from
HOW THE FENDER BASS CHANGED THE WORLD—"ST. JAMES"

BY JIM ROBERTS

The commercial viability of the Fender bass was by no means guaranteed, even after ten years on the market. There are no precise records of Fender's Precision Bass production in the 1950s, but we know the numbers were low. According to Richard R. Smith, who has scrutinized the early Fender sales orders, it appears that fewer than 200 P-Basses were made each year in the early '50s, with a gradual increase to annual production of perhaps 1,000 by the end of the decade.

By 1961, a few players (most of them converted guitarists) had begun to define a sound and an approach that distinguished the Fender bass from the upright. But the instrument was awaiting its first virtuoso—the player who would expand the range of creative possibilities and firmly establish the position of the electric bass in the musical world. He would arrive in the form of an unassuming studio musician working for a fledgling record label in Detroit: James Jamerson.

Jamerson was a bass player, not a guitarist. After dabbling with the piano as a child, he studied acoustic bass in high school. He was a quick learner, and before long he was playing jazz on the upright and trying to emulate such heroes as Paul Chambers and Ray Brown. Jamerson's ability as a club musician came to the attention of several local producers, including Motown's Berry Gordy, and James began to get calls for session work.

Jamerson started to work for Motown in 1959. He played his early sessions on the upright, but his approach was dramatically different from that of the era's other bassists. Allan "Dr. Licks" Slutsky, the author of the authoritative Jamerson biography, *Standing in the Shadows of Motown*, described his impact: "Although his early Motown bass work was nowhere near the mature late-'60s style that would ultimately evolve in masterpieces like 'Bernadette' and 'I Was Made to Love Her,' James was quickly setting himself apart from most of the bassists in the R&B industry. Gone were the stagnant two-beat, root-fifth patterns and post-'Under the Boardwalk' clichéd bass lines that occupied the bottom end of most R&B releases. Jamerson had modified them or replaced them with chromatic passing notes, Ray Brown-style walking bass lines, and syncopated eighth-note figures—all of which had previously been unheard of in popular music in the late '50s and early '60s."

Sometime in 1961, Jamerson began to play a Fender Precision Bass. A friend and fellow bassist, Horace "Chili" Ruth, had urged him to try the new instrument. Resistant at first, James eventually decided he liked the Fender well enough to try it in the studio. Although Motown's studio records do not provide any definitive information, Slutsky says he believes that "Strange I Know" by the Marvellettes was probably the first Motown recording Jamerson made with a Fender bass. It was released in 1962.

The first track where you can hear Jamerson's unique style begin to emerge is Marvin Gaye's "Pride and Joy," which was released in April 1963. (It went to No. 2 on the R&B charts and No. 10 on the Pop charts.) The tune begins with a walking bass intro over handclaps, and the bass line under the verse is a standard blues pattern. Although simple, it's played with great feel, and there are subtle embellishments and accents that

James Jamerson played the bass lines for dozens of Motown hits on one instrument: a sunburst '62 Fender Precision Bass known as "the Funk Machine." The instrument was completely stock and still had its chrome pickup cover and bridge cover (with foam string mute) in place. The strings were LaBella flatwounds—the older and deader, the better. The action was very high, probably because of Jamerson's background on the upright. The bass was stolen shortly before Jamerson's death and has never been recovered.

After Leo Fender sold his company to CBS in January 1965, the new management introduced a number of unusual instruments, including this 5-string bass. It added a high C string to the usual EADG and had only 15 frets. James Jamerson owned a Bass V and may have experimented with it occasionally in the studio.

give the groove life and energy. For the final chorus, Jamerson returns to the walking line, playing it with a relaxed, infectious swing and tossing in surprising cross-string rakes and melodic fills. The entire part builds and develops, as if it were a two-minute bass concerto (and the singer isn't bad, either).

Jamerson's style continued to evolve, and Motown's producers gave him increasing freedom to shape his parts. He took full advantage of the opportunity, and by the mid '60s Jamerson had elevated pop bass playing to an art form. As Slutsky explained it: "Through 1965, James probably had the funkiest and most melodic eighth-note bass style in the universe, but for some reason toward the end of the year, he exploded in a completely new direction. Sixteenth-notes, quarter-note triplets, open-string techniques, dissonant non-harmonic pitches, and syncopations off the 16th seemed to enter into his style almost overnight. It closely paralleled the change in the jazz world from Charlie Parker's eighth-note bebop style to the evolution of John Coltrane's 16th-note 'sheets of sound' approach. There is a distinct break from the bass lines Jamerson was playing in '64 and early '65 on tunes like 'Dancing in the Street' and 'Stop! In the Name of Love' to '66 and '67 masterpieces like 'Reach Out' and 'I'm Wondering.' Out of nowhere, James started playing almost as if he was the featured soloist.

Slutsky's book has transcriptions of 50 Jamerson bass lines, almost all of which are amazingly creative, even by contemporary standards. In a chapter called "An Appreciation of the Style," Anthony Jackson offers a detailed analysis of three songs,

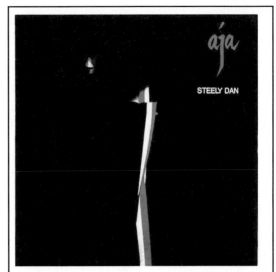

Chuck Rainey credits James Jamerson as his primary creative inspiration: "In terms of me playing bass, Jamerson gave me the keys to get into the house." A busy session player since the mid '60s, Rainey played his '57 Precision on hundreds of sessions with artists such as Aretha Franklin, Sam Cooke, King Curtis, Marvin Gaye, Donny Hathaway, and Roberta Flack. Some of his best work was done with Steely Dan, especially on the classic album *Aja*, which Rainey cites as a personal favorite.

While James Jamerson and his colleagues were making history in Detroit, another great rhythm section was doing groundbreaking work for Stax Records in Memphis. Duck Dunn was the bassist, and his name was better known than Jamerson's because the Stax rhythm section recorded on its own as Booker T. & the MG's. Dunn's stark, earthy lines are the driving force behind many great tracks by Otis Redding ("I've Been Loving You Too Long") and Sam & Dave ("Soul Man") as well as Booker T. & the M.G.'s instrumental hits like "Boot-Leg" and "Hip-Hug-Her."

Although the bassists changed regularly, the mid-'60s rhythm sections of James Brown set the standard for gutbucket grooves. Bernard Odum had one of the longest tenures and contributed to the recorded version of "Cold Sweat." Charles Sherrell, Tim Drummond, and Bootsy Collins also had significant stints with the Godfather of Soul. Their work has had an enduring influence on many styles, including contemporary hip-hop.

Just about any Atlantic Records soul session from the late '60s that didn't have Chuck Rainey or Tommy Cogbill on bass featured the impeccable grooves of Jerry Jemmott on his '65 Jazz Bass. Jerry's work graced classic albums by Wilson Pickett, Aretha Franklin, King Curtis, B.B. King, and many others. In a 1984 interview, Jaco Pastorius said, "He was my idol, making the sounds I wanted to make."

showing how Jamerson used unusual melodic and rhythmic devices to make his lines strong and distinctive. While influenced by Jamerson's knowledge of jazz, many of these ideas would be difficult to execute on the upright. They are truly *electric* bass lines, and they demonstrate the expressive capabilities of the instrument. "Perhaps the key word that sums up [Jamerson's] techniques," wrote Jackson, "is unpredictability. It was impossible to foresee what he would play." In contrast to the formulaic bass playing in pop music before then, Jamerson's work was a revelation.

And, because it was a vital component of a long string of hit records, Jamerson's playing reached the ears (and feet) of millions. It helped to break down the line that supposedly separated "Pop" (white) music from "R&B" (black) music. It is not an exaggeration to say that the immense popularity of Motown changed the course of American popular music and, in doing so, had a huge impact on the development of an entire generation. Certainly, there were many reasons for Motown's success—from Smokey Robinson's voice to Berry Gordy's business savvy—but much credit must go to James Jamerson and his '62 Precision Bass (known as "The Funk Machine"), as well as his colleagues in the great rhythm section known collectively as the Funk Brothers.

It is hugely ironic—and there were many ironies in Jamerson's life—that all of this happened without anyone knowing who this great bass player was. (Motown, like many other labels of that era, did not list the backing musicians on its records.) James finally received a credit in 1971, on Marvin Gaye's *What's Going On*, a landmark album that broke all of Motown's sales records.

Bob Babbitt began to do session work at Motown in 1967 as a "pinch hitter" for James Jamerson. He eventually contributed to dozens of hits by artists such as Stevie Wonder, the Temptations, Gladys Knight, and Marvin Gaye. His favorite recording bass for many years was a modified mid-'60s Precision.

But it would be years before Jamerson would be properly acknowledged for his accomplishments. Plagued by alcoholism and self-doubt, victimized by the shifting fortunes of the music industry, he died lonely and embittered in 1983. Years later, his Motown colleague Smokey Robinson paid tribute to him, saying: "He's really the father of the modern-day bass player. He had the purest fingering—all his notes were pure and true. No matter how fast he was playing them or whatever rhythmic pattern he was doing, you could hear the whole note. That was a big part of his sound. Even today, nobody plays like that."

Although he was known for many years only as "the Motown bass player" (or "the Tamla bass player," as the label was named on U.K. releases), Jamerson was highly influential among his fellow bassists. Now that we know his name, he has taken on the status of a patron saint—a player inspired by a vision of his instrument's potential whose work showed the way to those who followed, and who shared his gift in a selfless and almost self-sacrificing way.

As James Jamerson developed his virtuosic style in the early 1960s, there was a young English musician who listened closely and began to seek his own distinctive electric bass approach. While he was different in just about every important way from "the Tamla bass player," this left-handed guitarist-turned-bassist was perhaps the most gifted member of a rock & roll band whose popularity has never been exceeded—and whose creative influence is still powerful today.

Invent

This article speaks to the way technology shapes moments in history. What are some key historical moments where technology changed the way people lived their lives? Why do you think technology can have such an impact on the progression of human existence? Think about technological advancement in conjunction with artistic, philosophical, and religious progressions in history. What connections do you see there?

Compose

This essay provides one example of how advancements in technology (in this case the Fender bass) can spark musical revolutions. Take a moment to reflect on current advancements in music (in any form—from instruments to iPhones), and write a short paragraph in which you explore how a specific form of technology has (or could) bring about significant changes in music. Don't worry so much if your argument is foolproof, but do try to back up your case with some specific evidence.

In this chapter from *How the Fender Bass Changed the World*, Jim Roberts points to one individual, James Jamerson, as a catalyst in the music revolution of the 1960s—specifically as it relates to the music of Motown. All revolutions have key figures credited for significantly contributing to the paradigm shifts that accompany them. In small groups, discuss who you think the key figures might be in any given current music revolution. Feel free to discuss music "at large" and/or specific genres (i.e., Who do you think is leading the current revolutions in hip-hop, country, techno, dubstep, etc.?).

Who was Leo Fender, and why was his invention of the electric bass in 1951 so unique and influential? To answer that, do some research on the web, exploring who Leo Fender was and how vast his influence has been over the last 60+ years. Feel free to watch a few of the documentaries on him—available on YouTube (YouTube search: Leo Fender Bass). You can even take a tour of the Fender Factory back in 1959 and see how guitars were made during that time period (YouTube search: Fender Factory Tour 1959).

Justin Davidson has been the classical music and architecture critic at New York Magazine since 2007. Before that, he spent 12 years as classical music critic at Newsday, where he also wrote about architecture and was a regular commentator on cultural issues. He won a Pulitzer Prize for criticism in 2002, and an American Society of Newspaper Editors criticism (ASNE) award. He has contributed to The New Yorker, W magazine, Travel and Leisure, the Los Angeles Times, Slate magazine, and Salon, is a regular columnist for the website emusic, and has appeared on WNYC, NPR, and German radio programs.

BEETHOVEN'S KAPOW

By Justin Davidson

If I could crash any cultural event in history, it would be the night in April 1805 when a short man with a Kirk Douglas chin and a wrestler's build stomped onto the stage of the Theater an der Wien in Vienna. Ludwig van Beethoven, 34 years old and already well along the way to deafness, swiveled to face a group of tense musicians and whipped them into playing a pair of fist-on-the-table E-flat major chords (*blam! … blam!*), followed by a quietly rocking cello melody. If I listen hard enough, I can almost transport myself into that stuffy, stuccoed room. I inhale the smells of damp wool and kerosene and feel the first, transformative shock of Beethoven's Third Symphony, the "Eroica," as it exploded into the world.

Before it was a work of genius, the "Eroica" was a provocation, and I sometimes wonder how I would have reacted if I had been in the crowd on that night in 1805. I might have concurred with the critic who felt "crushed by a mass of unconnected and overloaded ideas and continuing tumult by all the instruments." The performance probably flirted with chaos. Beethoven himself conducted, and he was a volatile man who could barely hear. The band of musicians had never grappled with a score so mountainous and rugged, and the audience hadn't either. Someone yelled, "I'll give another kreutzer if the thing will only stop!" It's easy to dismiss that wag as a philistine, but the first performance, unlike most of the thousands upon thousands that followed, didn't take admiration for granted.

This week, Lincoln Center hosts the conductor Iván Fischer leading two ensembles—one period, the other modern—in a comparative festival of Beethoven's symphonies.

The Orchestra of the Age of Enlightenment plays the "Eroica," plus Symphonies Nos. 1, 2, 5, and 8, just as they purportedly sounded 200 years ago. The Budapest Festival Orchestra performs the remaining symphonies in their plusher, louder, and more modern incarnation. The difference between those styles is usually framed as a distinction between music's authentic past and its dynamic present, between scholarship and technology, the latest framing of a 40-year movement that goes by various cumbersome and misleading titles: Original Instruments, Early Music, Authentic Performance Practice. But in truth both paths pursue the same illusion: that a certified masterpiece has just come blaring out of the composer's brain.

Why do we reenact these rituals of revolution, when revolution is no longer at stake? How can an act of artistic radicalism retain the power to disturb after two centuries? What's left when surprise has been neutralized and influence absorbed? Beethoven toyed with expectations we do not have and dismantled conventions that no longer guide us. As a result, the "Eroica," which emerged with such blinding energy that some of its first listeners thought its composer must be insane, sounds like settled wisdom to us. His contemporaries had never experienced such wild, loud, assaultive sounds outside of combat. Our ears are attuned to a rougher sonic landscape: The construction site that edges Lincoln Center is far more raucous than whatever goes on in the hall.

If the composer flailed against the constraints of his world, today's Beethoven performers battle the legacy he bequeathed: the whole stultifying tradition of greatness. Conductors have various strategies for making even connoisseurs forget the scriptural familiarity of those notes. They can exaggerate idiosyncrasies or whisk up an irritatingly manic sense of excitement. They can buff the playing to a technocratic gleam and engineer an interpretation so faithful to the written score that it becomes fanatically neutral. Or they might emulate the corporate approach of Herbert von Karajan, who drew from his orchestras a rich, emulsified sound and treated Beethoven's symphonies as monuments to be gilded with fresh applications of elegance.

The most thrilling versions of the "Eroica" I've heard have felt like quests, crackling with desperate urgency. In the mid-nineties, John Eliot Gardiner led his private band, the Orchèstre Révolutionnaire et Romantique, in a complete cycle of Beethoven symphonies that enshrined their violent defiance. He achieved that effect through scrupulous historicism and tolerance for the technical imperfections inherent in period instruments. Natural horns occasionally bobbled a difficult passage. Gut-string violins struggled to balance wooden flutes that wandered out of tune. Even with a full-arm wallop, the timpanist could only eke a muffled thud from his early-nineteenth-century Viennese kettledrums. But those challenges added to the revolutionary élan, and to the exhilarating suspicion that at any moment the whole apparatus might fall apart.

Beethoven craved that sense of imminent collapse. As a pianist, he pummeled the keyboard and tried to force it into playing lower, higher, louder, and softer than it could. The "Eroica" rattled the Theater an der Wien, a grand and modern space by 1805 standards, but an ornate little shoebox when compared with, say, Carnegie Hall. There's a moment in the middle of the first movement, when the symphony shudders as if it were coming unglued. The pulse grinds down and the burbling theme stops short, overpowered by a chain of dissonant blasts that, in the first performance, must have ricocheted off the graceful walls and buzzed through the audience's bones. In the early nineteenth century, listening to orchestral music was a full-body experience.

But the epic scale of Beethoven's symphonies created a new, supersized infrastructure that gradually swallowed his music. Larger audiences and bigger orchestras required more spacious venues, where music reaches the ears only after picking up resonance and losing its edge. The most authentic, and exciting, way to hear Beethoven's symphonies would be in cramped rooms rather than in great, flattering halls. (The Lincoln Center concerts take place in the relatively cozy Alice Tully Hall.)

We can't unravel a history of listening, and the work can't easily slough off its encrustations of meaning. Beethoven's music comes to us at once impoverished by time and marinated in meanings: Wagner's analytic raptures, Schroeder's obsession in "Peanuts," the Morse code V-for-victory of the Fifth during the Battle of Britain, *A Clockwork Orange*, Bernstein's substitution of *Freiheit* (freedom) for *Freude* (joy) in the Ninth at the collapsing Berlin Wall, and so on. We also can't recapture the heat with which the nineteenth century debated the meaning of that cryptic subtitle. Is the hero Napoleon, the composer himself, or perhaps a more archetypal figure? A moral but unconventional loner? A vessel of humanity's most intense feelings? An artist-genius? It hardly matters now, when the whole notion of a hero-worshipping symphony seems impossibly hoary. What sort of figure would we enrobe in music of such complexity, fury, and moral struggle? Tiger Woods? David Petraeus?

For much of today's public, even the most thoroughly tilled symphonic turf has become unexplored terrain. The orchestral Establishment treats that widespread musical illiteracy as a disaster, but it's also a chance to give works of "Eroica"-like stature an infinite number of premieres. The fact that many audience members have never heard the piece should be a bracing thought for the players on the stage: To dispense revelation is a daunting responsibility.

Classical-music neophytes often worry that they don't have enough background to appreciate a performance, but the opposite is often true: They're the ones who listen without preconceptions and who are primed for danger and unpredictability. The "Eroica" was the first symphonic psychodrama, a chronicle of a character's interior battles. Already in the opening seconds, the restless theme spins away from its expected course to go skating through patches of harmonic uncertainty, disruptive syncopations, and asymmetrical phrases. Moods change with mercurial quickness. Beethoven knits his structure out of conflict and unease, turning unpleasant states of mind into artistic virtues.

If the first movement romanticizes anxiety, the second makes misery seem celestial. It is a funeral march, but the orchestration suggests it is an imagined event, a procession unfolding in the protagonist's mind. The sounds are softer, rounder, than a street parade. We hear no brass. Cellos and basses play the role of muffled drums. An oboe takes the place of a mournful bugle. The march coaxes intimate emotions into the public realm. If Beethoven's music still speaks to us now, it's because, like that roomful of startled Viennese two centuries ago, we want to hear suffering transfigured, too. Pain is ugly and joy fleeting, but each performance of the "Eroica" offers to shape everyday disorder of the mind into something luminous and sublime.

Whether the upcoming Beethoven festival does justice to Beethoven will not depend on the vintage of instruments or the historical purity of technique. Modern orchestras and period ensembles can both pluck excitement out of the past. What matters instead is whether Iván Fischer and his two groups are faithful to the intertwining of nuances and extremes. If the performers etch the contrasts between a lonesome horn and a full orchestral roar, if they savor the abyssal terror of a silence, snap off an accented chord before it becomes pillowy and fat, bring out the pleasurable sourness of dissonance, dispel complacency, and banish habit, then they just might summon the prickle and panic of that first night.

Invent

Davidson's essay concerns the question of authenticity and classical music in the modern age. In describing the two ways conductors might approach performing classical music, Davidson says that it's usually framed "as a distinction between music's authentic past and its dynamic present, between scholarship and technology." To what degree do you think that digital technology—and all its accompanying side effects—plays a role in the way classical music is consumed today? Do you think the sonic power of original classical music performances is impossible to convey in today's world of power speakers and amplification? How might classical music be helped by digital technology? In what way might digital technology hinder its purpose?

Using Spotify or iTunes, listen to Symphony No. 2 in E-flat Major (preferably through headphones) and jot down your thoughts and feelings during the process. Remember that, according to Davidson, not having heard the symphony before can aid in you having a more authentic experience as it allows you to "listen without preconceptions." What emotions does this music stir within you? What kind of experiences do you associate with the movements in the music? These are just a few questions you might consider as you write down your thoughts on the composition.

In small groups, choose different performances of "Eroica" to watch (there are many on YouTube). Feel free to pick performances that promise to be noticably different in their presentation. Take notes on the performance and how it shapes your experience as a viewer. Be prepared to report back to the class and compare your performance with others.

While classical music is rooted in acoustic performances, like all genres it has been forced to contend with modern audiences and digital technology. Investigate the ways in which digital technology has been incorporated into classical music, examining its positive and negative reception. For example, several universities, like Stanford, now have iPhone orchestras, and computer programs are now being written that can compose classical music. These are just a few areas worth investigation; there are many more.

Anthony Wing Kosner has successfully launched, rebranded, and managed a great variety of magazines, books, and websites during the last 20 years. He is a content strategist, designer, and developer who uses his experience as a magazine art director and web editor to help publishers, marketers, non-profits, and self-branded individuals tell their stories in words and images. He follows all of the technologies that relate to the content business and tries to identify the opportunities and pitfalls that these technologies pose. He is always looking to find connections between the worlds of neurology, economics, entertainment, travel and mobile technology.

GOTYE'S YOUTUBE ORCHESTRA REMIX: THE SWEETNESS OF THE OPEN SOURCE POP STAR

By Anthony Wing Kosner

In 2009, an artist named Kutiman launched a project called Thru-YOU (a play on YouTube) that aimed to show what open collaboration could be on the internet. He played the "YouTube Orchestra" for a series of video remixes that made the network effects of music video on the web powerfully clear.

Kutiman didn't just mash clips up. He meticulously combined and time-matched them into coherent (and very funky) compositions. His server crashed twice in the first days after the videos were posted. Since then, the videos have been viewed more than 10 million times (which no longer sounds like a lot!) and named one of the 50 Best Inventions of 2009 by Time magazine.

Sasha Frere-Jones of the *New Yorker* wrote, "What is the mark of Web success in 2009? A million page views in a week? A spike in Twitter mentions? Both are meaningful indices, but not quite as satisfying as traffic crashing your whole site. It's the Internet version of a standing ovation." And patron saint of opensource and author of REMIX, Lawrence Lessig, wrote of Thru-YOU, "Watch this, and you'll understand everything and more than what I try to explain in my book."

It is in this opensource spirit that Gotye—whose "Somebody That I Used To Know" video has now been played more than 300 million times—decided to honor the hundreds of cover versions and parodies of his über-viral hit.

"Reluctant as I am to add to the mountain of interpretations of 'Somebody That I Used To Know' seemingly taking over their own area of the internet," writes Gotye (aka Wouter "Wally" De Backer). "I couldn't resist the massive remixability that such a large, varied yet connected bundle of source material offered."

Gotye worked through a pile of original videos (links displayed below) and made his own quirky version of the song from remixed and overlayed bits of his fans' versions, to produce "Somebodies," (see above). "All audio and video in Somebodies is from the YouTube user videos featured, each of them a cover or parody of Somebody That I Used To Know. No extra sounds were added to the mix, but I used some EQ, filtering, pitch-shifting and time-stretching to make the music. I avoided using any existing remixes of the song, or any covers from tv talent shows."

He even apologizes for not being able to fit every single source video in, and calls out viralogist Tay Zonday's cover for special (non-inclusion) mention.

On a technical level, Gotye even shares the details of his toolkit, "I used KeepVid.com to download the YouTube videos, Ableton Live for audio stretching, pitch-shifting and the initial video editing, and Adobe's After Effects to put the final video together."

Not only is the resulting video fun to watch, but it also tells you a lot about the modesty and humility—and sweetness—of this ubiquitous pop star. He knows that his fans, and YouTube, are the source of his success and his response is to give back, to pay forward with his own mouse clicks.

I have written a lot (too much) about this particular song, and I really hope for everyone's sake that we find another one of his songs to love. Gotye is a master of grooves, perhaps more than hooks, so it is possible that nothing he does will ever top this hit. With "Somebodies," Gotye is letting us know that he wants to be an artist of the open internet, too.

Gotye's popularity is unarguably linked to the covers of his songs that appeared on YouTube (most notably Walk off the Earth's "Five People on One Guitar" version). How do you think YouTube has changed the way in which musicians reach their audience? What role do you think song covers and parodies play in drawing attention to any given artist? Before the Internet, the most popular parody artist was probably Weird Al Yankovic (Google him), but now parody bands like the Key of Awesome seem to be everywhere. Do you watch parody songs and videos on YouTube? If so, what do you enjoy most about them? How does parody function differently in a digital media savvy society than in a more literature-oriented one?

Write a parody of one your favorite song lyrics, trying to match the cadence and phrasing that the original does. Feel free to look up the qualities of a parody and model that in your own creation. Remember to focus on a theme for your lyrics. Be prepared to share your parody with someone else.

Form a small group and, using a video or phone camera, make a video (cover, parody, lip-synch) of a song. This may involve some time outside of class. It doesn't have to be fancy; it just needs to give you the experience of trying to make a parody or cover of a song. After you've made it, present it to the class and share the details of your experience. Feel free to upload it to YouTube. Who knows, maybe it will make you famous.

Via YouTube, watch the official video of Gotye's "Somebody that I Used to Know," Walk off the Earth's cover, then the video Kosner refers to in the above essay. Discuss the manner in which the song's influence spreads across race, nationality, gender, etc. Then, watch a few of the parodies (like the Key of Awesome's version).

Jacob Adams writes about music, books, and popular culture for the web magazines Spectrum Culture and PopMatters. He also teaches literature, composition, and communication studies at a public high school in the Chicago area. He holds degrees in English, music, and education from Indiana University. When he is not busy teaching and writing about all aspects of popular culture, he enjoys writing music and poetry.

A FIELD GUIDE TO THE INDIE MARKETPLACE

BY JACOB ADAMS

The indie dream looks something like this: some creative, free-spirited early twentysomethings move to an edgy, not-quite-yet-gentrified neighborhood in Brooklyn or Chicago or Portland or Austin where the rent is relatively low and the cultural opportunities are seemingly vast. They work some stupid, lifeless jobs during the day to make ends meet. At night, they write poetry and listen to obscure no-wave or avant-garde jazz groups on vinyl. Given their limited income, they shop at off-the-map thrift stores instead of trendy, name-brand clothing shops. Eventually, these kids find likeminded friends and start playing music together. The songs they write and perform are influenced by musicians of a wide range of genres, both past and present, yet there is an undeniable originality to their art. They pull together funds for some rudimentary recording equipment and, with the help of a basic laptop, make a "bedroom record," one low in audio fidelity but high in legitimate feeling. Using these tracks as a demo, they land some gigs at a couple area clubs. In time, they develop a small, yet passionate, fan base. Some local bloggers write positive reviews of their shows. The band throws their EP up on Bandcamp and makes a little extra cash from album sales. They are discovered and signed by a small, independent record label, but even as their music reaches a larger audience, they retain a "DIY" aesthetic. They go on mini-tours and play larger venues, but keep their day jobs so they don't have to sell out by sacrificing their art to TV commercials or mainstream Hollywood movie soundtracks.

This hypothetical band's fan base is culturally similar to the band members themselves. They live in major urban centers or smaller college towns. They spend a healthy chunk of their free time perusing blogs, hoping to latch on to some little-known band that will "change their lives." They avoid only listening to what's playing on mainstream radio, since this seems far too easy, and top-40 pop music is over-commercialized. They go to random shows at little venues in their city, preferring the intimacy of a small rock club to a large, impersonal stadium. Instead of downloading their favorite band's music from iTunes or illegally grabbing it for free from torrent sites, they are more likely to purchase the physical product on CD or vinyl from a locally-owned record shop. They happily believe that their idiosyncratic musical tastes exist outside of the influence of the musical PR machine. They love certain songs or albums simply because they love them, not because someone is telling them they *have* to love them. This is *their* music, and nobody can take it from them.

The indie dream, much like the ever-illusive American dream, exists more in the minds of true believers than in the physical world. Music produced in a capitalist society has never been, and will never be, completely liberated from the tight hands of commerce. Even the indie-est of indie musicians must deal with the day-to-day financial realities of recording, promoting, and distributing their music. With the advent of new technologies and music distribution models, these challenges are as profound as ever. Nevertheless, the idea of this thing called indie remains a powerful force in contemporary culture, one that continues to capture the imagination of young consumers and artists alike. In order to understand why indie maintains such cultural ubiquity, it is essential to first consider what the word actually means.

Ever since indie entered the popular consciousness, its meaning has been endlessly debated. Some use the word exclusively for music released by small record companies that operate without major corporate funding. In an interview for the influential music website *Pitchfork*, Britt Daniel, frontman for the band Spoon, affirms this definition of the term, noting that indie might be best understood as a condition of the marketplace rather than a designation of genre.[1] In this scenario, indie can be viewed as a cultural product of late capitalism. Young, idealistic people want to have some control over their own destinies. They may feel powerless in the realms of politics and economics, but why should they feel the same way about music? In a world of mass consumption, multinational corporations, and globalized labor, the indie dream emerged in the 1990s as a way for progressive musicians and conscientious fans to gain more autonomy over the way they create and consume art. Small labels such as Sub Pop, Matador, and Merge tried to nurture artists and give them the maximum possible leeway to be creative, in contrast to the oppressive, heavy-handed approach of corporate labels. This economic definition of indie seems simple enough, until one recognizes that plenty of artists, including Modest Mouse, The Shins, and the White Stripes, have made the switch from independent

---

1 Perrez, Rodrigo. "Spoon." *Pitchfork*. 1 Mar. 2003. Web. 15 Jan. 2013. <http://pitchfork.com/features/interviews/5901-spoon/>.

labels to the majors without giving up their indie designation. While fans of such bands often criticize them for the change—it's not uncommon to hear "indie kids" claim that these artists are "sell-outs"—these bands often continue to be labeled indie by critics and listeners alike. Conversely, a number of bands have spent most of their careers toiling away on major labels, yet fall naturally under the umbrella of what is normally considered indie. The music of Radiohead and Wilco, for example, has long played a central part in the conversation about independent music.

The scope of a band's live performance also has little bearing on that group's identification as indie. Arcade Fire and LCD Soundsystem have played increasingly larger venues, ultimately both selling out Madison Square Garden, yet many would still identify them as indie bands. For some, then, indie can be defined as a *genre* of music, not a strict term of commerce. It's not unusual for a young music fan, when asked what kind of bands she listens to, to say, "Oh, you know, I like *indie*." While one might think that artists referred to as indie would have some major musical characteristics in common, the label has been applied to acts as dissimilar as Brooklyn rock band The National, folk artist Sufjan Stevens, and rapper MF Doom. If indie is indeed a genre, it's one whose diversity renders it almost meaningless as a classifying term.

If the musical and economic definitions of indie are fundamentally flawed, its cultural meaning is even more problematic. As indie entered into the cultural lexicon, the term "hipster," originally used in the 1940s to refer to bebop-loving, beat poetry-writing, consciousness-expanding young urbanties, was resurrected and applied to a rising subculture of bohemians who listened to obscure music, sported vintage clothing, and embraced the irony of making decidedly "uncool" things seem "cool" (i.e. dark-rimmed glasses, trucker hats, and Pabst Blue Ribbon beer). The internet exploded simultaneously with awareness of this subculture among the general public. Stereotypes about hipsters have spread digitally at astounding rates since the early 2000s. Hipster has become more of a pejorative than an objectively descriptive term for a particular subculture. The image of a pretentious, overly self-conscious snob always one step ahead of everyone else and obsessed with letting you know that they have been listening to the coolest bands years before they were popular has become digitally ubiquitous. Blogs with titles such as Diehipster.com are full of diatribes against such individuals. The current TV show *Portlandia* on Independent Film Channel is in some ways a satirical culmination of all these stereotypes, although the program's criticism of all things hipster functions more like a gentle ribbing than outright invective, perhaps because stars and co-creators Carrie Brownstein and Fred Armisen identify themselves with the culture that they mock.[2] The association of indie with this controversial subculture runs the risk of trivializing the music, rendering it merely a cultural product to use to prove one's hipness rather than authentic art that is worth experiencing for its own sake.

2 Daley, David. "Portlandia" Stars: Why We Tease the Cool Kids." *Salon*. 1 Jan. 2012. Web. 15 Jan. 2013. <http://www.salon.com/2012/01/01/%E2%80%9Cportlandia%E2%80%9D_stars_why_we_tease_the_cool_kids/>.

Since the generic, economic, and cultural meanings of indie inadequately explain why the concept has such staying power, a different definition is needed. Perhaps indie is most usefully thought of as a sensibility or spirit. Those who identify as indie, no matter what type of music they listen to, what subcultures they identify with, or whether or not the artists they admire are signed to a major label, tend to share a common set of values. They respect artists who embrace such ideals as independence (evident in the word "indie"), open-mindedness, creativity, authenticity, sincerity, spontaneity, and integrity. Living in a mind-numbingly complex, fragmented world has driven those pursing the indie dream to seek out life in a spiritually deadened American popular culture.

The proliferation of the internet and its accompanying technologies over the past couple decades has helped spread this dream while simultaneously making it seem more and more out of reach by the second. On one hand, the web has exposed a greater number of people to music that normally wouldn't be accessible to them. Streaming services such as Spotify and Rhapsody allow instant access to an overwhelming musical library, affording consumers the opportunity to embrace the indie value of open-mindedness by exploring genres and artists that might normally be off their radar. There is a price to pay, though, for such convenience and endless possibility, since artists see very little revenue through such services, making it even harder for them to focus on creating art rather than scrapping for money.[3] This financial challenge leads independent artists to pursue websites like Bandcamp to give their fans direct access to music, offering downloads, streams, and purchases without the pesky "middle man" of a record company.

On the other hand, the positive effects of this wide availability of musical choices have been poisoned by an emerging indie PR machine not unlike that of the corporate pop world. With the expansion of social media, in-depth critical analysis of exciting, original music has often been replaced by bite-sized blurbs intended to promote hype for a product. The magazine *Spin*, long a bastion of respectable alternative journalism, has replaced many of their normal reviews from their website with 140-character Twitter assessments.[4] *Pitchfork*, which started as a relatively small, irreverent voice for underground music, has reached media powerhouse status. The site arguably has more influence today on the popularity and reception of new music, especially with the younger generations, than old print standbys such as *Rolling Stone*. While the site still covers a wide range of music, it also features multimedia content that serves more as advertisement for bands than critical engagement with art. Watching a rapper bragging about his bling or a punk group getting drunk on a boat does little to further musical discourse. Aggregate sites like *Hype Machine* compile links to streaming mp3s of new songs based upon their popularity, serving as de facto gatekeepers for what music should be considered "important" or "worth checking

3 Sydell, Laura. "How Musicians Make Money (By the Fraction of a Cent) on Spotify." *The Record: Music News from NPR*. National Public Radio, 26 Sept. 2012. Web. 15 Jan. 2013.

4 Powers, Ann, and Jacob Ganz. "Are 140-Character Reviews the Future of Music Criticism?." *The Record: Music News from NPR*. National Public Radio, 13 Jan. 2012. Web. 15 Jan. 2013.

out." The website *Hipster Runoff*, run by the pseudonymous Carles, satirizes the notion of "hype" and internet culture. Carles recently wrote a rather serious piece, though, in which he suggests that we are facing a "broken Indie Buzz Machine."[5] Many of the so-called indie blogs and webzines of today, rather than advocating for little-known artists that the writers find personally meaningful, function as tastemakers that effectively determine the "coolness" of a particular band. Because of this influence, indie now has a set of canonical artists and albums that you simply must be into to maintain your indie cred. There are thousands of indie blogs on the internet today, but a large majority cover the same agreed-upon artists because they have been deemed hip by the most influential media outlets. Judging by what one reads on the internet, indie often seems just as narrow and close-minded as mainstream music culture.

Unfortunately, it is more difficult today than ever to be truly indie, to retain independence and authenticity amidst the noise of emotionless irony and senseless hype. The question of how the powerful tools of technology can be used to move the music marketplace closer to indie ideals is an open one. Perhaps the best thing that could happen to indie culture as we know it is for artists and consumers to rededicate themselves to Ralph Waldo Emerson's assertion that "imitation is suicide" and stop worrying about what the most vocal tastemakers say is "cool." As long as media outlets prioritize search engine optimization over engaging, interesting content, the indie dream will be far from view. Imagine a website that covered not just the same guitar-driven bands that have been hyped to death on every other blog, but authentic music from scenes and genres often neglected in the indie conversation (say jazz and bluegrass, for example). What if bloggers' end-of-year lists consisted not just of the tired, predictable choices found on site after site, but music truly off the reader's radar? Perhaps the biggest current tastemakers could make a conscious effort to resist the seductive powers of the indie PR game, which often promotes the status quo, and actively seek out worthy emerging artists in local scenes across the country. One must believe that the indie dream, no matter how unhealthy its current state, will ultimately prevail as long as there are still musicians and consumers who believe that adventure and beauty can be found in their art. After all, optimism is an indie ideal as well.

---

5 Carles. "How Indie Finally OFFICIALLY Died: The Broken Indie Machine." *Hipster Runoff*. 5 Oct. 2012. Web. 15 Jan. 2013.

Invent

Consider the perspective of the author. Is this a completely objective piece, or is it more subjective? Is he reporting or advocating? Where does he come down on the benefits of indie music? Do you think he's a hipster? Why or why not?

Compose

For the next two days, keep a log of all the music you hear and where you hear it. Analyze that data to determine how the wide availability of music determines the music you most enjoy. How independent are your music choices? Where do you get your music from the most (iTunes, Pandora, YouTube, etc.)? Write up a small report in which you make a specific claim as to what the data suggests about your listening habits.

Collaborate

In a small group, make a list of your ten favorite artists and then compare that with your peers. How many are the same? Discuss to what degree you feel your musical choice is independent when compared to your peers.

Explore

1. Go to Pitchfork.com and analyze the way the site is put together (layout, presence of advertisement, design of the page, etc.). What does the design suggest about the independence of the site? Analyze the manner in which indie ideals are, or are not, at work on the site.

2. Go to YouTube, and watch Arcade Fire's acceptance speech at the Grammy's (YouTube search: Arcade Fire accepting Grammy). Notice that this "indie" band beat out four established mainstream artists for Album of the Year (Katy Perry, Eminem, Lady Antebellum, and Lady Gaga). Also watch their backstage interview (YouTube search: Arcade Fire backstage at Grammys). How does their reaction to this mainstream award reveal their indie approach to music and the mainstream music scene?

3. Go to www.hipsterrunoff.com, the website that Adams mentions, to take a look at the way in which hipsters are made fun of by its authors.

Jesse Walker is managing editor of Reason *magazine. He has written on topics ranging from pirate radio to copyright law to political paranoia, and is the author of* Rebels on the Air: An Alternative History of Radio in America *and* The United States of Paranoia: A Conspiracy Theory.

2010: THE YEAR JOHN CAGE BROKE— AMATEUR PRODUCERS AND UNEXPECTED MUSIC

BY JESSE WALKER

The week before Christmas, the number 21 spot on the British pop charts was held by a supergroup called Cage Against the Machine, a gang of pop stars who had gathered to record John Cage's 1952 composition "4' 33"." They had hoped to take the track to number one, thus denying the Christmas top spot to any alumnus of *The X Factor*, an *American Idol*-style show that the Cage crew despised. They failed at that, but it's still impressive that they made it halfway up the top 40, considering the track they chose to record.

"4' 33"" sounds like a joke the first time you hear it described: The musicians sit onstage doing nothing for four minutes and 33 seconds. The piece is sometimes described as four minutes and 33 seconds "of silence," but that isn't really right: The music consists of all the ambient noises in the concert hall that we usually filter out. Cage believed that every sound is musical. As he put it, "Music is everywhere, you just have to have the ears to hear it."

In 2010, that sounds less like a philosophical statement and more like a matter-of-fact description of one of the paths popular music has been taking. It's appropriate for Cage to enter the top 40 at the end of a year that saw a hit fashioned from a TV news report.

"The Bed Intruder Song," which crept into the *Billboard* Hot 100 in August and made it to number 3 on the iTunes R&B chart, was born when an Alabama man chased a would-be rapist out of his sister's room one night. Interviewed afterward by WAFF-TV, Antoine Dodson was still angry. "Well, obviously, we have a rapist in Lincoln Park," he exclaimed. "He's climbing in your windows, he's snatching your people up, trying to rape 'em, so you all need to hide your kids, hide your wife, and hide your husband 'cause they're raping everybody out here." His rant became a hit in that great repository of found footage, YouTube. And then the Gregory Brothers, the comedians behind the Auto-Tune the News series, remixed it into a song, with Dodson's monologue auto-tuned into lyrics. The Gregorys had been doing this to news reports and other footage since April 2009 and had gathered a substantial cult following, but this recording was their breakthrough into the mainstream.

Music is everywhere, you just have to have the ears to hear it. And if you *don't* have the ears to hear it, don't fret: Let a couple of comics add some auto-tune and an electronic beat, and you'll get there. Hard-core Cageans may call it a crutch, but the results are too fun for me to start complaining.

Not that many years ago, it was a cliché to accuse auto-tune of subverting good music by making everyone sound the same. Every variation from perfect pitch was being sanded away, the complaint went, all in the interest of creating conformist and predictable pop hits. Since then, though, it's become common to use auto-tune the opposite way: to distort voices rather than homogenizing them, to create new effects rather than replicating old ones. And what has happened to Antoine Dodson and the other stars of Auto-Tune the News undermines those old complaints even more thoroughly. Thanks to sampling, it was already possible to turn any sound in the world into a part of a song, from a dripping faucet to an air raid siren. Now, with auto-tune, anything anyone says can be turned into a lyrical performance. Cagean purists can quietly contemplate the music of rustling leaves and car alarms and the teenager across the street screaming at her parents; pop Cageans can feed those sounds into a computer and dance to the results.

And anyone with a laptop and the appropriate plug-ins can do this. That too marks a change. Producers used to be the shadowy illuminati of the music world. With occasional exceptions—Phil Spector, George Martin, Rick Rubin—they were nearly anonymous. Producers avoided the limelight while the musicians they worked with basked in stardom, even when the producer clearly bore more responsibility for a hit song's sound than the artist credited on the sleeve. In the disco era, an anonymous producer might hire anonymous session musicians and then release the results under the name of an entirely fictitious "group." In a culture fixated on "authenticity," that helped disco acquire its plastic reputation, though in retrospect the practice was no more inauthentic—and possibly more honest—than the customs of the rock world.

Now that the producer's tools are as widely distributed as electric guitars and drum kits, the picture looks a little different. The Gregory Brothers have split the profits from "The Bed Intruder Song" with Antoine Dodson, explaining that "He wrote the lyrics, he's the one who put it out there." That's very decent of them, and I in no way want to argue against their decision to do it. But as a simple matter of public perception, it's the Gregory Brothers, not Dodson, who are seen as the artists behind the song. (It helps that they inserted themselves into the recording, as they usually do—though if you ask me, their clips would be better if they left themselves out.) In the mash-up era, anyone on the Internet can be conscripted into a band; if you wanted to turn Dodson, the "Dude, You Have No Quran" guy, and the world leader of your choice into a viral-video supergroup, you could mash them up in your basement in an afternoon or two and then release the results online without the bandmates ever learning that they participated. Even if the song becomes a hit, they might not find out that they were a part of it.

If you listened to "4' 33"" on Christmas, anyone in earshot was unwittingly a part of a top 40 hit: your aunt banging around in the kitchen, your son playing a game in the living room, your dad washing his hands in the bathroom. The BBC refused to play "4' 33"" when it charted, on the grounds that "the majority of BBC Radio 1's listeners" would not be interested. But you don't need to rely on any DJ to hear Cage on the BBC, or on any other station in the world. Just turn the volume down as far as it will go, and listen intently for four minutes and 33 seconds.

Invent

John Cage's 1952 musical score, "4'33"," may seem strange to most people, but, as Walker points out, the composition is not simply four and a half minutes of silence. Rather, it's a song that focuses on the ambient noises in a concert hall. Do you agree that "every sound is musical"? Why or why not? What do you think makes something musical versus just being noise? Do you agree that current trends in music support this assertion? What do you think of Walker's argument that what Cage was after is now common in today's music?

Compose

Listen to a performance of Cage's "4'33"" composition and attend carefully to all the ambient noises you hear during the process. You can choose to listen to the piece in a concert hall or anywhere you like (even your classroom). Remember that the time (4'33") matters, so make sure and acquire an accurate recording of the piece (there are many online). Once done, freewrite about the experience and the process of listening to this composition. What did you notice? Where did your mind travel?

As a class or in small groups, watch a performance of "4'33"." Try to find one that is as close to the original intent as possible (i.e., in a concert hall). There are plenty of videos of live performances on YouTube. After watching the performance, jot down your thoughts on the performance. What stood out to you and why? Then, in small groups, discuss your findings with each other to see if there were any shared experiences. Next, watch a modern version (a dubstep remix version, for example). Discuss whether modern versions, removed from a concert hall, provide an experience similar to that which Cage had in mind. Talk about how Cage's attempt at making "noises" musical applies to the auto-tune phenomenon Walker discusses.

Via YouTube, watch the auto-tune songs and videos Walker alludes to in his essay (YouTube search: "The Bed Intruder Song" and "Dude, You have no Quran." Research the history of auto-tune and its initial foray into music. Who was the first to use it in pop music? Spend some time skimming the numerous articles on the Internet debating its use in pitch correction. What are the reasons most given for its necessity? What are the reasons some think it shouldn't be used at all?

Rod C. Taylor is the editor of (E)Tunes and an Assistant Professor of Literature and Writing at Tennessee State University, specializing in literature, writing, and popular music studies. In addition to his academic work, Rod has long been involved in music, both as a performer and as an academic. A bass player for over two decades, he has written numerous articles for a variety of music magazines, including Bass Player magazine, Bass Guitar Magazine, and No Treble. As a bassist, Rod has been fortunate enough to play and/or record with Krista Detor, Artemis Robison, Victor Wooten, Chuck Rainey, Steve Bailey, Stew McKinsey, Jake Adams, and a variety of other great musicians. When he's not teaching or writing, you're likely to find him recording in his home studio, located in Nashville, TN.

WINNERS AND LOSERS IN DIGITAL RECORDING

By Rod C. Taylor

Over the last few decades, digital technology has ushered in a variety of changes, all of which have greatly impacted the way music is created and consumed. In the world of music creation, that impact is most clearly manifested in the switch from analog to digital recording.[1] On the surface, it might seem like a simple change in the medium used by recording engineers, a minor modification in the way sound gets encoded for purposes of mass audio production. That's just the tip of the iceberg, however. As the ability to convert music into zeroes and ones emerged, so did a brave new world of sound recording, and the transformations in equipment and recording techniques have been numerous, intense, and on a scale that might never be repeated. To put it in some perspective, those who own an Apple computer have at their fingertips pre-installed free software that would put most analog studios from the 70s and 80s to shame in terms of its capabilities and ease of use. Similarly, on my iPhone I have a $4.99 recording app that easily outperforms my first analog studio interface, purchased in the early 90s—a Tascam 464 4-track that originally cost $1000.

---

1   In its most simple form, analog recording can be thought of as the transfer of sound wave signals into or onto a medium—most often as physical texture (as with records) or via magnetic tape (as with a cassette tape). Digital recording relies upon the converting of analog signals into discrete numbers, whereby they can be easily manipulated, replicated, and reproduced via computers and other digital interfaces.

While accessibility and economic feasibility of professional recording represents just two of the major shifts initiated by digital recording, they are surely two of the most obvious, and each spawned its own revolution in music. As recording equipment became more widely available and affordable, a new generation of musicians and recording engineers emerged, which, in turn, brought about further significant changes. Amateur home studios began popping up everywhere, allowing more and more musicians to

Tascam 464

produce their own CDs. Bands suddenly didn't need to purchase pro studio time to offer fans a copy of their music; they could just take that money and purchase their own studio gear. As you might imagine, as the demand for home studios grew, so did the availability of new (and less expensive) gear. Each reality fueled the other. One can think of the advent of digital recording as the first domino to fall in a long line of dominoes that, to this day, still continue to tumble in the recording industry.

New forms of technology, especially those that prove themselves truly revolutionary, tend to bring about two realities. In one, new knowledge is gained, new techniques discovered, new approaches embraced, and new equipment invented. In the other, existing knowledge quickly becomes irrelevant, specialized skill sets gained through years of study prove outdated, older approaches are set aside, and older equipment rendered obsolete. It happens so fast. One minute we're all writing letters and mailing them to our loved ones, and in the next email is invented and "snail mail" is passé. As indicated above, in these kinds of revolutions some things are gained and some things lost. In each case, you'll find some running as fast as the can toward the future and all it has to offer, while others cling with all their might to "the way things were."

Still, there are also those who try and find a balance in all of it, those who seek to take on the best the new technology has to offer, while bringing with them the best from the older devices and techniques. Such has been the case for many successful music producers, four of whom I interviewed in the summer of 2012 while visiting Nashville, Tennessee, a city I now call home. Each has a career that spans both analog and digital recording, and each has had to learn to navigate the changes in order to continue successfully making music. In talking with Mark Bright, Tommy Sims, Steve Taylor, and Richard Dodd, I learned that no matter how different producers are from one another (each is quite distinct in his focus), they tend to share similar attitudes when it comes to pondering what we've won and what we've lost with the arrival of digital recording. What follows are some excerpts from these interviews on just a few key areas that I discussed with each producer. To be clear, there are far more consequences, good and bad, related to the proliferation of digital recording than we will be discussing here, but I choose to focus on the ones that these producers felt most impacted their lives in the practical world of music recording. As you'll see, the influence of digital technology on the music business ranges from the psychological to mechanical—and everything in between.

© Tony Phipps

Mark Bright is one of the top country producers in Nashville. He has produced all of Carrie Underwood's albums (which have led to multiple Grammys), as well as the music of BlackHawk, Sara Evans, Lonestar, Scotty McCreery, Reba McEntire, Jo Dee Messina, and Rascal Flatts, to name just a few. Growing up in East Texas, Mark cut his recording teeth on a makeshift 8-track recording studio in the back of TV repair shop in Longview, Texas. That was around 1978, and Mark would learn much from that experience, and soon after he would choose to pursue recording as a career. In 1981, he moved to Nashville, TN, and over the next few decades would serve as both the Vice President of EMI Music Publishing and CEO of Word Entertainment. He would also start a couple of record labels, one of which launched the career of Rascall Flatts. Through it all, Mark continued to record and produce records, transitioning from analog recording to digital in the process. He feels strongly that his experience with both eras helped him gain a better understanding of how to make great records.

Mark Bright

"I feel like I gained something by starting in the analog era," Bright says. "I think you gain something else when you come into it with only digital recording, but it's a different learning curve. I think I gained a little bit more wisdom, however, because I benefited from the origins of analog and digital recording. Kids learning recording today are only going to learn the origins of digital recording."

© James Waddell

That's a sentiment shared by 5x Grammy Award winning mixing and mastering engineer/producer, Richard Dodd. Since his first big hit production, "Kung Fu Fighting" (1974), to his Grammy award winning work on Tom Petty's *Wildflowers* (1994), Dodd has proven himself to be both highly skilled and versatile in the field of audio engineering. In the last few years, Richard has switched to exclusively mastering albums in Nashville, and with much success. For example, he mastered all of Jason Aldean's Platinum albums, including ten of Jason's #1 hit singles. Like all successful

Richard Dodd

producers and engineers from the 60s and 70s, Dodd had to work with equipment that demanded he dedicated a lot of time to figuring out how to manipulate analog machines, but he has no regrets. "I can tell you that I'm very grateful for the fact that I had to learn the way I did, because I am able to apply so much of it to the methods I use in digital recording." The other producers interviewed feel likewise. Having learned "the hard way," they now work with digital technology more efficiently and artistically.

Steve Taylor

Digital technology also made recording far more affordable, an aspect producer and recording artist Steve Taylor celebrates. Taylor's career as an artist spans over two decades and has earned him two Grammy nominations for his albums *Meltdown* (1984) and *Squint* (1993) long with two Billboard Music Video Awards. Steve produced a variety of artists in the nineties, mostly notably Sixpence None the Richer (of "Kiss Me" and "There She Goes" fame), and the highly successful Christian rock band, Newsboys. He's also directed and produced numerous music videos and two feature films. Steve explains that in his early years as an artist there was always a gap between what he heard in his head and what he could afford to pay for in the studio. "I think that gap has shrunk over a time," he says, "largely due to the digital revolution. When I first started recording, the basic tools of recording—multi-track tapes, analog tapes, mixing boards, microphones—all if was very expensive. When it came time to record, it wasn't just the quality of musicians that mattered. It was the quality of the gear that they were using. So, if you wanted a certain sound, you knew that you were going to have to buy that piece of gear for five or ten thousand dollars, or you were going to have to rent it for three to five hundred dollars a day. So, from a creative standpoint, digital recording has been a good thing." Mark Bright agrees. "Frankly, analog recording was too costly for most people," he admits. "Just the expense of buying mounds and mounds of 2-inch tape to make a record was prohibitively expensive for most people, whereas opening up a MacBook Pro and turning on Logic or Garage Band is not."

Such affordability can have some drawbacks as well, as producer and multi-instrumentalist Tommy Sims points out. Over the past three decades, Sims has contributed in some way (either as musician, writer, vocalist, or producer) to more than 45 million records. Along the way, he's earned 4 Grammys, 3 Stellar Awards, 7 Dove Awards, multiple ASCAP Songwriter/Performance Awards, and the Nashville Bass Player of the Year Award. Credited on over 350 different albums, Tommy has worked with approximately 150 artists, from Bruce Springsteen and Bonnie Raitt to Taylor Swift and Michael McDonald. He's a man who loves using and supporting live instrumentation on albums. Still, he explains how the digital craze of the late eighties and nineties worked

Tommy Sims

against that approach, even if it was to his advantage. "When I moved to Nashville, one of my primary aspirations in music was to arrange, so in that sense digital technology was invaluable," Tommy says. "It was amazing to be able to buy these little boxes and various devices that could emulate real strings and real horns. I could effectively mock up all kinds of instruments with these various gadgets that every couple of years were getting better and better, and getting more authentic. It went from the cheesy digital patches to samplers, then to stereo samplers. Then it went from 16-bit samplers to 24-bit. It just kept growing and growing. All this was amazing for a guy like me in the line of work that I was in." As Tommy grew more skilled at using digital machine, his reputation as a producer and multi-instrumentalist grew as well. He reveals that his discomfort began when artists began seeing him as a one-man band, so to speak. They could just hire him and his digital machines, and no one else, for half the cost. That didn't sit well with his goals as a producer. "I always thought that when I got to produce I'd get to hire all these great musicians I'd grown up admiring, and I'd make records like that. But that's not what happened."

Such overreliance on digital instrumentation concerned him, and he now actively works to encourage more traditional instrumentation alongside the digital technology. But that approach came about through his personal trials as a young producer. For some time, he struggled with the trend to not use live instrumentation or band members on albums. "I remember going through much of the nineties pretty much in a real funk, in terms of producing," he explains. "I mean, I was riding a pretty strong wave career wise, but internally I was having a real struggle being a part of a genre or an industry that I felt was just killing itself—just absolutely, on purpose, fostering the extinction of something I considered so beautiful: that thing when four or five musicians get together and lay down a song in the studio, making something beautiful out of it." For the next few years following that realization, Tommy used his machines very little. "I just didn't care about the trend," he says. "I could write songs and make a living, but I didn't want to make those machine-oriented records. I only want to make records where people wanted to use real musicians." Tommy wasn't alone in this approach. Much of the music in the 90's and into the early 2000's featured digital, or "canned," instruments, and, like Tommy, a number of producers realized something valuable was being lost in the process and would later work hard to move live musicians back into the studio. But digitized instrumentation wasn't the only aspect of digital recording that gave producers and engineers pause.

For many, music recorded on digital devices, or through digital instruments, proved to be a bit *too* polished for their tastes. Mark Bright recalls his own reaction to the first time he experimented with digital recording: "I remember when Apple started coming out with basic Garage Band. I had just bought all this used—very used—analog recording equipment, and then I got my first Garage Band. At first, I thought, 'I'm never going to use that analog stuff again because this sounds twice as good.' It's so clean and quite. Then I started recognizing just *how* clean and quite. 'Wait a minute,' I told myself, 'it's too clean, too quiet.'" For Mark, recording needs to provide a certain amount of audible space, where one might be able to imagine the artist singing in a room. Similarly, the human voice needs to be able to reveal its organic qualities, and if the recording is too clean or too polished that becomes difficult to project. Through these kinds of experiences, producers and engineers began to realize that while digital technology made recording more affordable and much easier, certain aspects of the process that attributed to an album's success were being lost.

"We've lost the art of decision making, along with a willingness to commit," Richard Dodd argues. "With analog recording, you could not easily redo, undo, or adjust what you recorded. In some cases, since analog multi-tracks were often quite limited in the amount of tracks they could offer, producers were forced to make decisions regarding what instruments would share the same track. As a result, you had to make a decision and commit yourself to it," he points out. "Consequently, the final product, if multi-track and overdubs were involved, was an amalgam of decisions and corrections and acceptance of those decisions. Nowadays, we have undo and can just set it, hit play, drop in, record, and save it…play, drop in, record, save it, play, drop in record, and so on. It makes no difference. You just have to get a track close enough and then technology can repair it and change it and alter it to what you think it needs to be."

Steve Taylor argues that the ability to alter, correct, and change everything too easily takes away from the nervous energy that can occur when recording, something he feels can lead to creativity. "It would always happen in the studio when you had to make a decision," he explains. "Is the best take this one, or is it this one? We had to get rid of one of them to save space, so we had to choose. That creates a certain amount of angst, right? And nervousness—all because you've got to make decisions. And then you go to the digital world and it's a different thing because now you know there's no reason to erase anything, so you keep it all. No decision needed." As a result, Taylor sometimes finds himself dissatisfied by how long it can take to finish a project. "It shouldn't be taking this long," he says. "We just have too many options—the possibilities are limitless and sometime you end up not making decisions." One of the bad sides of digitalization, he argues, is that it can create kind of a laziness or attitude that one can always fix it later. "It lowers the stakes, the immediate stakes, and I'm not sure that's good for the creative process."

Focusing on the seemingly simple task of muting a portion of a recorded track, Richard Dodd supplies an example to drive home the difference between the decision making process when it comes to analog vs. digital recording:

> There's a massive difference between going to a track on the edit window of a computer program, selecting a portion of a track, and hitting "Command M" to mute it. With a tape machine, you would roll to the bit you didn't want to

hear, turn the tape oxide up, work out where track 3 would be with the part your wanted to mute. You would then physically cut that piece out of the tape and apply some rubbed splicing tape on the back side just to make sure it didn't fray the edges. Now the note is muted, for good. You're not going to undo that. There is no back up of that tape. You cannot make a mistake, you can't undo it, and you can't go to a copy. That's the amazing thing. How we existed day to week to month with one fragile master back then, I don't know. That would scare the pants off anyone nowadays."

Most producers seem to agree that the analog era forced engineers and producers to become adept at making quick judgment calls, knowing that they could not undo many of the decisions once they were made. Still, most appreciate the ease with which digital recording allows them to work with a recording and the degree to which it allows them flexibility in how they handle the master recordings. "Digital technology offers freedom on the front end," Mark Bright asserts. "You could suddenly take the whole project home with you and work as long as you wanted, and the tracks never fall off the tape or degenerate over time. That was always a real problem with analog tape when you were working for a long time on a record."

These types of changes to the way producers approach recording in the digital age extend beyond the control room, however, as new technology affects the way consumers listen to the music produced in the studios. As such, producers have had to come to grips with certain realities that are less than ideal, while also trying to make the best of it. Along with the iPod and other MP3 style devices, a host of new headphones and desktop speakers have emerged. As Mark Bright explains, the quality of those speakers must be considered as well when mixing and mastering any album. "I have to mix to the lowest common denominator and to the highest level I can, simultaneously. I want to make sure that the mix sounds good on a pair of computer speakers, a set of cheap headphones, and on a pair of $30,000 studio reference monitors. That's just the way it is. It's got to sound good on Dre's Beats, Apple's headphones (which are fairly terrible), and everything in between. If you've done the job right, what you've mixed is going to sound reasonably good through all those crummy speakers, sound magnificent through expensive speakers, and still be enjoyable on everything in between." Bright points out that he would love for everyone to listen through great speakers, but he accepts the fact that such a reality will never come to pass.

For Tommy Sims, as for the other Nashville producers, the key for navigating these changes, as well as the others we haven't discussed here, lies in understanding that digital technology, like its analog counterpart, is ultimately just a tool, and it's use (or abuse) depends upon the how producers, engineers, and musicians use it. "I recognize that technology is there to aid us in creating music, and it's not an enemy," Tommy says. "It's meant to be an ally, but every tool is about the hands in which we find it being used. I think now that's where I'm at. I'm trying to make it more of an individual thing; different records call for different things."

Each of these producers has had to, in some way, come to terms with what we've gained and lost with the proliferation of digital technology in the recording process. And each is still optimistic that there are more winners than losers in the process. For his part, Richard Dodd credits his continued success, at least in part, from not trying to recreate the past. "It's a crazy world now," he says. "It's very different, but I'm still optimistic about it. What hurts is when I try to make music like it was. That's painful, and that's when I get sad. But when I try to make the most of what it is, then I'm okay again. It's different. Very different." For Steve Taylor, the ability of digital software to "fix" anything and make it perfect has led to a devaluation of raw talent and authenticity in albums, but he sees the upside of that as well. "You know, perfection is no longer something to be desired because anybody can achieve it," he says. "If perfection can be achieved by anybody with a laptop, then what's the new goal? You really have no idea if you're hearing perfection or not if you're listening to a recording. I think that has increased the value of live performances in some ways, because now that's the only place we can go to see if we're hearing authentic musicianship."

Mark Bright remains inspired by his quest to continue to produce hit songs regardless of the changing digital landscape. "The thing that motivates me," he says "is when you have big hits created with the new technology in that given year." He's committed to embracing whatever changes come. "Technology changes so fast now. I tell you what, five years from now, CDs, MP3, YouTube, etc. won't be in the conversation. It will all be dead and done. It's going to be that new thing over there–some technology that's not even here now—that's going to take off like a rocket ship. And new hits will still come; new music will still be made. That's the exciting stuff. And guess what? It always happens. That's why I'm sitting down in the studio day in and day out, making something new that's fresh sounding, something that's going to sound amazing. And it gets me just completely jazzed up and excited to think that maybe it comes from my end of the pool." Tommy sees the need to navigate the digital and analog divide and its continued changes by taking the best of both, and—like Bright—he acknowledges that good music, regardless of the process, is still being produced, and that's a positive thing. "Even if there are fewer musicians involved in making a record, people are still making music," he says. "They're still writing songs, and they're still creating from that space, even if it's just one guy in the room with his laptop."

In the end, what these interviews demonstrate is that there is no substitute for the human element in the creation and production of music. No matter how easy technology makes it, producers like Bright, Sims, Taylor, and Dodd prove the irreplaceable role that the human heart, mind, and spirit plays in producing the music that moves us. With good music as the goal, then, it seems that despite what's been lost in the transition from analog to digital recording, we're all still winners.

Invent

Unless you're into music production, the topic of digital recording might at first seem irrelevant, but as you have seen in this essay, that is not the case. How might what happens in the professional studio affect your life as it pertains to music? Have you see any of the effects of the analog-to-digital transition that these producers speak to in the essay? If you listen to music from the 60s, 70s, or 80s, what kinds of sonic differences do you notice between that era and the one now?

Compose

In this essay, each producer reveals some of the challenges that he has faced in making the analog-to-digital transition. Pick a producer and write an informal response to their arguments. For instance, you might take on Tommy Sims's contention that live musicians in the studio are better than digital ones, or you might challenge Richard Dodd's and Steve Taylor's thoughts on the value of decision making in the production of music. Remember not to offer just your opinion, but rather support your view with examples, just as they did.

Collaborate

Divide into four groups, and have each select a different producer on which to focus their attention. Using the web, research your chosen subject and learn what you can about his or her history, projects, and musical taste. Don't forget to check YouTube. For example, on YouTube you can find a video interview of Mark Bright, in his studio, talking about the recording of Carrie Underwood's 2012 album, *Blown Away* (YouTube search: Mark Bright and Carrie Underwood Interview). Pay special attention to the aspects of the producers' lives or projects that demonstrate the kinds of things discussed in the essay. Check out Tommy Sims's recollection of listening to records (YouTube search: Get to know Tommy Sims), or Steve Taylor's Kickstarter video where he makes fun of having taken a long break from the rock music scene (YouTube search: Steve Taylor and the Perfect Foil Kickstarter). When you're done with your research, you might put together a short presentation for your classmates so they can benefit from your research.

Explore

Build your own studio! Do some research to learn what equipment a basic professional digital studio requires and then work to create that studio via online shopping. Using sites like Musiciansfriend.com, Americanmusical.com, or Sweetwater.com, you can find more than enough items to fulfill your mission. Be ready; there are many options. If you like, make it a contest with others in your class. First, try to create the cheapest, but still respectable, digital studio possible. Next, try and spend as much as possible, creating the most expensive studio you can. Create an itemized budget to keep track of what you are spending. When you are done, do a little more research to see what it would have cost to build similar size studios in the analog days. You'll probably have to be a little creative here as some modern options were not even available back then.

Rossen Ventzislavov received his Ph.D in Philosophy from The Graduate Center of the City University of New York, and is currently Assistant Professor in the Art History department. His doctoral thesis explored the normative, aesthetic, and substantive dimensions of the language of early analytic philosophy. His interests include aesthetics, the history of philosophy, continental thought, and critical theory. He has published work in the philosophy of architecture, the aesthetics of popular music, and the history of philosophy. His current research focuses on lyrical nonsense in music and on curatorial wisdom.

THE TIME IS NOW: ACCEPTANCE AND CONQUEST IN POP MUSIC

BY ROSSEN VENTZISLAVOV

But the merit of a work of art is not measured so much by the power with which the suggested feeling takes hold of us as by the richness of that feeling itself: in other words, besides degrees of intensity we instinctively distinguish degrees of depth or elevation.

— Henri Bergson

In what follows, I will try to critically discuss the underpinnings of contemporary pop culture from a very specific, and admittedly limited, angle. As a consumer of contemporary popular music, I have, on numerous occasions, encountered a curious tangle—any given work that belongs to this problematic class can invite aesthetic judgment of a seasoned, educated kind although simultaneously remaining immune to considerations of authenticity, originality, artistry, and longevity, all customary markers of aesthetics proper. This paradox teases out a new problem for aesthetics today—that of locating pop music in the listener's ear, sufficiently far from claims of understanding what we like and not too close to claims of liking what we have understood. The part of the proverbial beholder is assumed by the (willing) consumer of popular music, someone who *simply likes* what they hear or at least they think that they *simply* do. My interest here is less in the passive dynamics of such liking and consumption, and more in the active forces that create the conditions for these forms of listenership. The two dimensions in which my study will operate are thus, first, the element of conquest inherent in the proliferation of pop music and, second, the forceful illusion of authenticity that distinguishes most of the musical works in question. The corresponding questions I will try to answer will be: Can the infectious character of pop music's dissemination and acceptance be reconciled with some understanding of art writ large? And, does pop music's claim to authenticity square with authenticity as a proper aesthetic category? These matters, and especially the initial paradox I identify, would not gain any traction if it were an easy task to define pop music apart or even away from music-as-art. This, however, should be, and is, difficult when pop has voraciously adopted and intensified the relevance of the aesthetic categories that its very existence undermines. One solution to these tensions that I will suggest is to view pop music as an artistic event of a very strict temporal order—the short-term falling of tropes of various origin and aesthetic merit on uncritical ears. This vantage point may help lay the groundwork for an aesthetics of pop music that is not painfully at odds with traditional aesthetic judgment. In the few theoretical steps I will take toward this daunting goal I will refer to Denis Dutton's comprehensive essay "Authenticity in Art," to some of Deleuze and Guattari's work in *A Thousand Plateaus*, and, expectedly, to a few current examples of pop music.

Before I go forward, I will try to provide operational definitions for some of my key terms. I will use the expression "pop music" to refer to any musical work, which is intentionally produced for the widest audience possible, is purposely marketed as such, and is at least remotely successful in fulfilling this intention. To this I also add musical works that are not explicitly meant to reach a considerably wide audience but which by some whim of the zeitgeist, manage to do so. What this definition presupposes is a music market that involves the commercial transfer of hard or digital copies of musical recordings, organized live performances, and the dissemination of all manner of promotional materials. By "conquest" I mostly mean the tangible demographics of popularity (charts, sales statistics, media exposure, concert attendance, etc.) but also the dimension, internal to the individual experience of music, of surrendering to the perceived aesthetic or other value of any particular work, which I also identify as "liking." By "originality" I mean a loose, pre-aesthetic criterion of perceived difference and novelty in a work of pop music that in great part facilitates its conquest. These definitions, particularly the third one, are imperfect for two reasons—first, they reflect the general difficulty of placing pop music within a strict critical framework, and second, their limitations mirror the modest purposes of the present inquiry. If any of these difficulties are surmounted by its end, my paper will have achieved enough.

ACCEPTANCE-AS-TRANSACTION

As my main case study in pop music I have chosen Lady Gaga, an artist against whose hegemonic currency some of my notions are thrown into high relief. And here is the first difficulty: How do we tailor the term "artist" so as to include pop music personae such as Lady Gaga? I, as a frequent reader of various pop music reviews and articles, am well accustomed to the identification of such personae as artists, but at the same time often remain suspicious of their status as such. One reason might be the objective difficulty in locating the depth and elevation Bergson speaks about in most of their works. Another reason might be my reluctance to grant them access to what I have come to accept as the pantheon of art, a place to which Schiele, Chaucer, and Mozart, to name a few, do not require a visa. However, to draw the boundaries of this pantheon, I must be operating on assumptions of the historicity, aesthetic worth, and cultural significance that its rightful dwellers have been bestowed by many others before me. In this, I see two different kinds of acceptance emerging—acceptance-as-process and acceptance-as-transaction.

When Jay-Z raps in one of his songs "I'm not a businessman, I'm a business, man," he provides a clue as to what I mean by acceptance-as-transaction. Instances of such acceptance invariably externalize the criteria for liking or consuming music—we are *shown* or even more often directly *told* what to like (or do) through a taunt ("Who is the best rapper alive?"), a come-on ("Do I know you from somewhere?"), an order ("Free your mind and the rest will follow!") and, consequently, are left only the choice of a predetermined response. This call-and-response approach, also amply used in most live pop music performances, externalizes the simplicity and immediacy of the listening/watching experience. It is thus not unlike the acceptance of the terms of monetary transactions or any other transfer of rights. In contrast, the granting of acceptance-as-process is, as the name suggests, a gradual coming to terms with a work of art, but also with the conditions that define it as such. The greatest difference between the two kinds of acceptance is, as far as I can see, that the traditional acceptance-as-process requires some critical framework although acceptance-as-transaction seems to be comfortably effective without it.[2] But this is just the tip of a very peculiar iceberg.

Other factors which contribute to the transactional nature of pop music are its temporal specificity, the transparency of its production, delivery and success, and, last but not least, the immediacy of its aesthetic tropes. As to the first factor, pop music's temporal dynamics, it is clear that pop personae and their creative output always exist in the present tense. The requirement of longevity, so central to the appreciation and the acceptance of art proper, is here replaced by the imperative of current relevance, the cutting edge, or as in the title of one Lady Gaga song, "The Edge of Glory." The space this imperative carves out is often reducible to what economists identify as the "point-of-sale:" How else would Lady Gaga's "Edge of Glory" fare on the popular stage if it were not strategically removed in time from the chart successes (and sales receipts) of other pop acts' edges (e.g., Aerosmith) and glories (e.g., Bon Jovi)?

In the following passage, Johannes Eurich offers an important insight into the issue of music's incursion into the present moment: "Music is one of those objects of transition that create time and survive it. It is able to open up a world beyond the everyday where the need for interpreting identification of the individual is also accepted and answered as a new experience of the possibility to arrange it in a subjective way" (68). What this suggests is that music brings the temporal dimension of our existence to our attention.

Eurich associates this with a special brand of empowerment whereby the listener is afforded the ability to twist the temporal order into a subjective psychological diorama. My only objection to this picture is that, in the case of pop music specifically, the exploding of the moment is largely enacted *on* the listener rather than *by* her. In other words, the subjective re-arrangement of time that Eurich writes about is built into the experience of pop music by design and owes little to the listener's will or imagination. The reason for this is that pop music explicitly refuses, in Eurich's terms, to "survive time," to literally be remembered beyond its moment of glory, or to figuratively perpetuate itself as part of an individual's self-identification. Ultimately, if given the choice between permanence and transience, Lady Gaga may have better reasons to choose the latter.[3]

The transparency of the production, dissemination, and market success of pop music is another element of its transactional approach to acceptance. Since the advent of music television, all wheels and levers in the mechanism of pop music have apparently been laid bare. The audience is allowed into the recording studio, the pop persona's private life, and the record producer's mind. But even before music television, the what-you-see-is-what-you-get business model of pop music had been sufficiently externalized by the well-publicized concerns of public image, chart performance, ticket sales, etc. Examples that immediately come to mind are the established tradition of two pop entities battling it out at the charts (e.g., The Beatles/The Stones; Blur/Oasis; 50 Cent/Kanye West) and the frequent public feuds over dubious honors (e.g., Aretha Franklin's reclaiming of the title "The Queen of Soul" from Tina Turner after a recent telecast when said title was bestowed upon Turner by Beyoncé, a younger performer and obvious aspirant for the same honor). It is interesting that although openly laying a stake on art and artistry, such pop phenomena are in no way reliant on critical acclaim—quite the opposite; copyright controversy and critical failure are as likely to bring success as any substantive praise. Similarly, as the case of Lady Gaga suggests, musical mastery has no straightforward relation to a performer's standing on the market.[4] All pop music requires of itself is—quite literally—to colonize the public imagination.

The question of imagination is an important one for any approach to an aesthetics of pop music. Imagination is important because it seems to be integral in the manufacture of pop phenomena but almost never in our response to them. I recognize at least two ways in which the audience's imagination is colonized and rendered null—first, through pop music's use of every possible resource toward the creation and promotion of never-before-seen spectacle and, second, and more subtly, through the careful crafting of the outlandish pop personae themselves. As to the first, the example of Lady Gaga is again of great relevance—for her Los Angeles Museum of Contemporary Art's 30th Anniversary Gala performance, different aspects of her public performance were handled by conceptual artist Francesco Vezzoli, architect Frank Gehry, artist Damien Hirst, clothing designer Miuccia Prada, and movie director Baz Luhrmann to name a few. Even the wildest and most singularly creative audience member is bound to have been left speechless by such an ostentatious and variegated display of artistry. Fittingly, the song Lady Gaga debuted at the event was titled "Speechless," and the event itself was billed as "The Shortest Musical You Will Never See Again." All of the above are signifiers of exclusivity, but what is excluded, most significantly, is the possibility that somebody somewhere can even *come up* with an event more spectacular. This, of course, is not yet enough to qualify such spectacles as proper art, even though the ambition is certainly there.[5]

In his "Performance and the Postmodern in Pop Music," Tony Mitchell touches on the problem of the listener's imagination. One of his case studies is the postpunk band the Jesus and Mary Chain. Mitchell is interested in the fact that the band's work exemplifies the opposite of the tendency I have identified in pop—their music, lyrically and aesthetically, insists on leaving things to the fan's imagination. In the words of the band's singer Jim Reid, this alternative ethos is expressed as follows: "It would be possible to tell you what all the songs are about but there wouldn't be any point in it because, first of all, it encourages people not to figure it out for themselves, not to use their imagination, and also it could destroy anybody else's idea" (quoted in Mitchell 278). Needless to say, such sensitivity to the end-consumer's intelligence automatically disqualifies the respective band from the race at the pop charts.

Another instance of the co-optation of the public's imagination is the forging of pop personae. The latter is a complex process whereby fact and fiction concerning a star are introduced to the public at certain intervals, usually with a view to keeping interest in them alive, especially when there is a new product to promote. The age-old salesperson's formula that what we see is what we get is immediately applicable to the tactics of creating and selling a pop persona. For example, a performer like Marilyn Manson is compelled to insist that his persona fully permeates his being off-stage.[6] In addition to having, like Manson, chosen a culturally bipolar alias, Lady Gaga also likes to remind us that the extravagant trappings of her public engagements are a natural continuation of an equally strange private life.[7] The message in such pronouncements is that the pop persona is generously available as a reference point for the fans' self-identification—if the performer wears her alien fashions at home, her fans should feel free to do the same, too. With Lady Gaga in particular, the identification loop closes in even tighter through the exploitation of all manners of perceived social marginality. She refers to her fans as her "little monsters" and part of what draws them to her (and "Mother Monster" to them) is ostensibly the communal refusal of mainstream norms. This type of communion in pop music, as Ken McLeod argues, can be a healthy social factor.[8] But at the same time, it is always tempting to read other forms of conformity and marginalization within it.

ORIGINALITY AND AUTHENTICITY

A certain ambiguity about categories like originality and authenticity seems to pose further difficulties for the smooth identification of pop music as an art form. Lady Gaga is, in name and in person, both an explosion of idiosyncrasy and a veritable Frankenstein patched up from parts of easily identifiable pop cultural parentage. Her claim to artistry runs deep enough to include proclamations of association with an artist like Andy Warhol and, yet, the pronouncements she makes about art remain transparently glib: "Music is a lie. It is a lie. Art is a lie. You have to tell a lie that is so wonderful that your fans make it true" (quoted in Strauss 71–72). It would be glib in turn to dwell too long on the pronouncements of a pop persona. As to the lyrical content of Lady Gaga's songs, I readily defer to Nancy Bauer, whose June 20, 2010 entry, "Lady Power," to the *New York Times* philosophy blog *The Stone* persuasively argues that popularity and empowerment in the case of Lady Gaga all but equal intellectual maturity and responsibility.

Instead of asking what makes Lady Gaga original, we should pose the question: What makes people believe the lie and, as millions have done, almost make it true? A good answer is implied in cultural critic Theodor Adorno's critique of the commodity society. According to Adorno, in such a society the category of the new is "not a substantive but merely an apparent one," and "what is new about the commodities is their packaging" (qouted in Bürger 61). And indeed, Lady Gaga's appeal is not because of the substantive newness of what she does but to the adept repackaging of pop culture tropes and references. The general public's ignorance of these references is what accounts for buying into Lady Gaga's "art" and its purported originality. Without knowledge of the multiple personae of David Bowie, Bjork, Madonna, Marilyn Manson, Nina Hagen, Roisin Murphy, Peaches, Marc Bolan, Grace Jones, Alice Cooper, etc., one is much more likely to be seduced by the scandal, the androgyny, the fashions, and the crypto-intellectualism that we, in such a short time, have been conditioned to expect from Lady Gaga.

The tropes of pop are in fact so firmly in place that they often take precedence over what is supposed to be the main event, i.e., the music. Reviewers of Lady Gaga's work have noted the discrepancy between the relative blandness of her dance anthems and the borrowed piquancy of the rest of her presentation (Strauss 71). The music is also generic enough that a recent Lady Gaga release has garnered criticism for the uncanny similarity it bears to a popular hit from the early 1990s.[9] As a result of such observations, with which I mostly agree, Lady Gaga naturally becomes vulnerable to accusations of inauthenticity. It is a useful exercise to consider Denis Dutton's comprehensive study "Authenticity in Art" to try and establish whether or not any of the traditional applications of this aesthetic category are relevant to Lady Gaga and the larger culture within which she dwells.

Dutton's essay makes the distinction between nominal and expressive authenticity. The former is a category concerning "the correct identification of the origins, authorship, or provenance of an object, ensuring, as the term implies, that an object of aesthetic experience is properly named" (Dutton Part 1). The latter category covers what Dutton calls "committed, personal expression, being true musically to one's artistic self, rather than true to an historical tradition" (Dutton Part 3). As to the first criterion, nominal authenticity, there can be no clear-cut satisfaction in the case of pop music and certainly not at all in the case of Lady Gaga's oeuvre. Some examples Dutton gives of perceived violations of nominal authenticity are such that the work of Lady Gaga hardly passes even the most liberal sieve. If "forgery is defined as a work of art whose history of production is misrepresented by someone (not necessarily the artist) to an audience (possibly to a potential buyer of the work), normally for financial gain," then, at least by such standards, Lady Gaga's music and its presentation remain suspect (Dutton Part 2). In addition to the Frankensteinian efforts in borrowing from other performers to create the Lady Gaga persona and the direct musical derivations mentioned above,[10] recently even the origin of the moniker "Lady Gaga" has been disputed in the courts of law.[11] To put such violations in perspective, I would like to bring forward an example of pop appropriation that is as extreme as some Lady Gaga has been charged with, and yet retains an air of artistic ingenuity. The work in question is a song, "How Beautiful You Are," by goth-rock band The Cure, whose lyrics repeat the (translated) text of an 1869 poem by Charles Baudelaire almost verbatim. One thing that, in my mind, makes this particular case interesting is the fact that the band never signaled any explicit desire for chart domination with this, or any other of its songs. In addition, the stylistics of this band and its larger oeuvre presents an almost seamless fit for the mischievous, exploratory tone of Baudelaire's poem. As a result of this fortunate symbiosis, it becomes much more likely that a listener will feel invited to join in the performers' fascination with the French poet, than if the historical references were obfuscated by a screen of pretend originality done for the sake of winning the listener over at all costs. The Cure were not attempting a break-in at the pantheon, but rather humbly introducing one of its inhabitants to an unsuspecting public. This gesture might not pass Dutton's criterion of nominal authenticity, but it demonstrates that its violations can sometimes be tasteful affairs.

As to expressive authenticity, the case against Lady Gaga seems even stronger. The caveat that such authenticity is measured by personal expression, insofar as it is independent from a historical tradition, is truly damaging to any illusion of authenticity on the part of most pop personae. Again, Lady Gaga is special in the liberal amount she licentiously borrows from the pop music tradition, to the point that she readily identifies with a number of her ostensible precursors. In a single interview, she can claim the inheritance of Mick Jagger, David Bowie, and, most enthusiastically and arguably misguidedly, Andy Warhol. However legitimate such appropriations may be deemed elsewhere, they remain appropriations of the damaging kind in terms of expressive authenticity as Dutton sees it.

CONQUEST

And yet, Lady Gaga remains somehow bigger and more alluring than the sum of her parts. In defense of pop, then, what could be unequivocally said is that it simply somehow *works*. In trying to understand the efficiency of pop music and, as a corollary, its relation to art writ large, I find a passage from Deleuze and Guattari's *A Thousand Plateaus* especially helpful. Below, I will quote a lengthy portion of this passage and then will try to apply some of its insight to the issues already outlined:

> The artist: the first person to set out a boundary stone or to make a mark. Property, collective or individual, is derived from that even when it is in the service of war and oppression. Property is fundamentally artistic because art is fundamentally *poster*, *placard*. As Lorenz says, coral fish are posters. The expressive is primary in relation to the possessive; expressive qualities, or matters of expression, are necessarily appropriative and constitute a having more profound than being. Not in the sense that these qualities belong to a subject, but in the sense that they delineate a territory that will belong to the subject that carries or produces them. These qualities are signatures, but the signature, the proper name, is not the constituted mark of a subject, but the constituting mark of a domain, an abode. The signature is not an indication of a person; it is the chancy formation of a domain . . . The stagemaker practices *art brut*. Artists are stagemakers, even when they tear up their own posters. (Deleuze and Guattari 316)

It might be too generous a gesture to yet again search for signs of art in the debris of pop. From what Deleuze and Guattari give us, the proposition does not appear attractive either—although they do not specify their meaning, their use of "art" does not seem to stray from the traditionally accepted one.[12] Still, the philosophers' pluralism invites, or at least allows for, certain alternative readings. If we accept their understanding of art as an archetype of appropriation, it might become a little easier for us to accept pop music as art. The passage above attempts a reversal of the old Aristotelian dichotomy of nature versus art—if "coral fish are posters," then nature's wonders are derivable from the details of human expression. By means of this reversal Deleuze and Guattari try to develop the logic of appropriation to its constitutive limit—the conquest of art over tangible territories (an audience, a domain) becomes a conceptual conquering of being and nature. In order for any of these contentions to become relevant to pop music we have to shake the conceptual and ontological implications and look squarely into the territorial ones. And indeed, the notion of forceful conquest befits the image of the pop persona—a force whose expressive qualities do not have to, or as we have seen are very rarely able to, constitute a proper subject or even a proper name, but which invariably make it possible to carve out a domain. The domain here is of course that of sales, charts, concert attendance, and other such statistical signifiers. But, still, thinking about pop music and its successes in these Deleuzian terms seems to open a tangent of similarity between it and what the aesthete calls art.

CONCLUSION

What I would like to add to this picture is the consideration of velocity. It is a trivial observation that pop music has a short shelf life. What has been heretofore insufficiently explored, however, is the relation between this fact and the numerous problems one runs into when trying to locate pop music within a larger aesthetic framework. It is true that we simply like pop music when we like it at all. The uncritical qualifier "simply" is emphatically built into the experience of pop music and is integral to its conquering potential. As I have tried to argue, for all of this to become possible, the listener must necessarily be devoid of all outside references—she must necessarily be, as it were, caught by surprise. Lending one's ear to a tune in such circumstances is akin to having one's ear colonized. For what else could account for the customary succession of the celebratory rush, the instant identification with its purveyor, and, soon after, the cloying hangover of overexposure associated with our experience of a piece of pop music? The speed of pop contracts this succession to a point where one's attention becomes a function of a fast-moving market and not, as common sense would have it, vice versa. In fact, I would argue that one's attention is not one's own at all, but is rendered public through its conformity to a listening public and through its acceptance of publicly sanctioned tropes. And if this begins to smell a little too much like art, with all the trappings and determinations of an art world replaced by market forces, it is no coincidence that it does. Still, it is useful to remember with Arthur Danto that acceptance-as-process allows for the gradual accrual of a critical dimension into the experience and evaluation of art, while acceptance-as-transaction relies on the blitzkrieg tactics of conquest. The difference remains one of velocity—in order to make her mark, Lady Gaga has to crash and burn in the face of all traditional aesthetic considerations and she has to do it fast. If pop music is a kind of art, it is the kind that happens too fast for the art to be seen, heard, or remembered. This is, perhaps, how pop is afforded its young age and its old critics.

Notes

1. The first part of my title, "The Time is Now," is borrowed from the title of a pop song released in 2000 by the group Moloko.

2. In my understanding, acceptance-as-process neatly conforms to art critic Arthur Danto's concept of the art world as a historical and historicized condition for the validation of, as he calls it, "*the is of artistic identification*" (579).

3. "If you want melody and a cheerful embrace of the moment as it happens, Lady Gaga is a wise bet . . . .Germanotta knows that the one-hit wonders are weirder and cooler than the well-paid musicians who stretch their careers over seven years on the stage and twenty more behind it. Can she have it both ways?" (Frere-Jones, "Ladies")

4. "And there is one unexpected transgression that will carry Ms. Germanotta into middle age: she can sing and play piano like a pro. No matter how much high art and green vomit she shoehorns into her live shows, she always clears out fifteen minutes to sit by herself at the piano and sing into submission those audience members who still care about criticisms like 'prefabricated' and 'packaging.' Gaga is a musician, which is largely buried under the carnival float she has decided to run through pop music. It doesn't much matter, though. Madonna was less of a singer, but a clearer director, and had a sense for the pop single, which Gaga has

yet to match. Pop isn't classical or jazz, and as a primarily recorded form it doesn't reward the most gifted players. The song is the thing" (Frere-Jones, "Show Runners").

5. "She sprang up and surveyed her borrowed finery: the Gehry hat; a grayish satin dress with a skirt of chandelier crystals (designed by Vezzoli and Miuccia Prada, after the costume that Giorgio de Chirico made for Diaghilev's 'Le Bal'); a brass-and-crystal mask, by Baz Luhrmann and Catherine Martin; a pair of tall clear plastic boots with black buttons up the side. 'I helped design the shoes,' Gaga said. 'They're supposed to look like spats, and they're just under the knee, a bit more of a tea length.' She said she felt at home in the world of contemporary art. 'The objective is to always be making something that belongs in a museum. Even what I'm wearing right now.'" (Goodyear).

6. In his "'I'd Sell You Suicide:' Pop Music and Moral Panic in the Age of Marilyn Manson," Robert Wright discusses Manson's attitude towards his own pop persona: "Unlike Alice Cooper, for example, for whom the 'Alice' stage act was known by fans and critics alike to be wholly artificial, Manson refuses to distinguish between himself and his persona, and takes great delight in playing upon this ambiguity. In an interview, he said, 'When people sometimes misconceive us as being like Kiss or like Alice Cooper, or being a persona, I don't think they understand how deeply Marilyn Manson goes into my existence'" (377).

7. In the following, journalist Dana Goodyear finds Lady Gaga in her rehearsal trailer, considering the way her wardrobe straddles her lives both on and off the stage: "Inside, Gaga, who is twenty-three and speaks with a prim grandeur that might have come from watching old movies, sank into a nubby upholstered seat. 'I wear this all the time,' she said, yanking closed her gaping leotard. 'This is like my sweatpants'."

8. "As such, the use of alien tropes in popular music typically resists the bourgeois concept of normality which, in Adorno's words, leads to 'the very disintegration of the subject' (Adorno 1987, p. 171). Psychoanalytic theorists have also sought to explain 'Otherness' in terms of the 'non assimilable alien . . . monster' (Kristeva 1982, p. 11)" (McLeod 339).

9. The release in question, a song called "Alejandro," retains so much of the structure, rhythm, and melody of the song "Don't Turn Around," by early nineties pop group Ace of Base, that they can be effectively played simultaneously without any experience of disharmony in the listener. Examples of such direct transposition of the two pieces are by now ubiquitous on the Internet.

10. Dutton talks specifically about nominal authenticity in music but only with reference to the performing of the music of bygone eras. As such his analysis does not concern itself with the brutally fast turnaround of pop music, or the criteria for an authentic performance of it. It might also be useful to note that pop music subsists on intentional change, renditions, cover versions etc., all of which lie outside of Dutton's critical parameters.

11. On March 17, 2010, Rob Fusari, a former Lady Gaga collaborator and close friend, filed a lawsuit seeking financial reparations for reneging on contractual obligations. The document mentions inadequate distribution of credit for music written by the plaintiff, but also offers a version of the origin of Lady Gaga's stage alias that is different from the one she herself has popularized. Even without such complications, the name itself is redolent enough of a fairly recent pop phenomenon, specifically of the title of the song "Radio Gaga" by rock band Queen.

12. Among Deleuze and Guattari's numerous cultural references there are very few inclusions of pop cultural icons, and barely any of pop music personae.

Works Cited

Bauer, Nancy. "Lady Power." *The Stone, The New York Times Online*. June 20, 2010. Available at http://opinionator.blogs.nytimes.com/2010/06/20/ladypower/#more-52953. Accessed on December 9, 2011.

Bergson, Henri. *Time and Free Will; An Essay on the Immediate Data of Consciousness*. Translated by F. L. Pogson. New York: Dover Publications, 2001.

Bürger, Peter. *Theory of The Avant-Garde*. Translated by Michael Shaw as "Theory and History of Literature," Volume 4. Manchester: Manchester UP, 1984.

Danto, Arthur. "The Artworld." *The Journal of Philosophy*. American Philosophical Association Eastern Division Sixty-First AnnualMeeting. 61.19 (1964): 571–84.

Deleuze, Gilles, and Felix Guattari. *A Thousand Plateaus*. Translated by Brian Massumi. Minneapolis: U of Minnesota P, 1987.

Dutton, Dennis. "Authenticity in Art." *The Oxford Handbook of Aesthetics*. Ed. Jerrold Levinson. New York and Oxford: Oxford UP, 2003.

Eurich, Johannes. "Sociological Aspects and Ritual Similarities in the Relationship between Pop Music and Religion." *International Review of the Aesthetics and Sociology of Music* 34.1 (2003): 57–70.

Frere-Jones, Sasha. "Ladies Wild: How Not Dumb Is Gaga?" *The New Yorker* April 27, 2009. Available at http://www.newyorker.com/arts/critics/musical/2009/04/27/090427crmu_music_frerejones?currentPage=all. Accessed on December 9, 2011.

Frere-Jones, Sasha. "Show Runners, The Women of Pop." *The New Yorker* June 27, 2011. Available at http://www.newyorker.com/arts/critics/musical/2011/06/27/110627crmu_music_frerejones?currentPage=all Web. Accessed on December 9, 2011.

Goodyear, Dana. "Dept. of Hoopla: Celebromatic." *The New Yorker* November 30, 2009. Available at http://www.newyorker.com/talk/2009/11/30/091130ta_talk_goodyear. Accessed on December 9, 2011.

McLeod, Ken. "Space Oddities: Aliens, Futurism and Meaning in Popular Music." *Popular Music* 22.3 (2003): 337–55.

Mitchell, Tony. "Performance and the Postmodern in PopMusic." *Theatre Journal*, Performance in Context. 41.3 (1989): 273–93.

Strauss, Neil. "The Broken Heart & Violent Fantasies of Lady Gaga." *Rolling Stone Magazine* (1108/1109) (2010): 66–74.

Wright, Robert. "'I'd Sell You Suicide:' Pop Music and Moral Panic in the Age of Marilyn Manson," *Popular Music* 19.3 (2000): 365–85.

Invent

At the center of this article is a debate as to whether or not pop music can be considered art, at least in the traditional sense (i.e., it is original, authentic, requires special artistic skills, and has the chance for longevity). What do you think of these qualifications? Do you agree with these boundaries? Are there others that should be included? Do you think pop music expresses originality and authenticity? Do you think Ventzislavov is correct when he argues that "liking" pop music is a type of intellectual surrendering? What does that suggest about pop music fans?

Compose

In the second paragraph of his essay, Ventzislavov offers a number of "operational definitions," which he finds essential in making his argument regarding the conquest of pop music. His tendency to clearly define his terms continues throughout the essay as he makes his argument. Starting with that second paragraph, create a list of these essential terms, composing the definitions in your own words. Be aware, it might take a little work to get at the meaning of some of these terms, so feel free to freewrite as you come up with your own definitions. Some terms you might consider: pop music, conquest, originality, artist, liking, acceptance-as-process, nominal authenticity, expressive authenticity, velocity.

Collaborate

Working with a few classmates, make a list of who you think are the current top three pop stars. Using Ventzislavov's definitions of authenticity and originality, decide if any of these artists' music warrants consideration as art. Don't forget, as Ventzislavov points out, that there are two types of authenticity (nominal and expressive). To aid in this task, feel free to use the Internet to look at videos or listen to music. Either way, be prepared to make your case to the class.

Explore

Ventzislavov's argument depends upon various definitions regarding what constitutes a work of art. As you might expect, the definitions he works with are not the only ones that exist, and debates regarding the definition of "art" are plentiful, especially in our postmodern age. Research the history of how art has been defined and then explore the various ways in which our views of it have changed in the last sixty to seventy years. You might explore notions of art in ancient Greece, and then compare those views to that of modernism and postmodernism. When and where do the significant changes appear? Does a postmodern view of art undermine Ventzislavov's appeal to a traditional view of aesthetics? Are there certain historical events that greatly impact aesthetic philosophies (i.e., the Fall of Rome, the Enlightenment, Industrial Age, etc.)? What other questions arise when we examine the way aesthetic theory changes throughout history?

Alternatively, use the pop cultural definitions provide by Ventzislavov to explore another essay in this book, "Growing Up Gaga," by Vanessa Grigoriadis. See how his theories play out when reading about how Lady Gaga became a pop star.

Tom Ewing is the Chief Culture Officer at the market research agency BrainJuicer, where he works on the Labs team, helping translate the findings of decision science and psychology into methods that create business advantages for clients. He's operated as an Internet analyst, social media researcher, and writer for magazines such as Pitchfork.

SHINY SHINY—A FUTURE HISTORY OF THE CD REVIVAL

BY TOM EWING

This column originated as a reply to Marc Hogan's excellent piece on the return of cassette culture. I wanted to imagine whether "CD culture" might also return in the future, and if so, what might drive it and what it might involve. Immense thanks to Marc for his work on the original essay, and for the passion and hard work of the people he interviewed, who inspired this response.

The piece is dated March 2022, so with the exception of Oval, the people and situations described in this article do not as yet exist.

On March 5, 2021, a dozen or so British students held an afternoon party. They dressed up, they drank tea, they ate buttered scones with jam, and then they played some music. Nothing so unusual, but all the music was on CD, and the same CDs they played had just been used as dishes for the jam.

"We spread the jam on CDs, got people to spoon it onto their scones, and then wiped the CD down and played it while they ate," laughs Reece Maclay, who hosted the party and has since become part of a cultish global revival of interest in compact discs. The jam trick, he explains, was originally a way of demonstrating the durability of CDs when they were first introduced decades ago: Maclay had seen it on an old YouTube clip and became interested in the history of the recently obsolete medium. "CDs were so futuristic when they were invented! They looked so shiny, it must have been like they'd come off a spaceship. So colorful compared to records, too."

For people like Maclay, that futuristic aura hasn't quite gone away. "I remember playing with my dad's CDs when I was tiny, and then at school we'd put our projects on to CD-Rs to take home. But I never really owned any-- by the time I was getting into music nobody bought them." So when Britain's high street stores stopped stocking CDs five years ago, like most people, he never imagined he'd miss them. "Even Dad's getting rid of his now-- I told him about the club, and he thinks I'm demented."

"The Club" is the 74 Sessions, a monthly night in London dedicated to making and swapping CD-Rs, named after the original storage capacity of a disc in minutes. Maclay started the club last year, and the reception has delighted him. "The CD-Rs people bring are amazing," he beams, "There's so much care going into them-- because people are making something physical, something they can't change once they've burned it, they put a lot of effort into it."

At the club the best CD-Rs play while pictures and videos from other contributions run on wall screens. Originally the 74 Sessions was just about the music, but members started picking up junked computers for free and pulling 'found files' off them onto their CD-Rs, creating homebrew versions of the multi-media packages popular 25 years ago.

But for the fans, the music is still at the core. Unlike today's collaborative, crowdsourced, and automatically generated playlists, a CD's tracklisting is fixed, and the CD-burning scene is an opportunity for music lovers to show their deep individual loves of music, its sequencing and presentation. The 74 Sessions is one of many CD-burning clubs and groups-- some ban members from remixing or mashing up material, others ask people to theme their CD-Rs. Chantal Fielding, who runs the Prismatic Spray trading club out of Rochester, NY, loves the way CD-Rs make her focus her fandom. "You've got all this information, literally everything you look at you can find out everything about it right there, and for music that means there's no mystery anywhere. So saying no, you can't explore endlessly, you have to reduce it down-- it's powerful."

This kind of rigor doesn't always appeal-- artificial limits work only if everyone's happy to play along. "You get people coming in to the club", says Maclay, "looking around trying to work out who the playlist owner is, trying to send me their votes for the next song-- it's actually pretty fun to say no, sorry, it's not like that: we're playing a physical thing and we're not going to change the order. Once people get used to that they're fine with it."

The rejection of music's networked elements is something a lot of physical-music aficionados believe in fiercely. "If you're listening via the cloud, you're listening in public," says Fielding, "Your taste becomes something public. People get to comment on it, borrow it, interrupt it, make suggestions-- physical music is more yours, it happens off the grid."

This regard for privacy is easy to frame as elitist. Prismatic Spray members pledge to make one CD a month, burn a copy for every other member and then no more-- a model based on the "amateur press associations" of 20th century fandom. Membership is very limited, and the waiting list more than double the active contributors. Competition to make the best themed CD-R each month is fierce. "It's not elitist, but it's demanding," says Fielding, "When people just go along with each other's tags, they're not going to have any original perspectives. We're opposed to that."

CD fans talk a lot about mystery, and the format's capacity for hidden treasures-- the way you can hide multimedia content or "secret tracks" on a disc, for instance-- is a big part of its attraction compared to other physical formats like cassettes or vinyl. Inire Wolfe runs the Hall of Mirrors label, which specialises in limited-run CD releases where content is buried in a "secret architecture" of folders, split and unnamed files, anagrammatic tags, and other Easter eggs. "Finding the music," he says, "becomes a game."

Unlike Fielding's vision of CD-Rs as celebrations of individual taste, Wolfe works hard to include what he calls a "co-operative" element to his releases. Fans form a tight community, puzzling out the contents of each CD together. Some Hall of Mirrors tracks are split across different CD-Rs within the same release-- the idea is to physically swap objects to get the full work, so the CD is engineering new meetings between people who might have been to the same show. Other releases operate on the "*Zaireeka* principle"-- two or more people have to play the CDs at once to hear the tracks properly.

While earlier physical-music movements fought to preserve analog formats in the face of digitization, CD revivalists see music's physical existence as a rebuke to a world where people's digital presence has overtaken their physical one. "It's not just about the music," explains Wolfe. "Words like 'social' and 'sharing' became absolutely twisted. It used to mean things people did together, now it's about how well you fit into algorithms. We leave snail trails of data everywhere, and all 'social' means now is that two trails have crossed and somebody's making money off it. Forcing people to collaborate for a fuller experience helps restore some of the real idea of 'social.'"

It's easy and lazy to lump people like Wolfe in with cassette and vinyl fandoms, but the artistic roots are different. Wolfe sees CD-R revivalists as part of a 'post-social' wave of digital mischief-makers and situation-builders, in the tradition not of industrial or noise culture but of Fluxus and Neoism. He's sympathetic to "troll artists" like bot-creators and recommendation-scramblers. A friend of his was involved with the 'artificial hipster' Karen Eliot, a digital taste bundle whose infiltration of music friendship networks in 2020 caused scores of trusted playlist generators to start throwing in 00s tracks like "Starstrukk" and "My Humps".

The sound on most CDs Wolfe releases is deliberately low-bitrate, with a glossy, uneasy, skinny sheen that's a stark contrast to the lossless warmth of most streamed music. Some fans call lo-bit music "ghostwave", because, as Hall Of Mirrors act Cursor Daly puts it, "you start listening to stuff that isn't there, phantom sound-- your ears are filling in the gaps. Below 128 kbps you're essentially hallucinating sound, no two people hear the same thing. Loads of CD nerds were neuroscience majors."

Like most CD artists, Daly loves to play with the effect of the technological process on music: In an age where the smooth user experience and the invisible interface is everything, CD acts are tinkerers, worshippers of the glitch and the bug. The one older act they constantly reference is Oval, a German 90s techno group that made records by deliberately damaging and abusing CDs then taping the results, drawing the listener's attention to the beauty hidden in digital error.

The music on Hall of Mirrors owes more of a philosophical than a sonic debt to Oval: Daly makes lo-bit R&B and Scando-pop, reflecting the era he's hoping to evoke. The CD's final peak in the late 90s coincided with a pop explosion, and alongside its more artistic justifications the CD revival rides on conflicted nostalgia for mass media itself. "Music ought to be larger than life, inescapable!" says Daly, "But now the people who make it don't even matter, it's just about which of your friends are into it and then you forget it the week after. People used to know when they watched a video that everyone else in the world might be watching! Now it's just everybody else in your world. It feels like a lot, but somewhere inside we know it's not the same."

Daly's is passed around the same networks and subject to the same spikes and troughs of popularity as anyone else's. But for him CDs are a statement of value and subversive aspiration. "My friends and I sneak into stores that used to be big music retailers years ago and put our CDs on the shelves. We even got an old shrinkwrapping machine from eBay so we can make them look right. We've been thrown out so often, banned. The stores hate us because people get excited and say 'Oh, how much is this thing?' Of course if you scan the code on the CD you get the music free, but having it sitting there between two boxes of diapers really surprises people. It's a way of saying—this stuff, physical music, used to be mainstream, not just something collectors care about."

Back in London, wiping strawberry jam from a CD, Reece Maclay agrees. "All the music I've ever known I got free, and I didn't know what owning or paying for music was all about-- not that most CD labels charge anything but voluntary fees anyway. But all this isn't just about trying to turn the clock back 'cause we liked mix CDs when we were kids. CDs started to die when people stopped wanting to pay for a product, and then social media and music streams came along and let people stop paying for it all legally, and the product vanished. But when you can't see what the product is and someone's still making money, then the product is you."

The term "physical-music" appears in various forms throughout Ewing's essay. More than likely, much of your life has involved purchasing, downloading, and playing non-physical music (i.e., MP3 files). What value do you think is attached to purchasing, owning, and playing music via a physical medium (record, cassette, or CD)? What do you think Ewing's point is with this humorous projection into the future of music listening?

In this essay, Ewing makes a number of references to the benefits of listening to music in a set order, as it was originally presented via the artist. He also makes a point to celebrate the individuality associated with creating your own mix CDs, where the "tracklisting is fixed," privileging it over "today's collaborative, crowdsourced, and automatically generated playlist." What do you think of this assertion? Do you think creating your own playlists is better than allowing Pandora, Spotify, or iTunes to do it for you based on your listening style? Write a couple of paragraphs where you explore the advantages and disadvantages of each method.

Take on the task of creating one of the CD compilations suggested in this futuristic world. You can do this as individuals or as a group. Come up with a list of songs, and then follow the guidelines of the "74 Sessions" club, as outlined in the essay. Burn your CD (remember to follow the 128k format), and bring it back to your class for your own "74 Session" party.

Look up and read the article Ewing refers to as the inspiration to his own (Google: Marc Hogan's "This is Not a Mixtape"). Research the timelines of the various music formats and their popularity in culture (from records to 8-tracks to cassettes to CDs). Analyze your research to see if you can find other technological advancements that seemed to accompany the shifts in the popularity of these various formats.

Eric Harvey has written for Pitchfork *since 2007. His reviews and essays on music, technology, and culture have also appeared in* Spin, The Village Voice, Rolling Stone, Atlantic.com, Convergence, *and the book* Managing Media Work. *He is currently an Assistant Professor of Communication at Weber State University.*

MP3: THE MEANING OF FORMAT

By Eric Harvey

MP3s have embedded themselves into daily musical life so thoroughly that they're taken for granted. They don't call attention to themselves as aesthetic objects like records; instead, we interact with them as files, documents, icons. They're infinitely duplicable and available in seemingly infinite numbers. At the same time, however, MP3s are intensely controversial. More than a decade after the government took down Napster, these digital objects remain at the center of intense debates about morality and musical value; they've eradicated the scarcity of music recordings, doing away with more than a century of economic and social realities about how, when, and where music can be accessed. And, if you listen to certain types of music or talk to certain people about them, MP3s sound quite horrible.

In his new book, *MP3: The Meaning of a Format*, McGill University professor Jonathan Sterne exhaustively and eloquently traces the history of the MP3 from the initial hearing model developed in Bell Labs to the current debates about piracy. As the author argues, each time we rip a CD to our hard drives, we're not only saving space in our living rooms or ensuring we have the appropriate gym soundtrack, but also reaffirming a fundamental idea about the limits of human perception.

"With an MP3, you're not going to have the same enjoyment that vinyl collectors talk about in terms of physicality, though, for a lot of people, that pleasure has been transferred to computer electronics."

Pitchfork: People often describe MP3s as "dematerialized" or "invisible" music. You argue that they're actually "things" comparable with CDs, though.

JS: They're just different *kinds* of things. You can hold an MP3 in your hand, you just need some kind of container for it; Apple developed an entire campaign about the thousands of songs you can hold in your hand. There's a materiality to them because you run out of space on your hard drive, or you can or can't stream them depending on bandwidth. But the important thing is that their materiality comes with completely different affordances than something like a CD.

With an MP3, you're obviously not going to have the same enjoyment that vinyl collectors talk about in terms of the physicality of the medium. Although for a lot of people, that pleasure has been directly transferred to computer electronics. The whole fashionable-portable-audio-player phenomena is very much of a piece with the enjoyment of records, except that it's not a subcultural phenomenon, and certainly doesn't lend itself to the same kind of aestheticism that comes with being a record collector. But the flipside, in a way, is that MP3s are closer to what I would call the social demand for music-- the desire to be with music, to move with it and share it. They're much closer to that than a record is.

Pitchfork: One of the book's best chapters is about the tests audio engineers ran in 1990 and 1991 to determine the standard for quality.

JS: Actually, the story of music testing comes from a longer history of industrial testing called hedonics, which I trace back to World War II. Hedonics was developed as a part of industrial psychology to try to measure and test pleasure and displeasure. For instance, if you're packing string beans in cans for G.I.s, how disgusting do they have to be before people won't eat them? Or on the flip side, a company like Frito Lay has chip testers at the ends of their production lines. The question isn't, "How tasty is this potato chip?" But: "How does the taste of this potato chip compare with the standard potato chip?"

This was the mode of testing that was used with the MP3. So the first question is, "What's the difference between one of several possible new coding schemes and CD-quality audio?" It's always relative to other audio. Really, it's just different flavors of processing, which is the defining characteristic of contemporary music aesthetics. So much stuff we hear now is so heavily processed. If you heard an unprocessed voice in a music recording, you would think it was wrong, because it didn't have dynamic range compression, it isn't heavily edited, there isn't any artificial reverberation added. It would sound strange to most listeners.

The MPEG listening tests used a variety of recordings: some castanets, a Suzanne Vega or Tracy Chapman tune, Ornette Coleman, a solo bass guitar piece, examples of male and female speech. The testers would listen to each of these recordings, flip back and forth between different coding schemes and the original recording without knowing which was which, trying to determine the difference. They'd do it over and over for hours-- the process is quite exhausting and unpleasant. If a tester was correct more often than they would be if they were guessing, the researchers would know there was a perceivable difference.

The question that immediately arises is: Would you get different results with different music and with different listeners? In the case of the MPEG test listeners, we're talking about professional engineers, people who work for audio companies, or people who work for radio stations. If you look at the aesthetics of the recordings, they all conform to this sanctioned radio aesthetic in terms of how recordings are made and what they sound like. I wasn't able to hear all the recordings, but if you listen to the commercial stuff, everything's recorded in exactly the way you'd expect an engineer at a radio station in 1991 to classify as "well-recorded." There isn't anything too esoteric or strange.

So by choosing mainstream music as the tests for MPEG audio, they actually produced a format that doesn't conform to universals of human hearing, but does conform very well to the record industry. In other words, a small number of mastering engineers have determined what good recordings will sound like.

Pitchfork: In the popular history of MP3s, Suzanne Vega's a cappella version of "Tom's Diner" is situated as the key musical moment in the engineering of the format. But you dispute the validity of that argument.

JS: The Vega recording is super interesting because if you listen to the recording in headphones or at a high volume on good speakers, you can hear a massive echo in the background at certain points, especially at the ending of phrases. In the first verse, listen for the sound after "dinner," "corner," "argue," "somebody," and "in." That's because she's singing very close to the mic and they're using a lot of dynamic range compression. That goes with the aesthetics of the time. So even this a cappella recording that's talked about as "pure" and "natural" and "organic" is this highly processed artifact, and the referent of perceptually coded audio is not Suzanne Vega singing in a room, but Suzanne Vega singing on a very well produced record.

Pitchfork: A lot of people cite piracy as the reason why MP3s became the ubiquitous medium for 21st-century music. But you broaden that out and consider some other factors that contributed to the format's ubiquity.

JS: Absolutely. Obviously, filesharing and unauthorized copying is a factor-- when I say "piracy," I really mean unauthorized copying, because piracy is not a real thing. In fact, it's a crazy term because it combines people in their rooms downloading music with armed thieves in boats off the coast of eastern Africa. So really we're talking about an industry that wants to limit copying as much as possible and control the means of purchase, use, and recirculation in problematic ways.

The MP3 took off after an Australian hacker cracked a piece of encoding software that the Fraunhofer Institute, which owns a lot of the patents for the MP3, created. It gets re-released for free, and people start using the software to rip MP3s from their CDs. Within a year or two, because they're so common, companies like Microsoft and Apple are signing deals with Fraunhofer, and by the time Napster takes off, anyone with a computer could use software to rip a CD to MP3.

That's part of the story, but there's a much more important part. When we think about music piracy or unauthorized copying, we normally think about it in terms of a record industry and an end user. But I actually think there's a more important relationship involving the conduit industries, which are as much media industries as the recording industry. These people benefit tremendously from file sharing. My favorite example of this comes from 2001, when Sony Music (the record label) joins a suit against Napster put forward by the Recording Industry Association of America at the same time Sony (the consumer electronics manufacturer) releases a CD player that can play MP3s. Where do you think those MP3s come from? You could say the same thing for the initial iPod.

Maybe now that the iTunes store is old enough, there are people in the world who have bought everything natively digital and didn't rip or download anything. But for a very long time in the 2000s, the ISPs, people selling hard drives, people selling bandwidth, people selling music playback gadgets, and even people selling new computers all benefitted greatly from file sharing. They had a huge economic interest in it. This is a big debate in Silicon Valley; the Free Culture movement. Content provision is something that helps amplify search engines, ISPs, and other companies that depend on people going out and finding content to make money.

"Music piracy is not a real thing. In fact, it's a crazy term because it combines people in their rooms downloading music with armed thieves in boats off the coast of eastern Africa."

Pitchfork: What do you see as the future of the MP3, if not, as you say in your book, the *end* of the MP3?

JS: Well, I think it's going to be around for a while, because people have very large music collections in MP3 format that they may or may not have bought. And if they didn't buy them, are they then going to spend a lot of money to replace them the way baby boomers did with CDs and LPs? It's a much tougher sell.

There are competitors to the MP3, some of which are open source like .ogg, which is a great alternative because it is completely open, but it also means that content industries like Apple are quite hostile to it because they see it as an indirect threat. MP3s are with us as long as we're using computers and the same kinds of music platforms we're using today. When the next telecommunications infrastructure comes along—with new devices and new ways of engaging with music—that's when the dominance of the MP3 and compressed audio in general will be challenged.

Invent

You will notice that this essay appears in the form of a short interview with the author of *MP3: The Meaning of Format,* by Jonathan Sterne. Imagine you are going to interview someone about his or her views on musical formats. Who would you choose to interview and why? What kinds of questions would you ask? What would you want to know? What should you cover in that interview?

Compose

After pondering the task of interviewing someone on the formats of music (see above), conduct an interview outside of class with someone and then write up a short article that, to some degree, mimics the one you have just read.

Collaborate

In this interview, Jonathan Sterne makes several big claims about MP3s that are worthy of discussion. In small groups, discuss your feelings on any of the following claims and be prepared to explain your responses to the class:

1. "With an MP3, you're not going to have the same enjoyment that vinyl collectors talk about in terms of physicality, though, for a lot of people, that pleasure has been transferred to computer electronics."

2. "If you heard an unprocessed voice in a music recording, you would think it was wrong, because it didn't have dynamic range compression, it isn't heavily edited, there isn't any artificial reverberation added. It would sound strange to most listeners."

3. "A small number of mastering engineers have determined what good recordings will sound like."

Explore

Sterne's full-length book on the history of the MP3 is 360 pages long. You're probably glad you only had to read a short interview on the topic, but you can still learn a lot more about it without having to read the whole book. Often, researching the context for any given book helps in our own research. For example, start by exploring the biography of the author. Examine his online biography and the other books he has written, attending carefully to his credentials in the academic community. What can you discover from exploring the background of the author in this case? Research the critical reviews of the book and see what you can learn from the topic just from reading them (Google: Critical reviews MP3: the Meaning of Format). Examine the table of contents and see what topics might interest you if you were to check the book out for your own research.

Victor Wooten is a five-time Grammy Award winning bass guitarist. He has been hailed as an innovator, composer, arranger, producer, author, teacher, vocalist, and multi-instrumentalist. In 2008, Wooten surprised critics with The Music Lesson, a book that contains many of the lessons, ideas, and ways of thinking about music that have made him famous, but in the form of a story about a struggling young musician who wanted music to be his life and wanted his life to be great.

excerpt from
THE MUSIC LESSON: A SPIRITUAL SEARCH FOR GROWTH THROUGH MUSIC—"THE FIRST MEASURE: GROOVE"

By Victor Lemonte Wooten

You should never lose the groove in order to find a note.

I'd been working in the Nashville music scene for many years and not once I had seen him. I was a known player around town and had played in many bands and no one had ever mentioned his name. Although I hoped to make a decent living playing music, keeping my head above water on a consistent level was always a struggle, and the present struggle was rapidly getting the best of me. Maybe that's what brought him out.

I was out of work but determined not to take a job waiting tables like so many musicians in town were forced to do. My landlord had just called to remind me that the end of the month was only a few days away, and with no gigs lined up, I was in no rush to return his call. My girlfriend, well, no need to lie about that; I didn't have one.

As much as I tried, I could never seem to break into the recording session scene. The few sessions I'd done never generated any return calls, and whenever I lost a gig with a club band, I rarely knew why. I was a good bass player—not the best, but good—so I couldn't understand why anyone wouldn't want me in his band.

Without a steady gig, and not knowing what to do, I decided to start practicing more. I didn't like practicing (and still don't), but I knew that I had to change something. It was either magically get better, alter my playing style, or move to another town and start all over. Realizing the gravity of my situation, I decided to practice.

Did I mention that I hate practicing? I never know what to practice or why I'm practicing it. I also get sleepy in the middle of the process.

So there I was at home, painstakingly working on scales and modes and not knowing why. I just knew that my previous teachers had told me to do so. All the books I'd ever read said the same thing, so that's what I was doing.

I was at my lowest point emotionally because I wasn't getting anywhere with my playing and I wasn't satisfied with my current playing situation. My home life and my love life, well, my whole life in general, wasn't in the best of shape.

The rain beating down on the metal siding of my duplex, coupled with the monotony of playing scales, was lulling me to sleep. It was during one of my sleeping sessions, I mean practice sessions, that I first met him; or, more accurately, when he first showed up. And that is exactly what he did. He showed up, uninvited! At least, I thought he was uninvited. He had a different story. He said that I'd actually called him. I'm still confused by that statement, but somehow, for some reason, there he was in my house.

I have no idea how long the stranger had been standing there looking down on me. The fact that he was completely dry when it was raining outside made me wonder if he'd been there awhile. The strangest part of all is that . . . I didn't want him to leave.

From my position on the couch, he appeared quite tall and mysterious. He was wearing a blue NASA-style jumpsuit and a black motorcycle helmet. And even though his eyes were hidden, I could feel them penetrating deep into my mind as though he was looking for the proper place to begin.

"How'd you get in here?" I asked, startled, half asleep, and wondering why I wasn't angry at his intrusion.

"You asked me to come."

"I did?"

"Yes."

"But how'd you get in here? Who let you in?"

"You did."

"Oh really! Did I give you a key?"

"I don't need a key."

"Who are you?"

"I am your teacher."

"My teacher?"

"Yes."

"My teacher of what?"

"Nothing."

"Nothing? Well, then, what are you supposed to teach me?"

"What do you want to learn?"

"Lots of things. What can you teach me?"

"Nothing!"

"What do you mean 'nothing'?"

"Exactly that, nothing."

This was typical of conversations to come, but at that time, I didn't know what to make of him and I needed a straightforward answer.

"You have to do better than that. You showed up in my house unannounced; I think I deserve some kind of explanation."

Tilting his head, he looked at me through the face shield of his helmet and replied, "I teach nothing because there is nothing to be taught. You already know everything you need to know, but you asked me to come, so here I am."

"But you said that you're my teacher."

"Yes, I did, but try to understand. 'Teacher' is just a title. I cannot teach you because no one can teach another person anything."

"What do you mean by that?"

"You can only teach yourself. Until we live in a day where I can physically implant knowledge into your head, I can teach you nothing. I can only *show* you things."

"What can you 'show' me?"

"Anything."

"Show me everything then," I replied.

"That would take a while. It might be easier if we pick a subject."

"Okay, how about music?"

"Perfect! Music! Shall we begin?"

I didn't know if I was ready to begin anything with this character. I already told you he was wearing a blue jumpsuit and a black motorcycle helmet (yes, he was still wearing the helmet), but did I mention that he was carrying a skateboard under his left arm and a burlap bag over his shoulder? I imagined him riding his skateboard down the street, through the rain, in his getup.

I didn't know what I was getting myself into. I also couldn't tell if he was really serious or not. For all I knew, he could've been there to rob me. But I didn't think so. There was a lot I didn't know, but I decided to play along anyway. There was an intriguing quality about him, and I wanted to know more.

"Wait a minute. If you're not a teacher, what are you? What should I call you?"

"Michael. Call me Michael," he answered as he removed his helmet and offered me his hand.

I remember his bright blue eyes as hypnotic. They had an immediate effect on me. Somehow, I sensed they could see beneath the surface, and I was fearful of what he might uncover. I struggled to stay in control.

Not bothering to move from my reclined position on the couch, I allowed his hand to dangle in the air. Asserting what I thought was dominance, I responded in a cocky tone, "Okay, Michael, what can you teach me about music?"

"Nothing. I already told you that," he answered, retracting his hand. "I tried teaching many times before. Once as an Apache medicine man in New Jersey and twice as a Yogi in India. I even tried teaching while flying biplanes in Illinois. This time around, I am living the laws of Music. Some may call me a teacher, but I don't teach; I show."

This guy was full of . . . well, something. I couldn't quite make him out. *Is this a joke?* I thought. *Is he an actor? He said that he is living the 'laws of Music.' What does that mean? Music has rules, that I know, but laws? It's not like we're talking about the law of gravity or the speed of light or—*

"Science," he commented, interrupting my thoughts. "Music is bigger than you think."

"Science," I said to myself. That's exactly what I was gonna say. How did he do that? Coincidence? Must've been.

"*Mu*," he continued, "is an ancient word for 'mother,' and *sic* is just an abbreviation for the word 'science.' So, put together, *Music* means 'the mother of all sciences.' So you see, Music is important. I can show this science to you if you'd like. Is it something you would like to see?

Even though he was talking like a crazy man, he had my undivided attention. But I didn't want to give in too soon. I also figured that since it was my house, I should be the one asking the questions. I reclined even more and laced my fingers behind my head. Next, I put my legs in a crossed position and tried to act cool. He gave a slight smile as if he was ready to counter my every move.

"What instrument do you play?" I asked.

He turned and took a seat in the chair across from me. Laying his skateboard in his lap, he tucked his hair behind his right ear and took a breath before responding.

"I play Music, not instruments."

"What do you mean by that?" I asked, losing my imagined control of the conversation.

"I am a musician!" he answered. He placed his hand on his chest to emphasize his point before gesturing at me. "You are just a bass player. That means you play the bass guitar. A true musician, like me, plays Music and uses particular instruments as tools to do so. I know that Music is inside me and not inside the instrument. This understanding allows me to use any instrument, or no instrument at all, to play my Music. I am a true musician, and one day, you too shall be."

He spoke with confidence, and I was trying to find a way to strip him of it.

"Are you saying that you can play any instrument?" I asked.

"Of course I can, and so can you! It is this knowing that separates us. A true writer can write using a typewriter, a pen, a pencil, or anything else that he chooses. You wouldn't call him a pencil writer, would you? Your understanding that the writing utensil is just a tool allows you to see past it and into the truth of what he is—a writer. The story is in the writer, is it not? Or is it in the pencil? Your problem is this: You have been trying to tell your story *with* a bass guitar instead of *through* it."

I liked what he was saying, and that bothered me. Trying to hold on to my resistance, I struggled to find the holes in his argument. The more I lay there thinking about what he'd said, the more interested I became in Michael and his ideas, and the less interested I became in finding the holes.

He definitely had a unique way of looking at things. Yes, he had shown up uninvited, and I probably should've been upset about that. At first, I was, but suddenly, I wanted more. I wanted to hear him talk. If he could help me become a better bass player, I was ready to let him. Maybe.

"Do you know what it means to be a bass guitarist?" he asked.

The question was a strange one. I didn't know how to answer, so I didn't.

"The bass guitar is the honorable instrument," he declared.

"What do you mean?"

"It is understated and underappreciated, yet it plays the most important role. The bass is the link between harmony and rhythm. It is the foundation of a band. It is what all the other instruments stand upon, but it is rarely recognized as that."

I struggled between getting sucked in by his words and trying to keep my dominance over the situation. He was winning.

"The foundation of any building has to be the strongest part," he continued, "but you will never hear anyone walk into a building and say, 'My, what a nice foundation.' Unless the foundation is weak, it will go unnoticed. People will walk all over it and never acknowledge that it is there. The Life of a true bass guitarist is the same."

"Wow! That's pretty cool! I never thought of it that way before."

"Why not?" he asked.

I was disappointed in my outburst. I didn't want to show my enthusiasm just yet, so I regained my composure and answered more calmly. "I don't know. I guess no one ever taught me music this way before."

"Therein lies your first problem," he stated.

"Problem? What do you mean by that?"

"You still think that you can be taught."

Not knowing what to say, I stared at the floor in silence for a long while. The stranger remained quiet as well, allowing me time to digest his words. I wasn't sure what he was talking about. I mean, we're all taught at some point in our lives, aren't we? I can remember taking music lessons as a kid, and I definitely had a teacher. I'd even taught music lessons myself when I first moved to town. Realizing, again, that I'd totally lost control of our dialogue, I found myself getting worked up.

I was reclined on the couch with my bass in my lap, trying to figure out something to say. He was sitting there in front of me in what I would eventually think of as "his chair."

I could tell he was looking directly at me, but I dared not look back. For some reason, I didn't want him to know how uncomfortable I was.

Remember: It had just been a few minutes since I was . . . uh . . . practicing. My mind was in a daze, my thoughts were racing, and there was a stranger in my house.

I reflected on grade school and all my teachers and all the summer music camps I'd attended when I used to play cello. How about all the music books or even the metaphysical books I'd read over the years? They were interesting, but none of them had prepared me for this.

Neither my mom nor my dad played a musical instrument, but they were very musical, more musical than some musicians I know. They sang in church and there was always a record playing on their stereo at home. They also helped spark my interest by taking me to concerts when I was young and supported my musical interest by offering to pay for lessons if I wanted them. I can't say they taught me how to play music, but they surely supported my decision to play. Hearing it around the house was such a major part of my childhood that it was like a second language to me.

"Language, that's good," Michael spoke out of the blue, as if reading my thoughts.

"What?" I replied in disbelief.

"Language, that's a good one."

"Wait a minute! Can you read—"

"Music?" he interrupted with a sly smile. "Of course I can. Can't you?"

"That's not what I was gonna say," I muttered.

Knowing where I was heading, he steered the conversation by asking, "Is Music a language?"

"I would say so."

"Then why don't you treat it like one?"

"What do you mean?"

"What language do you speak the best?" he asked.

"English," I answered.

"Are you better at English than you are at Music?"

"Much!" I answered, not knowing where he was headed.

"At what age did you get really good at English?"

"I would say by about age four or five I was fluent."

"And at what age did you get really good at Music?"

"I'm still working on it," I answered in total seriousness.

"So it took you only four or five years to get really good at English, but even though you've been speaking Music for almost four times as long, you're still not really good at it yet?"

"Well, I guess not," I answered, finally realizing his point. I hadn't looked at it from that perspective.

"Why not?" Michael asked.

"I don't know why. Maybe I just haven't practiced enough." I was frustrated by the question.

"How much did you practice English?"

"All the time," I answered, but then I thought about it. "Well, I didn't really practice English; I just spoke it a lot."

"Bingo!" he replied, "That is why you speak that language naturally."

"So, are you saying that I should stop practicing music?" I asked sarcastically, trying to regain some ground.

"I'm not saying that you should or shouldn't do anything. I'm just comparing the two languages and your processes of learning them. If Music and English are both languages, then why not apply the process used to get good at one of them to the other?"

Realizing I'd totally lost my ability to direct the conversation, I finally relaxed and gave in.

"How do I do that?" I asked.

"How *do* you do that?" was his reply.

I had to think for a minute, but I soon came up with an answer.

"Well, when I was young, I was surrounded by people who spoke English. I was probably hearing it even before I was born. So, since I've heard people speaking English every day of my life, it was easy for me to pick up because it was always around. How's that?"

"It's a start; keep going."

"Okay. Because I heard English every day, speaking it came naturally to me." I was talking more quickly and with more confidence. "It wasn't something I ever thought about. It wasn't something I ever really practiced. I just did it. I just listened to it and spoke it. And the more I spoke it, the better I got."

"That's brilliant! See, you do understand. I like the part about it coming naturally to you. I must be a good teacher," he said smiling.

"Comedian? Yes! Teacher? I'm not so sure," I retorted, joining in on the fun.

"How can we apply this approach to Music?" Michael inquired.

"I'm not so sure," I answered. "I am around music most of the time. It's hard to go anywhere without hearing some type of music playing in the background. So that part of it is similar to English, but I know that there's still something missing. There has to be something else that keeps me from being just as good at music as I am at English."

I thought for a moment.

"Oh, I know. I speak English every day. I'm always talking, but I'm not always playing. I don't play music every day. If I played my bass every day, I'd be just as good. Is that it?"

"Did you speak English every day when you were a baby?" he asked.

"Well, not exactly." Apparently there was more.

"Do you need to speak English every day to get better at it?" he asked.

"No, I don't."

"Then what's missing?"

"I don't know." My frustration grew. "Just tell me."

"Jamming!" he stated with a slight nod of his head.

"What?"

"Jamming," he repeated. "That is the missing element. When you were a baby, you were allowed to jam with the English language. From day one, not only were you allowed to jam, you were encouraged to. And better yet, you didn't just jam; you jammed with professionals. Just about everyone you communicated with when you were a baby was already a master of the English language. And because of that, you are now a master."

"A master?" I inquired.

"A genuine master," he confirmed. "The only reason you are not called a master is that everyone else is just as good at it as you are. Everyone is a master. Think about it. If you were as good at Music as you are at English, you would surely be considered a master. Would you not?"

"Oh my God! You're right!" Another unintended outburst. The words just leapt from my mouth, seemingly of their own free will. What he was saying made so much sense. I was surprised I'd never recognized it before.

"Thanks for the compliment, but please keep listening," the stranger continued. "There are only two elements that allowed you to become a master of the English language at such a young age. Only two: being surrounded by it, and jamming with it. That's it! English came quickly and easily to you, and from what you told me, you were also surrounded by Music, so it must be jamming that makes the difference.

"Imagine if we allowed beginners to jam with professionals on a daily basis. Do you think it would take them twenty years to get good? Absolutely not! It wouldn't even take them ten. They would be great by the time they were musically four or five years old.

"Instead, we keep the beginners in the beginning level class for a few years before we let them move up to the intermediate level class. After a few more years at that level, they may move up to the advanced level class, but they still have to work up through the ranks of that class before they are really considered advanced level players. Once they stay at that level for a few years, we turn them loose, so that they can go pay their dues elsewhere. Think about it. After all these years of training, you still have to pay dues. When it comes to learning a language, what does paying dues mean? How many dues did you have to pay while learning English?"

Michael had interesting things to say. Abandoning my need for dominance, I sat up on the couch. The only way I can explain it is that I wanted to get closer to what he was saying. I wanted him to keep talking, all day if he was willing, but he paused as if inviting me to say something.

"I see your point," I replied, "but not all of us have access to professional musicians. I can't just call up Herbie Hancock or Mike Stern and say, 'Hey, I'm coming over. Wanna jam?' So what now? What am I supposed to do if I don't have professionals to play with every day?"

"You could have chosen to be born into a family of professional musicians," he answered without a smile, making it hard for me to tell if he was serious or not.

"It's too late for that now," I replied.

"I guess so. There is always next time. Still, there are professionals you can bring here to you."

"Really now? How am I supposed to do that?" I wasn't following his logic.

"Who would you like to jam with?" he asked.

"Well, I've always wanted to play with Miles Davis," I answered with a smile. I was only half joking.

Placing his skateboard on the floor, he rode over to my bookshelf and pulled out a Miles Davis CD, as if he'd placed it there himself. I didn't think much about it then. He put the CD in the player, pressed *play*, and nodded his head toward me.

"What do you want me to do?" I asked.

"Play," he answered.

"What am I supposed to play?"

"What is Miles asking you?"

"What do you mean, 'What is Miles asking me?'"

"I thought you said Music is a language. Are you telling me that you can't understand what Miles is asking you to play?"

"Um, I don't know," I sighed. I was slightly embarrassed by the question.

He turned off the CD player and picked up my acoustic guitar, which was sitting in the corner being used as a coat rack. The guitar was an old, beat-up, pawn shop special that hadn't been played, or even tuned, for I don't know how long. It didn't even have a brand name. I called it a "Majapan" guitar because it was made in Japan. Years earlier, I had a pickup installed inside, but I rarely plugged it in. That guitar was unplayable, or so I thought.

He sat down, placed his foot on top of his skateboard, and without the slightest bit of hesitation, began to produce the most amazing sounds. The music that poured out from beneath Michael's fingers was astounding. It was . . . well . . . it was Miles Davis!

"Play," he ordered.

"What key are you in?" I asked as I picked up my bass.

Ignoring my question, he looked me straight in the eyes and repeated himself in a stern voice, "Play!"

I recognized the song right away. It was "So What" from the *Kind of Blue* album, but I had no clue as to the key he was playing in. I fumbled around for a while until I finally found it, and as soon as I did, Michael stopped playing.

"Where are you from?" he asked abruptly.

"Virginia," I replied.

Immediately, he started playing again as if he didn't care about my answer, but this time, he was in a different key.

"Play!" he instructed again.

"What key?" I repeated.

He stopped playing, this time asking me for my shoe size.

"Nine and a half," I replied, more than a bit confused.

"Play!" he commanded in a stronger voice, as he continued strumming the guitar.

I knew better than to ask for the key, so once again, I fumbled around until I found it. And, once again, as soon as I did, he stopped.

"What kind of bass is that?" he inquired for some unknown reason.

"A violin-shaped Univox. It's a copy of a—"

Not letting me complete my sentence, he spoke firmly.

"Why is it that when I ask you a verbal question, your answer is immediate and direct? But when I ask you this—" he started playing again in a different key, "you don't seem to know how to answer. Don't you know this song?"

"Yes, I do, but—"

"Well, what's stopping you? Play!" he nearly shouted.

"But I need to find the key first!" I tried to hide my frustration, but he sensed it, and didn't seem to care.

"Oh, I see. You can't play Music until you first find the key. Very elementary." He stood up and walked over to where I was sitting. I guess it was so he could talk down to me. "What do you need a key for? I didn't even need a key to get into your house. Do you think your listeners have time to wait for you to find the key?"

"Well, usually I know the key before I start playing," I responded with hesitation.

"Do you always know what you're gonna say before you start talking?"

"No."

"And does that stop you from talking?"

"Not usually."

"Okay, then, play!"

He sat back down and, again, started playing in yet another key. For the first time, he seemed a little irritated, which didn't make things any easier for me. I took a deep breath and jumped right in, playing along with him as best as I could.

I fumbled around trying to find the root note so I could figure out something good to play but quickly got frustrated and put the bass down.

"That was horrible," I mumbled.

"You could use some help, but we'll get there," he replied in a gentle voice. He was smiling now, as if pleased with me all of a sudden. "What were you thinking about when you were playing?"

"I was trying to find the right key."

"And you need to find the right key before you can play Music?"

"It helps."

"Why?"

"I need to find the right key so that I can play the right notes."

"I see. Notes are so important that all Music stops until you find the right ones?"

"I didn't say that."

"Yes, you did. You said it clearly with your bass."

"Well tell me, then; when should I find the right notes?"

"You shouldn't."

"I shouldn't?"

"No! Not at first anyway. There is something more important you should find first."

"And what is that?"

"The *groove!*"

"The groove? Wait a minute. So the first thing I should do is find the groove when I start playing?" That was news to me.

"No! You should find the groove *before* you start playing. It doesn't matter whether you know the song or not. If you need to, let a few measures go by while you figure out what the groove is saying. Once you find the groove, it doesn't matter what note comes out; it will 'feel' right to the listener. People generally feel Music before they listen to it anyway. If finding the key is so important to you, at least find it while you groove."

I wanted to say something, but I couldn't think of a way to prove him wrong. I just stared at him while I fidgeted with my bass.

"Forget about your instrument," he said, staring back at me. "Forget about the key. Forget about technique. Hear and feel the groove. Then allow yourself to become part of Music."

Still holding the guitar, he started playing again. He leaned forward and nodded. Realizing I was not going to win the staring contest, I closed my eyes and waited, trying to figure out what to do. I decided to give in and do what he had suggested—listen. I listened to the groove.

Then a strange thing happened. Listening to the groove allowed me to hear more of the music. All of a sudden, along with Michael's guitar part, I could hear the drums, then the piano. I could hear Miles's trumpet too. I could even hear myself playing the bass, even though I wasn't holding it yet.

As if he was listening to what I was hearing, he spoke, more softly this time, "Play."

Without opening my eyes, I picked up my bass and started playing. I don't know if the first note I played was the right one or not, but it surely sounded good. Really good. I was shocked. I didn't want to lose the feeling, so I kept playing. I was lost in the music. The thought of a blue-eyed stranger in my house was no longer an issue. I was jamming with Miles Davis!

I opened my eyes to see that Michael had stopped playing and had already put the guitar down. He was applauding me, yelling, "Bravo! Bravo!"

I was proud of myself. "How did I do that?" I asked.

"How *did* you do that?" Michael repeated, forcing me to answer my own question once again.

"I don't quite know, but it sounded good to me. I just grooved, I guess. I didn't think about the notes at all, but everything I played seemed to work."

"That's right. Everything worked because you grooved before you started playing," he added.

"Groove before I play." I resolved to commit this new concept to memory.

"I have a saying," Michael said, "and I think you should remember it. It goes like this: 'Never lose the groove in order to find a note.'"

"I like that, and I think I understand it. Are you saying that grooving is more important than playing the right notes?"

"Don't jump to conclusions prematurely. All the elements of Music are equally important, or not."

"The 'elements of music'? What are you talking about? What is that?"

"The elements of Music are the individual parts that make up Music as a whole. Many musicians like yourself struggle because you are not familiar enough with all the elements. You rely mostly on one or two of them when you play. Doing that is a great recipe for frustration. A musician like me, who appropriately uses all the elements, will be one of the greats even though he may not be aware of the fact that he is using them. Actually, it would be nearly impossible to become a great musician without using all of these elements."

What he was saying was interesting even though I didn't totally understand the concept. "Elements" was not a term I usually associated with music.

"Can you please tell me more about these elements and how to use them?" That was something I had to know more about.

He flashed a sly smile, leaned forward, and whispered,

"Why do you think I am here?"

Invent

In many ways, this chapter from Wooten's book focuses on teaching and learning, and it asks readers to reexamine the way music is often taught in schools. Take a moment and reflect on how you've either experienced or observed music being taught. How do Michael's suggestions about teaching music push against traditional methods of music education? What benefits do you think one can gain from trying a non-traditional approach? How might Michael's ideas about music education apply to all education? What are some possible disadvantages you might experience if you tried to learn music exactly like you learned your native language?

Compose

Recall a time where you tried to learn to play an instrument, or a specific song on an instrument, or a particular technique. How did you go about learning? Did you use a book, DVD, YouTube videos, a friend, professional instructor—or perhaps a strange visitor who just appeared in your room? Freewrite about that experience, detailing the process and how successful you felt it was. Imagine how it might have been better and include that information as well.

Collaborate

Michael makes a number of statements about teaching and learning in this chapter that have been both celebrated and challenged in the musical world since the book's initial publication. Some educators have formally adopted these ideas while others have rejected them. In small groups, first identify all the claims regarding teaching or learning made in this chapter (for example, "You can only teach yourself"). Make a list of these claims and then, playing the skeptic, evaluate each one, testing its validity in various "real world" scenarios. Regardless of whether each claim proves itself to be 100% correct, what might be gained in adopting each one for a certain period of time when trying to learn something new? Be prepared to share your answers with the rest of the class. Alternatively, you might also have a classmate come to class with an instrument (or two) and provide a lesson for the class, after which you can all discuss these same concepts.

Explore

This book was published a few years after YouTube was invented. YouTube has become a leading method of music education in our current digital age, largely due to the vast amount of material on it and the ease with which one can access any number of lessons and instructors. *The Music Lesson*, however, presents us with a one-on-one teacher/student scenario, a model that seems to become more rare with the current generation than previous ones. Research various models of musical education, paying particular attention to the various differences in the philosophies behind why certain methods are used (i.e., learning from one's environment is at the core of the Suzuki Method of music education.). Also, explore the various discussions on the Internet regarding the increase in YouTube music education. What are the perceived problems at the center of the various arguments surrounding the use of video instruction?

Matthew D. Thibeault is an Assistant Professor of Music Education and Assistant Professor of Curriculum and Instruction (Affiliate) at the University Of Illinois. He publishes in the areas of media, general music, and technology. During the 2012-2013 school year, Thibeault was a Faculty Fellow at the Illinois Program for Research in the Humanities. He was the 2013 recipient of the Outstanding Emerging Researcher Award presented by the Center for Music Education Research at the University of South Florida. Thibeault also leads the Homebrew Ukulele Union, a group devoted to participatory music making in the Champaign-Urbana community. You can find him at www.matthewthibeault.com

HIP-HOP, DIGITAL MEDIA, AND THE CHANGING FACE OF MUSIC EDUCATION

By Matthew D. Thibeault

Here's a story you can share with your students: A young man wants to make hip-hop music and share it with the world. Devoted, he constantly writes and records raps on top of his friend's beats, sharing the songs via the Internet. He also lifts beats from other people, using digital software to sample and loop the beats from other popular songs, over which he records new rhymes. He even samples some of his own rhymes, reinserting and developing them into new songs that he releases. He dreams of taking all he has learned to put out an album on a major label that goes to the top of the charts, with all the kids around the country and especially where he grew up infatuated with every song he releases.

It's a true story about Dwayne Carter Jr., a rapper most music educators probably don't know but beloved throughout the world as Lil Wayne, or Weezy, or a host of other nicknames. Although he released music on a label for nearly a decade, during 2007 virtually all of his work was released solely online through a series of free downloads and illegal leaks. He was astonishingly prolific, often recording three or four new songs a day (Frere-Jones, 2007). He recorded so many songs that *Vibe* magazine felt the need to assist their readers in weeding through them with their November 2007 cover story, "The 77 Best Weezy Songs of 2007." Many of Wayne's songs were built on the beats of other artists, including a double CD set called *Da Drought 3*. This album consisted entirely of Lil Wayne's new versions of hip-hop hits by other artists, 29 tracks that in many instances are more highly regarded than the original songs he built on. This level of output led

Pitchfork reviewer Ryan Dombal to write, "He's given away more worthwhile free music online than most artists of his stature ever release officially" (Dombal, 2008).

All these albums were unofficially leaked or posted on the Internet, provided to fans at no charge, but Lil Wayne did profit indirectly. He used the ideas and feedback he collected when he went into the studio, recording *Tha Carter III*. Released in June of 2008, it went on to sell 2.88 million copies, making it the top selling recording of the year in the United States, enough for nearly 1% of the population or 2.5% of all households to own one (Hasty, 2008).

Critics overwhelmingly proclaimed Lil Wayne the top rapper in the hip-hop game, and the album and his work leading up to it were universally regarded as some of the most important hip-hop music available (Christgau, 2008). His fans, including young students and teachers in his hometown of New Orleans, obsessed over everything he released. One of the richest portraits of a teacher connecting with his students through music can be found in, "I Will Forever Remain Faithful," David Ramsey's (2009) essay, with a title drawn from a Lil Wayne line. The author details the incredible challenges in his first year teaching in post-Katrina New Orleans, where he was assessed by his students through his answers to questions about where he was from, whether he had "a lady," and whether he listened to "that Weezy." The article is structured around a series of quotes from Lil Wayne as Ramsey details how students loaned him stacks of Lil Wayne's mixtapes and he found that, "My kids sang his songs in class, in the hallways, before school, after school. I had a student who would rap a Lil Wayne line if he didn't know the answer to a question" (p. 8). Lil Wayne, the young man who dreamed of making it big had more than arrived, becoming a global phenomenon.

I expect most readers found much of the previous description of Lil Wayne's creative practice alien to their own ideas about teaching music. Many traditional musicians can't imagine being an artist who samples recordings, who makes his music exclusively in the studio rather than in face-to-face performance, who predominantly performs via the Internet, who gives away his recordings, and who raps instead of playing an instrument or singing in Western art style. I also expect that some educators would not like Lil Wayne's recordings if they listened to them, and they're often as explicit as old blues singers. Nevertheless, his work is a concrete example of the mainstream level of hip-hop, as well as some of the new musical practices that are emerging from digital media: new ways to be a musician, new ways to perform, and new music that is fundamentally different from what is offered in most music education programs. Throughout the rest of this article, I will lay out some of the big ideas at play and some of the leading scholars who are addressing these ideas.

HIP-HOP AS POSTPERFORMANCE MUSICAL PRACTICE

If it were merely the case that hip-hop were another musical culture, and that music teachers should try to teach them all, I think it would be hard to convince teachers to spend the time and energy it takes to credibly present hip-hop to their students. Instead, I would like to build a case that hip-hop exemplifies and uniquely embodies important and growing trends all educators should consider. Hip-hop may well be the best way to explore and understand trends in music, musician, and audience that will have profound educational implications.

These trends cluster around the notion that musical practice has entered an age I describe as "postperformance" (Thibeault, in press). Simply stated, musical experience through in-person performance by musicians is becoming an increasingly small part of our lives, with most musical experiences had through recordings. These recordings consist of musical materials edited and synthesized to a degree that calls into question their status as a performance. Just as tonality moved from being the only musical reality to an option with the rise of atonal music in the early 20th century, I believe that performance has moved from being the only way to present music to become one among many options that also include recording, computer synthesis, sampling, remixing, and more. Coming to terms with this reality will help the profession alter and broaden the variety of ways to share music.

Even for devoted performers such as my students, nearly all their musical experience comes through recorded sound. All commercial recordings are heavily edited and consist of the best of multiple takes (yes, even classical recordings), and many more recordings consist of music that is only remotely connected to live performance—whether synthesized, remixed, digitally generated, and so on. As Sasha Frere-Jones (2008), music critic of *The New Yorker*, writes, "In reality, the unsullied object is the Sasquatch of music. Even a purely live recording is a distortion and paraphrasing of an acoustic event." These ideas, clustered around the implications of recorded music and the reproducibility of music are key in the emerging field of "sound studies" (Sterne, 2003), scholarship around remixing (Lessig, 2008) and the convergence culture made ubiquitous through digital media (Jenkins, 2006; Manovich, 2002), but they date all the way back to Walter Benjamin's classic essay "The Work of Art in the Age of Mechanical Reproduction" (Benjamin, 1935/1986), as well as "Art and Civilization," the final chapter of John Dewey's (1934/1980) *Art as Experience*.

SOME MORE IDEAS AND RESOURCES FOR TEACHING WITH HIP-HOP

Sampling and remixing not only provide hip-hop an efficient way to create a new track on which to write new rhymes, they also bring along their own aesthetic dimensions. Sampling allows us to bring musicians from across space and time to be part of our own artistic process, and even if a drummer could perform and record a beat from a James Brown track, as Mark Katz (2004) writes that, "to do so would be to miss the point of hip-hop sampling completely" (p. 145). Juxtaposing, manipulating, and repurposing samples carry a special artistic weight.

Repetition is also a device within hip-hop that scholars have explored. Musicologist Susan McClary (1998) connects the repetitive structures of time found in hip-hop with minimalism, suggesting that hip-hop and minimalism should be understood as reactions to the prior dominance of epic narrative music such as the symphonies of Mahler and Beethoven. Robert Fink (2005) points out that to live in our corporate-manufactured age is to be deeply immersed in a minimalist aesthetic, from rows of desks in schools and Suzuki violin concerts, to endless supermarket aisles filled with repetitious packaging. Sampling also invites liberal doses of corporate and popular culture, distant from most music education but common to many arts, with the writer David Foster Wallace saying of popular culture references,

"Me and a lot of other young writers I know, we use these references sort of the way romantic poets use lakes and trees" (Lipsky, 2010). Digitally produced music, then, captures and embodies something of the way that we live our lives, something of the digital corporate landscape in which we find ourselves immersed. Hip-hop offers opportunities to reconsider what it is to be alive right now, surrounded by repetition, and mass production, and sampled soundbites.

In addition to the broader ideas previously presented, hip-hop culture and music are specifically the subjects of much important and valuable scholarly work. Teachers who find themselves without background or interest in hip-hop can easily consult some of the following resources, many of which can be screened and shared in part with students of all ages. For the elementary school practitioner, I know of no better volume than *Hip-Hop Speaks to Children: A Celebration of Poetry With a Beat*, a book/CD collection of poetry edited by Nikki Giovanni (2008). I have reviewed this book elsewhere in depth (Thibeault, 2010). The quality of the illustrations are superb and the recorded examples both valid and valuable. The book also conveys a convincing overall frame that places hip-hop as part of the rich vein of 20th-century African American artistic culture and a direct descendent of the Harlem Renaissance.

Films and books remain wonderful ways to connect with hip-hop culture, and there are plenty of outstanding examples. The early years of hip-hop, when it existed in the South Bronx, are on view in the classic film *Wild Style* (Ahearn, 1982). The culture of hip-hop "writers," graffiti artists whose work arose during the 1970s in New York, can be seen in action in the wonderful documentary *Style Wars* (Silver & Chalfant, 2004), and are beautifully photographed by the artist Henry Chalfant in his book *Subway Art* (Chalfant & Cooper, 1984). For those interested in exploring the turntable as a musical instrument, the movie *Scratch* is indispensable (Pray, 2001), along with a wonderful chapter by Mark Katz on DJ Battling (Katz, 2004). Terry Gross recorded a series of interviews with hip-hop pioneers such as Kool Herc and Grandmaster Flash that can be listened to online as part of Fresh Air's 2005 "Hip-Hop Week" (Gross, 2005). Jeff Chang (2005) provides an indispensable history, *Can't Stop, Won't Stop: A History of the Hip-Hop Generation*, a wonderful supplement to the still-invaluable *Rap Attack 3* (Toop, 2000). A selection of essays dealing with hip-hop, *Critical Minded: New Approaches to Hip Hop Studies*, contains many valuable readings (Hisama & Rapport, 2005). For those interested in the linguistic aspects of hip-hop, Stanford professor H. Samy Alim has authored/coauthored several valuable books (Alim, 2004, 2006; Spady, Meghelli, & Alim, 2006).

Hip-hop is here to stay and impossible to dismiss as a fad given its nearly 40-year history as well as dominance in both the music industry and public imagination. If more music teachers take time to understand this musical culture and some of the larger trends it exemplifies, they likely will reach more students, especially those who presently choose not to participate in our music programs. Digital media and the musical creations it foments will undoubtedly continue to grow and take on an increasing prominence within the larger culture and our school music programs. It would be welcome if school music programs reflected these developments, creating a new generation of artists as prolific and inventive as Lil Wayne.

References

Ahearn, C. (Writer). (1982). Wild style [DVD]: Rhino.

Alim, H. S. (2004). *You know my steez: An ethnographic and sociolinguistic study of styleshifting in a Black American speech community*. Durham, NC: Duke University Press.

Alim, H. S. (2006). *Roc the mic right: The language of hip hop culture*. New York, NY: Routledge.

Benjamin, W. (1986). The work of art in the age of mechanical reproduction (H. Zohn, Trans.). In H. Arendt (Ed.), *Illuminations* (pp. 217-252). New York, NY: Schocken Books. (Original work published 1935)

Chalfant, H., & Cooper, M. (1984). *Subway art*. New York, NY: Rinehart & Winston.

Chang, J. (2005). *Can't stop won't stop: A history of the hip-hop generation*. New York, NY: St. Martin's Press.

Christgau, R. (2008). *Review: Da Drought 3*. Retrieved from http://www.robertchristgau.com/get_artist.php?name=Lil+Wayne

Dewey, J. (1980). *Art as experience*. New York: Perigree Books. (Original work published 1934).

Dombal, R. (2008). *Pitchfork album reviews: Lil Wayne Tha Carter III*. Retrieved from http://pitchfork.com/reviews/albums/11608-tha-carter-iii/

Fink, R. (2005). *Repeating ourselves: American minimal music as cultural practice*. Berkeley: University of California Press.

Frere-Jones, S. (2007, August 13). High and mighty: Lil Wayne takes over hip-hop. *The New Yorker*. Retrieved from http://www.newyorker.com/arts/critics/musical/2007/08/13/070813crmu_music_frerejones

Frere-Jones, S. (2008). *The gerbil's revenge: Auto-Tune corrects a singer's pitch. It also distorts—a grand tradition in pop.* Retrieved from http://www.newyorker.com/arts/critics/musical/2008/06/09/080609crmu_music_frerejones

Giovanni, N. (2008). *Hip-hop speaks to children: A celebration of poetry with a beat.* Naperville, IL: Sourcebooks Jabberwocky.

Gross, T. (2005, August 29). DJ and hip-hop pioneer Grandmaster Flash. *NPR Music.* Retrieved from http://www.npr.org/templates/story/story.php?storyId=15729080

Hasty, K. (2008, December 31). Taylor Swift reigns again on Billboard 200. *Billboard Underground.* Retrieved from http://www.billboard.com/column/taylor-swift-reigns-againon-billboard-200-1003926053.story?tag=nextart

Hisama, E. M., & Rapport, E. (Eds.). (2005). *Critical minded:New approaches to hip hop studies.* Brooklyn, NY: Institute for Studies in American Music.

Jenkins, H. (2006). *Convergence culture: Where old and new media collide.* New York, NY: New York University Press.

Katz, M. (2004). *Capturing sound: How technology has changed music.* Berkeley: University of California Press.

Lessig, L. (2008). *Remix: Making art and commerce thrive in the hybrid economy.* New York, NY: Penguin.

Lipsky, D. (2010). *Although of course you end up becoming yourself: A road trip with David Foster Wallace.* New York, NY: Broadway Books.

Manovich, L. (2002). *The language of new media.* Cambridge: MIT Press.

McClary, S. (1998). *Rap, minimalism, and structures of time in late twentieth-century culture.* Lincoln: College of Fine and Performing Arts, University of Nebraska-Lincoln.

Pray, D. (Writer). (2001). Scratch [DVD]. USA: PALM. Downloaded from gmt.sagepub.com at Stanford University Medical Center on January 17, 2013

Ramsey, D. (2009). I will forever remain faithful: How Lil Wayne helped me survive my first year teaching in New Orleans. In G. Marcus & D. Carr (Eds.), *Best music writing 2009* (pp. 3-14). Cambridge, MA: Da Capo Press.

Silver, T., & Chalfant, H. (2004). Style wars [DVD]. Los Angeles, CA: Public Art Films.

Spady, J. G., Meghelli, S., & Alim, H. S. (2006). *Tha global cipha: Hip hop culture and consciousness.* Philadelphia, PA: Black History Museum Press.

Sterne, J. (2003). *The audible past: Cultural origins of sound reproduction.* Durham, NC: Duke University Press.

Thibeault, M. D. (2010). [Review of the book *Hip hop speaks to children: A celebration of poetry with a beat*, by N. Giovanni]. *Orff Echo, XLII*(2), 35.

Thibeault, M. D. (in press). Media and music in a postperformance world. In G. McPherson & G. Welch (Eds.), *The Oxford handbook of music education*. Oxford, England: Oxford University Press.

Toop, D. (2000). *Rap attack 3: African rap to global hip hop* (3rd rev., expanded and updated ed.). London, England: Serpent's Tail.

Invent

Thibeault's essay appears in a journal for music educators, and, as such, his readers are likely music teachers. In this essay, he argues that hip-hop "exemplifies and uniquely embodies important and growing trends all educators should consider." He points out, however, that much of music education follows a very traditional path and often centers on traditional music. Do you think there is a place for modern music in music education programs? If so, what styles do you think would best work in the music classroom (i.e., pop, metal, hip-hop, rock, etc.)? Do you think music educators need to be fans of the music styles they use in teaching musical concepts? What might be the advantages of teaching music through a modern style like hip-hop? What might be the challenges to teaching this way? Have you experienced a music education at some point that broke from tradition in this way?

Compose

Thibeault argues that formal music education could benefit from its teachers attending to hip-hop and all it has to offer the music classroom. Likewise, in his essay "Groove," Victor Lemonte Wooten challenges the traditional music education classroom, arguing that music education should extend beyond the classroom, offering its student less formal experiences. Thibeault offers his thoughts via an academic essay, and Wooten presents his views through a story, but both authors argue that traditional notions of music education need to adapt, and each is careful to make clear that they wish to augment—not eradicate—traditional music pedagogy. Examining both essays, make a list of the similar ways in which both men approach music and music education. What do these two educators (one a music education professor and the other a Grammy-Award winning musician) have in common?

As stated above, in this essay, Thibeault argues that music teachers need to embrace hip-hop in the classroom, not just because it's a growing music genre but rather because it is "the best way to explore and understand trends in music, musicians, and audience..." As a small group, pick a trend that hip-hop embodies (hint—Thibeault mentions several in his essay). Prepare a lesson on that trend that you will then teach to your classmates. Make sure to utilize multi-media elements in your lesson (i.e., don't just tell your students; show them). After your lesson, allow for some time to reflect on how hip-hop helped you in teaching about the trend. Do you think Thibeault is correct in his argument that this genre provides a unique way to teach music?

1. In this essay, Thibeault touches on numerous musical phenomena associated with hip-hop, one of which is sampling. While it's easy to think sampling has always existed in its present form, that is not the case. Research the history of sampling in hip-hop, exploring how the technique has changed over the decades and what other aspects of music have affected the way in which it is approached (i.e., analog vs. digital, legal consequences of sampling, mashups, etc.).

2. Alternatively, look at the history of music education, investigating key moments where traditional music pedagogy resisted new ways of imagining the music classroom. What modern musical teaching methods exist now that have generated controversy?

Steve Lawson is a bassist, composer, improviser, teacher, and author. His solo career began in 1999 and has resulted in more than 25 acclaimed solo and collaborative albums. Steve Lawson has toured extensively across Europe and the US and has lectured on performance, improvisation, and the changes in the music industries brought about by the Internet at universities and colleges for over a decade. His first novel, Rock and Roll Is Dead came out in 2009. This essay first appeared on his personal blog in 2010.

MUSIC IS WORTHLESS

By Steve Lawson

The BBC have an article today, in which they report on Rob Dickins, former head of Warner Music UK, saying that albums should cost a £1.

It's a fairly radical step, and there's some merit in what he says, as a response to currently-illegal downloading, within a fixed price market.

However, what's missing from this is the simple fact that music is worthless. 'Music' as in noises that fit within the 'organised sound' definition that most of us recognise as music, has no inherent value at all. All the value is contextual. It can be invested, it can be enhanced, it can even be manufactured counter to any previously measured notions of 'quality' with a particular idiom, but it's not innate. Noise is not a saleable commodity.

So, we're back to the point I've been making time and time again. The financial value of music is entirely based on the listeners sense of gratitude for it—that gratitude can be

- to the music itself for existing
- to the artist for making it
- to the person who introduced it to them and to the community/culture that fosters its existence.

And there are three entirely natural ways for that gratitude to be expressed:

- Sharing
- Saying Thank You
- Paying for it

The problem facing those who 'set prices for download music' is that the price/value/gratitude matrix is impossible to second-guess. And fixed prices completely mess it up. A fixed price becomes a game of brinkmanship between artist and listener. The calculation of value is done without any room for altruism, for a sense of sponsoring or fostering art, for being a patron of the continuation of the art that we love.

The stats are there to back it up. My own experience with download sales has been that some people are happy to pay £20 for a download album of music that they love by someone whose work they want to see continue. They are almost always people who I have had contact with, that could be described as friends, but often that friendship came out of them listening to my music, being introduced to it by some other means.

I know that Zoe Keating has had a (small) number of people pay $100 for her latest album. Why? Because they have the means to and it's a great way of demonstrating their love for her art in the face of a music industrial environment that is trying to force people to pay amounts that have no bearing on the cost of releasing music to the artist, or the value of that music to the listener.

Big Music—the major industrial model for releasing recorded music—is broken. It's been broken for decades.

Now is the best time ever to be a musician making music and finding an appreciative audience for that music. The story telling that goes on around the creation of music and its inspiration is the best possible way of investing potential value in the experience of listening to it, and of encouraging people to go against the economic norms of the day and think about what music means to them and how much they are willing to pay to reflect that value to them, as their part in the ongoing financial viability of spending time making music.

It's beautiful. It's magical, it's a chance to take art and tell stories about it, to get excited about things being wonderful and meaningful rather than spending HOURS talking about just how fucked up the latest crop of contestants are on *The Apprentice*. Or how bad the singers are on *X-Factor*.

Take great things, share them, be grateful for their existence and their role in making the world a nicer place.

Here's some music that I love, that's I'm proud of, that I'd love you to hear. You can listen to it all here, you can download it, share it with your friends on Facebook or twitter, bookmark it for later, and if you want to you can pay whatever it's worth to you. If you want to prove Rob Dickins' point, pay a pound for it. If you want to get into a 'whose listeners pay the most' competition with Zoe Keating, feel free to pay $101. I'm happy either way.

This essay concerns the value that individuals place on music. How do you decide how much you are going to pay for music? How much is too much for your favorite artist's new album? Do you think everyone should have to pay the same amount for the music they own? If so, how do you think we should determine the value of that music? Who should determine that value? What does the price a society is willing to pay for music say about the value it places on the musical arts?

Think back to the first time you remember paying for music with your own money. Write a paragraph or two about that experience. Provide plenty of details regarding the music you bought, how much you paid, why you were willing to give up your money for it, and how you felt after you purchased it.

Lawson's main contention seems to reject the idea that the price point for music should be static. In fact, insisting that music is noise and "noise is not a saleable commodity," he argues that the value of music can be expressed in gratitude, which can be demonstrated in a variety of ways, of which payment is just one. In small groups, discuss whether you think this approach to the value of music is realistic on a large scale. In other words, do you think it would work if all artists adopted this approach to music and allowed their audiences to pay or not to pay for it as they saw fit? Why or why not?

Research the history of pay-what-you-want models in music, exploring who has tried it (for example, Radiohead did so with their 2007 *In Rainbows* album), the success or failure of this model, and organizations dedicated to allowing full access to creative works (think Napster, Creative Commons, etc.). Also, look up the article to which Lawson refers in his opening sentence (Google: Album Price Should Drop to £1, by Ian Youngs). After reading Youngs's essay, go back and revisit Lawson's to see how well you think he challenges Youngs's ideas.

XTC was a new wave/alternative rock band from England, formed in 1972, but most popular between 1979 and 1982. Their album Go 2 was released in 1978 and featured an all-text record jacket cover. Radiohead is a modern English rock band, formed in 1985 and led by front man Thom Yorke. Their debut album was released in 1993, and their popularity continues to grow. Hail to the Thief was released in 2003, the final album with their major record label, EMI. The album cover, along with some of the songs, expressed the band's response to The War on Terror.

ALBUM ART: *GO 2 BY XTC AND HAIL TO THE THIEF BY RADIOHEAD*

By Radiohead, XTC

```
This is a RECORD COVER. This writing is the DESIGN upon the
record cover. The DESIGN is to help SELL the record. We hope
to draw your attention to it and encourage you to pick it up.
When you have done that maybe you'll be persuaded to listen to
the music - in this case XTC's Go 2 album. Then we want you
to BUY it. The idea being that the more of you that buy this
record the more money Virgin Records, the manager Ian Reid and
XTC themselves will make. To the aforementioned this is known
as PLEASURE. A good cover DESIGN is one that attracts more
buyers and gives more pleasure. This writing is trying to pull
you in much like an eye-catching picture. It is designed to get
you to READ IT. This is called luring the VICTIM, and you are
the VICTIM. But if you have a free mind you should STOP READING
NOW! because all we are attempting to do is to get you to read
on. Yet this is a DOUBLE BIND because if you indeed stop you'll
be doing what we tell you, and if you read on you'll be doing what
we've wanted all along. And the more you read on the more you're
falling for this simple device of telling you exactly how a good
commercial design works. They're TRICKS and this is the worst
TRICK of all since it's describing the TRICK whilst trying to
TRICK you, and if you've read this far then you're TRICKED but
you wouldn't have known this unless you'd read this far. At
least we're telling you directly instead of seducing you with
a beautiful or haunting visual that may never tell you. We're
letting you know that you ought to buy this record because in
essence it's a PRODUCT and PRODUCTS are to be consumed and you
are a consumer and this is a good PRODUCT. We could have
written the band's name in special lettering so that it stood
out and you'd see it before you'd read any of this writing and
possibly have bought it anyway. What we are really suggesting
is that you are FOOLISH to buy or not buy an album merely as a
consequence of the design on its cover. This is a con because
if you agree then you'll probably like this writing - which is
the cover design - and hence the album inside. But we've just
warned you against that. The con is a con. A good cover design
could be considered as one that gets you to buy the record, but
that never actually happens to YOU because YOU know it's just a
design for the cover. And this is the RECORD COVER.
```

XTC's album begins with the statement, "This is a RECORD COVER." From that point on, the text concerns itself with self-reflective comments on commercialism, the music industry, and the money record executives make off their artists. What are your thoughts regarding the commercialization of music? What kind of control do you think record companies should have when it comes to the music we listen to? What does the XTC album cover suggest about the money that the record companies make off artists' music?

Carefully read the two album covers, making separate lists of the key words that appear on each. Start with the bold words for XTC, but don't restrict yourself to those. Look for repeated words or synonyms (words with similar meanings). Once you've compiled the lists, compose a paragraph for each record that summarizes the argument you think each cover makes.

Design your own album cover! Form small groups and discuss the two album covers and their potential meanings. Both operate as a form of protest, and you should first identify and understand how each album cover presents its message. Next, as a group, decide on a topic you want to protest through your album cover and begin to work on your design. Feel free to utilize design software on a computer. Remember to privilege text in some fashion, as our examples do. Feel free, however, to get creative with your use of images, etc.

A lot has changed in the record industry since XTC's *Go 2* in 1978, and even since Radiohead's *Hail to the Thief* in 2003. Explore the history of the relationship between record companies, their artists, and consumers. How has it all changed? What have been the catalysts for such changes (hint: think Napster)? Focus on the time between the mid–70s and now. Much has been written about this topic, so you should have no trouble finding material to aid in your inquiry, and much of its history can be found on the Internet. Also, note that Greg Kot's article in this book provides a good summary of what has transpired from the late 90s until now.

Pieter Bruegel (1525–1569) was a Flemish Renaissance painter, famous for his landscapes and peasant scenes. W. H. Auden (1907–1973) was a celebrated British modernist poet whose poems often explored moral, religious, and political issues. William Carlos Williams (1883–1963) was an American poet, who chose to focus on his literary career in the evenings after working all day as a doctor. He was closely associated with imagism, a modernist movement that privileged clear and precise language and imagery. Krista Detor (b.1969) is an internationally acclaimed singer songwriter from Bloomington, Indiana, whose lyrics, often in narrative form, explore various aspects of the human condition and touch on elements of both modernism and postmodernism.

LANDSCAPE WITH THE FALL OF ICARUS (C.1558), "MUSEE DES BEAUX ARTS" (1940), "LANDSCAPE WITH THE FALL OF ICARUS" (1960), "ICARUS" (2007)

BY PIETER BRUEGEL, W.H. AUDEN, WILLIAM CARLOS WILLIAMS, KRISTA DETOR

THE FALL OF ICARUS

Pieter Bruegel

Landscape with the Fall of Icarus. 1558. Oil on canvas. Musees royaux des Beaux-Arts de Belgique, Brussels.

MUSEE DES BEAUX ARTS

W. H. Auden

About suffering they were never wrong,
The old Masters: how well they understood
Its human position: how it takes place
While someone else is eating or opening a window or just walking dully along;
How, when the aged are reverently, passionately waiting
For the miraculous birth, there always must be
Children who did not specially want it to happen, skating
On a pond at the edge of the wood:
They never forgot
That even the dreadful martyrdom must run its course
Anyhow in a corner, some untidy spot
Where the dogs go on with their doggy life and the torturer's horse
Scratches its innocent behind on a tree.

In Breughel's Icarus, for instance: how everything turns away
Quite leisurely from the disaster; the ploughman may
Have heard the splash, the forsaken cry,
But for him it was not an important failure; the sun shone
As it had to on the white legs disappearing into the green
Water, and the expensive delicate ship that must have seen
Something amazing, a boy falling out of the sky,
Had somewhere to get to and sailed calmly on.

LANDSCAPE WITH THE FALL OF ICARUS

William Carlos Williams

According to Brueghel
when Icarus fell
it was spring

a farmer was ploughing
his field
the whole pageantry

of the year was
awake tingling
near

the edge of the sea
concerned
with itself

sweating in the sun
that melted
the wings' wax

unsignificantly
off the coast
there was

a splash quite unnoticed
this was
Icarus drowning

ICARUS

Krista Detor

Spent the night under the dogstar chasing my tail
All out of things to say—No one to tell anyway

And the ambulance sped down the road in search of a heart
Whose beating had stopped—A life interrupted

Statements were taken and solemnly filed in a drawer
I wish I had known, she said, that he'd go off alone, she said

And Icarus fell while no one was looking
We had places to go, and what could we do
He fell out of the sky, disappeared in the blue unending

Maybe it's better there on the other side
I hope that it is, for my sake and for his

It's got to be greener, she said, when they'd left with their lights
All gone on their way—Nobody to save today

He should have known better than flying so close to the sun
The wings couldn't hold, but he never did what he was told

And Icarus fell while no one was looking
We had places to go, and what could we do
He fell out of the sky and disappeared in the blue forever

I could have saved him, I could have, just one minute more
Had I thought of it then, but you know how it's been,
All this thinking I do lately takes all of my attention.

A minute has passed since the words dropped right off of the page
Nobody to catch them—May I live to at least forget him…

While Icarus fell and no one was looking
We had places to go, and what could we do
He fell out of the sky and disappeared in the blue unending
Blue unending … sea

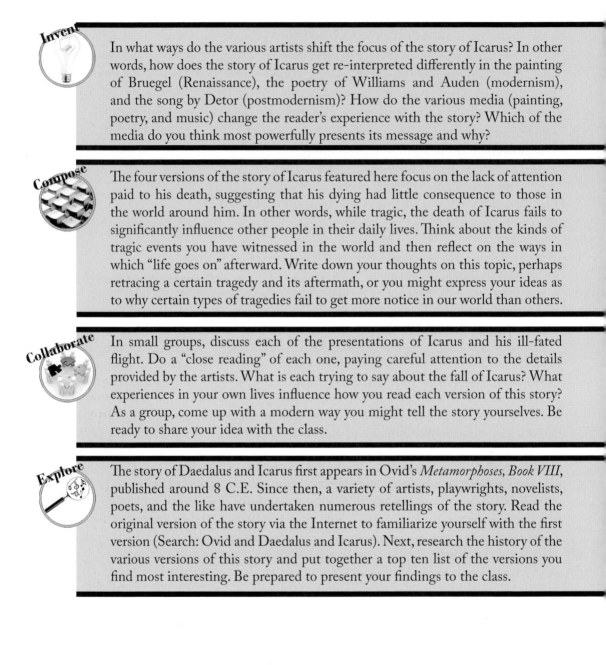

Invent

In what ways do the various artists shift the focus of the story of Icarus? In other words, how does the story of Icarus get re-interpreted differently in the painting of Bruegel (Renaissance), the poetry of Williams and Auden (modernism), and the song by Detor (postmodernism)? How do the various media (painting, poetry, and music) change the reader's experience with the story? Which of the media do you think most powerfully presents its message and why?

Compose

The four versions of the story of Icarus featured here focus on the lack of attention paid to his death, suggesting that his dying had little consequence to those in the world around him. In other words, while tragic, the death of Icarus fails to significantly influence other people in their daily lives. Think about the kinds of tragic events you have witnessed in the world and then reflect on the ways in which "life goes on" afterward. Write down your thoughts on this topic, perhaps retracing a certain tragedy and its aftermath, or you might express your ideas as to why certain types of tragedies fail to get more notice in our world than others.

Collaborate

In small groups, discuss each of the presentations of Icarus and his ill-fated flight. Do a "close reading" of each one, paying careful attention to the details provided by the artists. What is each trying to say about the fall of Icarus? What experiences in your own lives influence how you read each version of this story? As a group, come up with a modern way you might tell the story yourselves. Be ready to share your idea with the class.

Explore

The story of Daedalus and Icarus first appears in Ovid's *Metamorphoses, Book VIII*, published around 8 C.E. Since then, a variety of artists, playwrights, novelists, poets, and the like have undertaken numerous retellings of the story. Read the original version of the story via the Internet to familiarize yourself with the first version (Search: Ovid and Daedalus and Icarus). Next, research the history of the various versions of this story and put together a top ten list of the versions you find most interesting. Be prepared to present your findings to the class.

Gary Marcus is an award-winning professor of psychology and director of the NYU Center for Language and Music, where he studies evolution, language, and cognitive development. He has written four books about the origins and development of mind and brain, including the New York Times Bestseller, Guitar Zero, and Kluge: The Haphazard Evolution of The Human Mind, which was a New York Times Book Review Editors' Choice. He is also the editor of the Norton Psychology Reader and author of numerous science publications in leading journals such as Science, and Nature. His essays have appeared in forums such as Wired, Discover, the Wall Street Journal, and the New York Times.

excerpt from
GUITAR ZERO—"LEARNING TO CRAWL"

By Gary Marcus

Even before a baby first sees the light of day, he or she is likely to have been surrounded by music for months. To be sure, the sound quality is kind of dismal. Bass sounds are relatively audible, but most of the treble gets lost in the amniotic fluid that surrounds the growing fetus; it is almost as if the baby were listening to music from the bottom of a swimming pool. Still, lo-fi is better than no-fi. The process of learning about sound and music starts long before the baby begins to breathe on its own. Even putting aside whatever filtered sounds pass through from the outside world, there's plenty to listen to: heartbeats, breathing, and the regular modulations of the expecting mother's voice, which travels on the inside in part through bone conduction. And by the end of the final trimester, the growing fetus begins to take in at least some of what comes through.

Whether as a product of genes or early experience, or (more likely) both, some of the precursors of human musicality emerge very early in life. But how much of music is wired into our genomes? And how much of our musicality is hard-won, through lessons, practice, and listening?

It is very popular these days to talk about humans as if we were born with a "music instinct," akin to the language instinct that Noam Chomsky and Steven Pinker suggest we are born with.

But what is popular is not always true. At first glance, the notion that we might be born with a music instinct seems pretty plausible. In one study, for example, the Hungarian neuroscientist István Winkler showed that the brains of sleeping newborns could make a first step toward recognizing so-called relative pitch, in which music is understood not in terms of exact frequencies but in terms of the gaps between notes. When infants heard large musical leaps amid a series of smaller leaps, their brains displayed a common measure of surprise.

In another study, Winkler and his associates showed that the brains of awake newborns responded differently to the sudden absence of bass kick drum in an otherwise repetitive four-beat-long drum pattern. In a third study, they found that infants' brains appear to recognize changes in timbre, or when a single pitch is played by more than one instrument. We also know newborns can distinguish consonance (in which the notes of a chord blend together smoothly) from dissonance (in which the notes of a chord clash). But these rudiments aren't the same as a genuine understanding of music, which unfolds more slowly, over the weeks, months, and years that are yet to come.

Another early milestone arrives by about the age of two months, a first aesthetic preference: by then, infants have begun to *prefer* listening to consonance rather than dissonance, and not just to distinguish between the two. (Intriguingly, one study suggests that infant chimpanzees, too, may prefer consonance to dissonance, even though their overall interest level in music is low, perhaps suggesting that the difference between consonance and dissonance has more to do with the dynamics of how primate brains work than with anything intrinsic to music per se.)

By around six or seven months, infants start to become sensitive to the shapes of melodies. Given enough exposure, they can detect when a note has changed, recognize a short melody even when it has been transposed upward or downward in pitch, and sometimes remember melodies for weeks.

In some ways, young infants can even find themselves ahead of adults, especially in making fine auditory distinctions. One study, for instance, suggests that ten-month-olds are better able than adults to notice deviations in rhythms that aren't common in their own culture, a finding that has a direct parallel in language, where young infants are sensitive to some linguistic distinctions that adults in their cultures can't recognize. Young Japanese children, for example, might distinguish the sounds of *l* versus *r* where their parents can't.

A few researchers have even argued that babies are born with perfect or absolute pitch, that is, the capacity to recognize the exact frequency of any given note, at least in relatively unmusical sequences of notes. But such observations are controversial, and babies certainly don't have absolute pitch in the sense that some trained musicians do. Trained adults with absolute pitch can not only recognize a note but name it; no infant can do the same. (And of course many infants grow up to be tone-deaf or rhythmically impaired, perhaps because of a confluence of genes and inadequate musical experience—whereas virtually all normal children manage to master their native language.)

Where does all of this leave the idea of a music instinct? Although for most kids, most of the time, the rudiments of both rhythm and pitch are in place by the end of the first year of life, a small initial sensitivity to rhythm and pitch does not a symphony make. When it comes to the notion of humans being born with a "music instinct," there are in fact several reasons for skepticism.

First and foremost is the fact that no matter which rudiments of music might be inborn, for most people it is a long, hard slog from there to anything recognizable as systematic music. Even if it takes your average baby only a few months to recognize some of the basic rhythms of his or her own culture's music, most children don't really work out the fact that there are discrete notes until they are at least two—if then. Notwithstanding the occasional five-year-old prodigy who possesses the rare phenomenon of perfect pitch and manages to learn to play piano by ear, most children struggle early on.

When it comes to singing, for example, toddlers often warble between notes without landing in any particular spot, yielding a kind of out-of-tuneness that sounds a bit like a beginning violinist. Eventually, most (but not all) kids start to grasp the general contours of songs, such as when a song starts high and ends low, but even then most kids often miss many of the individual notes. (In my own case, pitch was a complete mystery; I remembered songs by their lyrics, but I was largely oblivious to the tune.)

It also takes our ears years to develop. Even basics, like recognizing that major chords tend to sound happier and minor chords sound sad, can take many kids until the end of the preschool years. More subtle capacities, like detecting chords that are merely unexpected rather than blatantly out of key, develop at an even slower pace. Children also have trouble paying attention to a background harmony that looms behind a foreground melody and may not even notice if the background harmony is dissonant.

Rhythm is no easier, as anyone who's ever been to a nursery school Christmas pageant can attest. Although babies can bop along to music by the time they're seven months old, they can't bop *in time* to music until a few years later. In the final analysis, children's first efforts to sing, which is often their first attempt at producing music, are often admirable but rarely especially musical. Even when children reach grade school, about half still understand only the broad contours of songs, rather than seeing songs as collections of specific pitches; a precise sense of melody comes late, in grade school for many children (and much later, if ever, for people less gifted). Mastering the ability to stay in key often takes years. In the polite but damning words of one academic article, "children enter school with a clear disposition towards learning the words of songs [that] is not matched by an ability to learn and reproduce the melodic components of [those] songs." And for some of us, these struggles persist well into adulthood. When I started this whole project, my wife described my efforts at singing as "cute but tuneless." (As I later discovered, I was not alone: at least 10 to 15 percent of the population never learn to sing in key.)

Compared with some other creatures, such as songbirds like the zebra finch, human beings just aren't that impressive in their early years. By the time a young zebra finch reaches the age of ninety days, it has learned to sing its own song, styled on one it hears from a tutor, with a solid sense of rhythm and pitch—and the young zebra finch manages all of this without any obvious correction or feedback. Few humans can say the same. Whereas nearly every three-year-old masters his or her native language, there are plenty of thirty-three-year-olds who can't sing their way out of a paper bag. There is also some evidence, for example, that birds have a better sense of pitch than most humans. At the same time, humans can lead perfectly normal lives without being musical. Theodore Roosevelt, twenty-sixth president of the United States, is said to have been amusical, and Sigmund Freud may have been, too. A male zebra finch that was unable to sing would be hard-pressed to find a mate.

All of this is a bit bad for the hypothesis that we are born with a music instinct. Even worse is the enormous challenge that most of us face in our efforts to master musical instruments. Although there are legions of six-year-olds trying to play violin, the vast majority don't sound that good to anyone but their blood relatives. Drummers typically take years to learn to move their limbs independently, and guitarists (as I was starting to realize) take many moons to learn to change chords smoothly. Humans clearly have much more innate interest in music than do chimpanzees or monkeys, but compared with your average starling or mockingbird, human children are nowhere near the front of the class.

Where we excel is later; if we humans set our minds to it, we can do almost anything intellectual better than our animal kin. Drawing on our gifts of language, culture, teaching, and leisure time, we can get really good at something if we work hard at it; no songbird will ever compose the symphonies of Bach or Beethoven. But saying that the most talented among us can produce great works of art if they devote their lives to that pursuit is not the same thing as saying that the average Joe is genuinely born with a gift for music. A good analogy might be skiing: human beings can surely learn to zip down bumpy snow-covered hills at high speeds—if they put the practice in—but that doesn't mean we are born knowing how to carve around moguls.

In hindsight, the idea that the conventions of music are largely learned rather than hardwired shouldn't entirely come as a surprise. In linguistics, there are many candidates for detailed and specific aspects of language that might be cross-culturally universal, like parts of speech. In music, by contrast, universals are few and far between—and often very weak. Most music may, for example, revolve around some sort of central sound, but the Western notion of "tonality" is hardly typical. Scales generally contain no more than six or seven notes (possibly as a function of human memory limitations), but the common chromatic scale has twelve, and some composers have experimented with dividing the scale into nineteen equal divisions. Most music is organized around rhythms, but recitatives are not. Even something as seemingly basic as a melody in which notes change from one pitch to another over the course of a song is not common to all forms of music; some music is based almost entirely around rhythm, with pitch at most an afterthought. Indeed, some of the things that modern listeners take for granted—like major and minor chords, and the whole notion of harmony—are absent in many of the world's musical systems. There's a case to be made for a strong universal grammar, but there may be little that is specifically innate about music.

If music is something that we learn, rather than something that falls directly out of a hardwired instinct, that still doesn't mean that babies must start their musical voyages from scratch. Among all the species on our planet, humans are special in many ways; we may not be the strongest or the fastest, but we are exceptionally good at repurposing old bits of brain tissue toward new tasks. Reading, for example, is not innate, and was not directly selected for over the course of our evolution; it's only about five thousand years old, and our species has a history that goes back millions of years. But reading *draws on* a set of circuits that predate reading itself, like circuits for detecting the sounds of words, recognizing fine visual detail, and drawing connections between different senses.

When we listen to music, we start with circuits in the temporal cortex of the brain (more or less behind the ear) that we share with virtually all other primates, ranging from monkeys to chimpanzees. Whether you are predator or prey, a good sense of pitch and of how sounds change over time can help you navigate and identify danger. Consistent with this notion of our brain repurposing old circuitry for music is the fact that the brain's tools for acoustic differentiation are far more precise than would be necessary for music alone. The upshot is that even if we aren't born to listen to music, we are well stocked with tools that can help make that job manageable.

In all probability, humans' capacity for acquiring music probably derives not just from good ears but also from a trio of other talents. The first is a general ability to soak up knowledge through culture and teaching, accompanied by a sometimes leisurely lifestyle that allows us the time to master new skills—from making stone tools (as our ancestors did) to playing Tetris to driving cars with a manual transmission. The second is a neural architecture, shared with other mammals, that inherently seeks links between different types of sensory information, such as sound and motion. Babies, for instance, can recognize when a vowel that they listen to matches (or fails to match) the mouth movements of an accompanying face.

The third? Our gift for language.

Language, like music, depends heavily on rhythm, and also on the ability to compensate for differences in pitch. We need to recognize words, for example, at whatever pitch they are uttered, whether in a low baritone (think Darth Vader) or in a Mickey Mouse falsetto. Our ability to transpose music—to recognize a melody sung in two different keys—could well be a by-product of our inborn capacity to recognize speech, rather than a direct product of some sort of musical evolution. The same may turn out to be true for rhythm and pitch.

A logical question, then, is about which comes first in the lifetime of an individual child, does language precede music or the other way around?

Surprisingly, only two studies have directly asked this question. The first showed that, given a choice, infants prefer their own mother's voice to instrumental music. The only other study comes from my own lab and equally attests to children's chief attraction being to speech rather than to music. In our experiments, we had an ongoing project studying seven-month-old infants and how they come to recognize abstract patterns, such as the *abb* pattern that is present in a string of syllables like *la ta ta*. When it comes to speech, infants are quick learners: after just two minutes of hearing a *la ta ta, ga na na* soundtrack, they can easily distinguish *wo fe fe* (same old *abb* story) from *wo fe wo* (new *aba* structure).

But after a series of studies looking at speech, we tried music and, somewhat to our own surprise, discovered that babies weren't nearly as good at detecting comparable patterns in music. Sequences of musical notes like C, D, D thoroughly engaged the infants, but nonetheless infants couldn't grasp the patterns when they consisted of musical notes, unless they'd had a chance to hear the speech syllables first. Speech, not music, appears to be the sound that holds the greatest initial interest for infants.

If there is one part of music that might be pre-wired and specifically tied to music, it would probably be the connection between rhythm and motion. When we hear music, our bodies want to dance, and that's true even for some of the youngest children anybody's studied. In one fascinating study, the developmental psychologist Laurel Trainor bounced seven-month-old babies at regular rhythmic intervals and discovered that they paid more attention to rhythmical patterns that coincided with patterns of bouncing than to rhythmical patterns that didn't coincide with the bouncing. But even here, it's not clear that what's going on is genuinely special to music, as opposed to being part of a more general tendency that I alluded to before, known as cross-modal matching: no matter what the stimulus, babies like it when information in any two senses goes together (such as when a set of sounds click in synchrony with a set of flashing lights). The coupling between music and motion may just be one more specific instantiation of this broader tendency, rather than a reflection of any sort of special-purpose hardware for music.

The proof lies in the pudding of the human brain. If humans really were born with a specific instinct for music, we might expect to find a specific hunk of brain tissue to be tuned to music and nothing else, much as a spot near the bottom of the brain known as the fusiform gyrus responds more to faces than to any other kinds of stimuli.

Instead, the many brain-imaging studies of music done in the last decade all point to a rather different direction: not toward a single specialized music area, but toward a vast mélange of brain regions—the prefrontal cortex, a portion of the temporal lobe known as the superior temporal gyrus, Broca's area, the planum temporale, the amygdala—not one of which appears to be dedicated full-time to music. Instead, virtually everything that plays a role in music has a separate "day job"; when the brain listens to music, it moonlights in a second career for which it did not originally evolve.

Broca's area, for example, is a key player in music, but if that area has a principal function, it's as a center for language. Ditto for the planum temporale, which lies within Wernicke's area. The superior temporal gyrus is indispensable in music, but it is essential for all kinds of auditory analyses, whether we are listening to speech or music or the blips and bangs of a video game. The cerebellum clearly plays a role in musical rhythm, but it's been known for years that the cerebellum is a key player in all kinds of movements, musical or otherwise. The amygdala matters for the perception of musical emotion, but you don't need to have music to have an amygdala; the amygdala is implicated in everything from fear to lust and anxiety, in a vast range of (mostly nonmusical) species. Unexpected chords might trigger the amygdala, but so will electric shocks. In no way is the amygdala, or any of the other regions I just discussed, specifically tailored to music; if there is a music-specific region in the brain, nobody has yet been able to identify it. Every brain area that I have mentioned—the amygdala, the superior temporal gyrus, the planum temporale—evolved long before human beings did and is found in many nonmusical species.

The same kind of argument can be made if you look at the development of the brain, rather than its anatomy. People develop more gray matter when they develop skill in music, for example, but gray matter has also been shown to increase as people learn to juggle or learn to type. Gray-matter increase is a diagnostic of learning in general, not a specific sign of learning music in particular. The brain can certainly acquire a facility for music, but that doesn't mean it specifically evolved for that purpose.

The bottom line is that some parts of our biology are all but inevitable, like the branching part of our lungs and the fact that we have two eyes. But the musical mind is not. A musical mind develops only if we put in years of hard work, or at least active listening, in which parts of the brain that evolved for other purposes such as language, skill learning, and auditory analysis are gradually co-opted into doing something new.

To the degree that we ultimately become musical, it is because we have the capacity to slowly and laboriously tune broad ensembles of neural circuitry over time, through deliberate practice, and not because the circuitry of music is all there from the outset.

Invent

What are your thoughts on the popular notion that some people are "born musical"? Do you believe that some people are born genetically predisposed to be more musical than others? What makes us think some people have inherited their musicality? If Marcus is right and musicality is achieved primarily through long hours and hard work, how might that change the way we view the musical heroes we all idolize?

Compose

Take a moment to compose a list of the top five musical instruments you would like to know how to play, ranking them from 1-5, with "1" representing the one you would like to play the most. Then, rank them according to how difficult you think it would be to learn to play each, with "1" representing the most difficult and "5" representing the easiest. After you've composed the list, review Marcus's argument regarding musical skill development and see if his insight would lead you to rearrange the list in any way.

Collaborate

In small groups, share your earliest memories of music. When and where do you recall hearing your first song? What was the first song you can remember singing? What was your earliest experience with any kind of training in music? Try to think of the methods by which you learned to sing or play an instrument—as a child or adult. See how well that experience matches up with the developmental process outlined by Marcus.

Explore

The book this essay comes from, *Guitar Zero*, chronicles the author's own journey in learning to play guitar at age 40, and he uses his experience to test various theories regarding cognitive development and musicality. As an individual or in a group, take on the task of teaching yourself a new instrument or musical skill. You might attempt to learn to play the guitar or drums, or you might work on singing a few particular tunes. Make it your goal to improve, however much, over the course of a week. Keep a journal during the week, taking note of how much time you spend and what specifics steps you take to improve.

Robert Christgau is an American essayist and music journalist and is known as the "Dean of American Rock Critics." He was one of the earliest rock critics, beginning his career in 1967, writing for Esquire. *He was music editor for the* Village Voice *for 37 years, during which time he created the annual Pazz & Jop poll. He's taught in a variety of colleges and universities and continues to teach music history in the Clive Davis Department of Recorded Music. He contributes regularly to* All Things Considered *on NPR.*

PAISLEY'S PROGRESS

BY ROBERT CHRISTGAU

Fifteen seconds of tune-up precede a partying rock riff that's corny even by Nashville standards. But it sure does rock, and soon it takes on virtuoso flourishes. Finally, 40 seconds in, there's a rather un-Nashville lyric: "She's got Brazilian leather boots on the pedal of her German car/Listenin' to the Beatles singin' 'Back in the U.S.S.R.'" Thus begins the lead and title cut of Brad Paisley's *American Saturday Night*. So optimistic it's intrepid and shameless at the same time, *American Saturday Night* rejects the anxious escapism and dark undercurrents of actually existing country, pop, and rock convention. As it strives to touch every human being in a nation Paisley knows is less unified and forward- looking than he pretends, the farthest it deviates from message is two breakup songs of uncommon tenderness and dignity. There's not a bum track on it—unless you're one of those sophisticates who's a priori nauseated by tunes more memorable than striking, lyrics that parse, pitch-corrected vocal harmonies, waveform compression, and strawberry ice cream.

Serving up an enjoyably crafted, commercially successful album in the warm months of every odd year, Brad Paisley has tasted fine to me since 1999, when I admired how confidently he opened for Loretta Lynn at Town Hall. A 26-year-old newcomer riding a good little debut few in Manhattan knew existed, he seemed more at home than she did. But I never expected he'd headline Madison Square Garden a decade later. As happens in Nashville, the hits that kept on coming were soon indistinguishable from genre exercises. Beyond the funny stuff—great in "Me Neither," where he disavows a series of lame pickup lines as each is shot down, not so great in "Celebrity," where he lobs paintballs at a reality-show jerkola—what stood out most was his guitar, which got a showcase instrumental every time out. Genre exercises work fine in the country market as such, where "repository of tradition" is part of the job description. But the real America—right, I'm being arch, punch in "the typical American music consumer" if you like—expects forceful identities from its standard-bearers, and that goes double for dudes from the sticks.

So although Paisley was my favorite young male country artist, I pigeonholed him as a likable pro, thought of him seldom, and didn't notice when he got married in 2003. From the perspective of *American Saturday Night*, however, the marriage was a turning point. According to publicity myth, which I'm happy to believe, New York-born actress Kimberly Williams appeared to the young West Virginian as in a dream way back in 1995, when he went to see *Father of the Bride II* in the vain hope that he'd run into his high school sweetheart and was entranced by Williams's portrayal of the bride. After obsessing for a good long dry spell, during which he gathered material for songs like "Me Neither," Paisley invited Williams to co-star in the 2002 "I'm Gonna Miss Her" video, where the girl demands that Paisley choose between fishing and her and he chooses fishing. In the real America, however, he got both — far from giving up fishing after he tied the knot, he took the missis camping. The couple split their life between a farm near Nashville and a house in Malibu. They have two sons, the oldest born in 2007 and christened William Huckleberry—Huck for short.

Those nauseated by meet-cute stories should rest assured that a political angle is coming, one that culminated in Paisley entertaining an Obama soiree with bluegrass progressive Allison Krauss, his duet partner on the atypically tragic 2004 "Whiskey Lullaby," and Charley Pride, country music's only African-American star ever. (Paisley's Twitter response to the invite: "Sure we'll play? what time? Now where's your house again? 1600 Pennsylvania? Got it . . . do you have a p.a.? What about food?") Politics got me started on this album—the lead track, which only begins celebrating the ongoing mongrelization of America with the lines I quoted, and then "Welcome to the Future," inspired by Barack Obama's victory and going out on a cross-burning tale in which a high school football star tries to date the homecoming queen. But the politics that kept me going were sexual politics, which proceed from a marriage that helped him put the genre exercise behind.

Paisley is remarkable among country stars for writing his own songs. But of course, that doesn't mean they're autobiographical. For one thing, he almost invariably collaborates, usually with buddies he's known since winning an ASCAP fellowship to Belmont University in Nashville. Paisley's 1999 breakthrough "He Didn't Have to Be," for instance, is based on Kelley Lovelace's experience as a stepfather, not either man's experience as a stepson. But don't think Paisley was just making nice when he promoted the artistic benefits of marriage to *Good Housekeeping*: "Before, I had nothing to write about but failed relationships and life on the road. Now, I feel emotions more deeply in every sense."

There have always been country guys women swoon for—like Garth Brooks, paunch and all. And in a time when bad-ass macho powered Nashville new jacks like Montgomery

Gentry and Toby Keith, Paisley's romantic come-ons had an appealing self- deprecation about them. But 2005's *Mud on the Tires* delivered something stronger: "Waitin' on a Woman," a song about how long they spend getting dressed, gender-based mortality rates, and if you stretch a little the elusiveness of female orgasm. Since then, Paisley has made the woman-friendly a mission—in a narrative voice more definitively his own.

That voice emerged on the two lookbacks at his naive youth that anchored 2007's *5th Gear*: "All I Wanted Was a Car," which does its partying with a fiddle and sets up "Letter to Me," where an older and wiser Brad assures his teenage self that the bad stuff is temporary, though he really should learn Spanish and give Aunt Rita some extra hugs. Both songs promised domestic satisfactions that included an SUV in the driveway. Deeper in came "If Love Was a Plane," about an American divorce rate Paisley reckons at 60 percent, and "It Did," about the ongoing perfection of love. Even the broad-jumping punch line of "Ticks"—"I'd like to walk you/Through a field of wild flowers/And I'd like to check you for ticks"—is more the kind of thing a husband murmurs to his wife on a fishing trip than a practical way for a singles-bar jerkola to get a butterfly tattoo into his vehicle.

5th Gear is the work of a master craftsman inspired to think about the shape of his life. Among its genre pieces are several born B sides and a soppy love duet with Carrie Underwood. But it establishes the foundation of a forceful identity. *American Saturday Night*'s politics help flesh out that identity, but an even bigger breakthrough is a maturing craftsmanship that's learned how to address familiar themes in unfamiliar ways. If the breakup tales don't suit his happily married persona, their calm, loving substratum does. The marriage proposal "I Hope That's Me" knows it's him, promising the kindness already in place; "You Do the Math" works the same for sex. There's a lookback that mourns a grandpa as it fulfills Paisley's one- Christian-track-per-album quota, and another that looks ahead to Huck's mistakes. The boys'-day-out rumpus "Catch All the Fish" is counterbalanced by the almost metaphysical "Water." And then there are the three feminist songs.

Ideologues, cynics, and disappointed office seekers may balk at this characterization, especially as regards "Then." Its narrative hooked to the endlessly evolving refrain "I Thought I Loved You Then," the album's first single updates "It Did." My wife Carola and I, together 30 years longer than Brad and Kimberly, had had a bad day when Paisley played the Garden October 21, but not with each other, and as he topped the show off by explaining how now he loved his spouse even more, we gripped each other's arms like teenagers in love. Avers Ms. Carola Dibbell, author of the groundbreaking "Inside Was Us: Women and Punk": "He notices all the things about marriage women are always complaining men don't notice." Given how many hits Paisley has, we forgave the omission of "She's Her Own Woman," a theme only strengthened by its unbraggadocios "and she's mine." But Carola was disappointed when the concert went out on Don Henley's "The Boys of Summer" instead of brandishing "The Pants," the subject of which is who wears them: "In the top drawer of her dresser there's some panties/Go try on that purple pair with the lacy frill/With your big old thighs I bet you can't get in 'em/With that attitude of yours, hell, I bet you never will."

Complete with the rowdy male choral farewell "You wear the pants/Buddy good for you/ We're so impressed/Whoop-de-doo," "The Pants" is a typically sidelong gambit from an artist who knows how to sell simple truths to a resistant audience—a master of the catchy chorus, the phrase ratcheted up a notch, the joke only a teabagging jerkola could resent. And though that's easier with marriage songs, those soppy country staples that sometimes come as well- honed as Loretta Lynn's "One's on the Way" or Garth Brooks's "Unanswered Prayers," no country artist has ever been sharper about what connubial bliss entails. In part because it's untainted by the dread sentimentality and in part because it comes less naturally, the political stuff gets ink, as when Paisley got to tell *The Los Angeles Times*: "You can name the reasons why you feel America is the greatest country in the world, but the fact of the matter is that pretty much anything you name, aside from American Indian customs, was not indigenous—it was brought here." Note, however, that the title track of Tim McGraw's new *Southern Voice* is in-your-face biracial, that Toby Keith's new *American Ride* highlights a heartbroken tribute to his departed African-American buddy Wayman Tisdale—and that both trend-spotters, avowed Democrats unlike the "staunchly moderate" Paisley, purveyed jingoistic trash post-9/11. I say Paisley's sidelong pro-Obama songs proceed from a less opportunistic place, and that that place owes his particular marriage big-time.

It's not just that Kimberly Williams donated the max to Obama, but that this New Yorker was the woman a clear-eyed, fair-minded dude from the sticks wanted to share his life with—and even more important, helped turn that life into an American dream come true, a dream the marriage embodies and signifies. Paisley isn't pie-eyed. He tells the world that if love was a plane no one would get on; he even took marital counseling with his prospective bride. Yet by some grace of upbringing, good sense, and body chemistry, success has only intensified an optimism that preceded and enabled it. The dark and the anxious seem foreign to him, yet he's never smug—he's so self-deprecating, so funny. I've watched too many kids grow up to think all their lives turn out like "Letter to Me." But Paisley evinces so much more reach and imagination than the hard- ass thrice-removed of roots-rock convention. I love Johnny Cash. I love the Drive-By Truckers. But right now, as a decent, intellectually gifted chief executive struggles to keep hope alive, I love and need Brad Paisley even more.

The Madison Square Garden show was a two-hour knockout— amazing video, and even when Paisley was catching his breath and making jokes, he never stopped extracting riffs from his guitar, like Jimi Hendrix at the dinner table. But the top balconies were empty, and though "Welcome to the Future" went number 10 country—doubly remarkable given a shamelessly and intrepidly multicultural video that a priori nauseated some of his market—its sales didn't approach those of "Then." Like Paisley's nine previous singles, "Then" went number one, a record. Admittedly, Paisley shares that record with the anodyne likes of Alabama and Ronnie Milsap. But if us sophisticates don't figure out that optimism isn't always anodyne, this nation will never be as unified and forward-looking as we supposedly want—and hope.

The "music review" genre has been around for a long time. Thanks to the Internet, it is even more widespread these days and remains a popular and influential genre. As with all good writing, a music review is crafted with a specific audience in mind. Who do you think the audience is for this review? What clues lead you to that conclusion? In general, what is the rhetorical purpose of a review, and what do you think Christgau's purpose here is specifically? What role do you think Christgau's fame as a writer and music critic play in achieving that purpose?

Issues concerning class, race, gender, disability, and nationalism are all touched on in this song, its video, and in this essay. Pick one of these topics that you feel connects with you in some way and write about an experience where you witnessed discrimination or felt discriminated against for any one of these reasons. Write about the context, the events that occurred, and the way you felt afterwards.

Look up Paisley's "Welcome to the Future" video on YouTube (YouTube search: Welcome to the Future) and, as a class, watch it. While watching, take note of the use of American iconography, images of multiculturalism, physical disability, and gender. In small groups, discuss the effect of these images on you as a viewer. How do they connect with the message of the song? How does the video present Paisley's thoughts on class, race, gender, disability, and nationalism? The verses of the song each present a different message. What is the message for each verse, and how does the video help present it?

Country music used to be about simple folks singing about simple things (or at least that's the way most people remember it). In the digital age, all that has changed. Now country artists travel the world more regularly, come from a variety of cities (big and small), and sing about a variety of life experiences. With the aid of YouTube, take some time and explore country music from the 1950s to the present and see how all these aspects have evolved. For example, compare the image of country music via Country Music Hall of Fame artist Conway Twitty, as presented in his video, "Hello Darlin'" (YouTube search: Conway Twitty Hello Darlin') to that presented by Paisley in "Welcome to the Future." How are they different? What kind of changes do such differences represent?

NASHVILLE SKYLINE: SEARCHING FOR THE HEART OF COUNTRY

By Chet Flippo

Where is the heart and the soul and the core of country music these days? Is it in Taylor Swift's on-the-road-around-the-world-empire dressing room? Is it in Garth Brooks's come-back Las Vegas dressing room? Is it in Miranda Lambert's glitzy dressing room at the Bridgestone Arena the night of the CMA Awards show, where she has a record nine CMA nominations?

Or is it in Dale Watson's lonely tour bus on the road in a midnight parking lot of a dark, bare-bones honky-tonk out in the boonies? Or in the hazy back of Jamey Johnson's tour bus sitting somewhere in lower Alabama? Or in the ghost-riders-in-the-sky tour bus that Willie Nelson will forever preside over?

Or is it in Robert's Western Wear or in Tootsie's Orchid Lounge on Lower Broad in Nashville where the pickers will eternally play for the tip jar? Is it at the Station Inn, which increasingly resembles Fort Apache, as Gulch chic-ness surrounds and overruns it?

Is it in the ghost-laden Ryman Auditorium? Or at the Grand Ole Opry? Or maybe at Billy Bob's Texas? Or in Gruene Hall? Maybe on George Strait's ranch? Is it maybe hiding at the end of a dirt road in some small town? Is it in mega-mogul-manager Irving Azoff's back pocket as he shuttles from venue to venue and from act to act and from new country acquisition to new country acquisition?

Or is it in a small, intimate club where a flower like Caitlin Rose blooms? Or in a rowdy Texas honky-tonk where the sassy Sunny Sweeney shows off her sugarbritches? Is it inside Zac Brown's cap?

Is it in some country star's Tweets, for God's sake?

Maybe, to lift a line from the Gatlin Brothers' song "All the Gold in California," the heart of country is actually "in a bank in the middle of Beverly Hills in somebody else's name."

Just where the hell is it?

I don't really know. No one does. And no one has even really known at any given time. And what's scary is that, these days, no one I know who has any sense knows either. The heart used to be at the center of the major Nashville record labels. And at the major recording studios. No more, no more. They're long ago eroding.

Country music is a wildly erratic radar screen these days. Random, unexpected blips are popping up all over the place and with no consistent patterns. May as well study tornado paths. The music is all over the map. So are the artists. And so is the audience.

But, if you sit back and reflect and study the music's recent and even ancient history, there's really no reason for panic.

It is ultimately in the listeners' hands. It's the fans, the true believers, who will choose their music. Each person's country is in the heart.

But it's also in marketing departments' hands. The breakdown of the sales pattern for Taylor Swift's first-week sales of more than 1 million copies of *Speak Now* is very revealing about present-day music marketing strategy. *Billboard* breaks the sales down thusly: Target, 350,000 units; iTunes, 220,000 units; Walmart, about 190,000 units; Amazon and Costco, each at about 40,000; Best Buy at about 35,000; and Starbucks at about 28,000. Starbucks was one of several nontraditional retailers pushing the album. Radio Shack will be another to be added.

Hot Topic stores, which mainly skew toward rock, moved about 5,000 copies. It has also been sold in Justice clothing stores for girls and in Rite Aid.

A Scholastic promo event also generated preorders and sales through schools. iTunes and Amazon also had preorder campaigns.

Big Machine set the CD's list price at $18.98, flying in the face of conventional wisdom that albums should list at $10. But it cut deals to get the pricing it needed for the physical CD.

Digital also heavily discounted the album -- the media delivery company digital priced the *Speak Now* download at $4, and then Amazon lowered its download to $3.99. Amazon's price for the physical CD was $8. Walmart.com set the CD album price at $7.78. J&R Music World priced it in-store and online at $6.99.

To her credit, Swift also insisted that *Speak Now* also be released as a vinyl record album.

But these million-plus sales numbers come after the world had decided that CDs and long, multi-song albums were quant artifacts of the past. With Taylor Swift, it seems that all things are possible. Her fans voted with their wallets and purses. Heart and soul of country, though? The listeners will decide that.

Invent

Flippo fills the first half of his essay with a string of rhetorical questions. Why do you think he chooses to begin his essay this way? What effect does that have on a reader? How do these questions affect the tone of the essay as it proceeds?

Compose

In some ways, Flippo seems to be lamenting a time when country music was more regional and easily identifiable. Such concern is not uncommon in our current era, as genre identification becomes more problematic due to wider circulation, more diverse audiences, and the fact that music rooted in particular regions is becoming less attached to a particular area and shared experience. These and other similar trends have led to a phenomenon known as "genre-bending." It's due in small part to the digital dissemination of music, as Flippo suggests with his example of Taylor Swift's *Speak Now* album. Identify a genre in your music collection that you think struggles a bit with its identity for any reason (hip-hop, indie, folk, jazz, etc.). Write a paragraph or two in which you explain why you think the "heart" of that genre is hard to identify. Be sure to provide concrete examples.

Collaborate

In the end, Flippo argues that finding the heart of country is "ultimately in the listeners' hands." In small groups, discuss the growing popularity of country music and the degree to which you think fans are in control of a genre and its identity. Discuss how much you think fans of a particular genre should be able to personally relate to that genre. Is there an authentic country music fan that is better than another fan? Feel free to take up another genre for this discussion.

Flippo partitions the bulk of his questions at the beginning of the essay into separate paragraphs, suggesting a connection among the information provided in each set of questions. Research the people and places mentioned in the questions and work to identify the connecting threads. For example, in the third paragraph he mentions Robert's Western Wear, Tootsie's Orchid Lounge, and the Station Inn—all older, well-established downtown Nashville music venues, each with a rich, local history. Feel free to use Google Earth to check out the locations and take a virtual tour of these locations and Nashville's famous Broadway street.

Alex Kasner is currently pursuing a J.D. at Stanford Law School, where he is the Managing Editor of the Stanford Law & Policy Review, *a Bradley Fellow for Constitutional Law, and a past law clerk at the Department of Justice's Civil Appellate Division. He has written for the* Stanford Journal of Complex Litigation *and the* Stanford Journal of International Relations, *and received the Firestone Medal for his undergraduate honors thesis. As an undergraduate at Stanford, Alex was President of the Stanford Wind Ensemble, playing alto and baritone saxophone, and he continues to compose for piano and saxophone and play bass guitar on the side. Alex wrote the following essay while a student in Rod Taylor's music themed writing and rhetoric course at Stanford University in 2010.*

ASPIRING TO ART: THE CONCEPT ALBUM, ARTISTRY IN MUSIC, AND AUDIENCE ARTIST INTERPLAY

BY ALEX KASNER

In the opening pages of Ayn Rand's *Atlas Shrugged*, Dagny Taggart anxiously pulls at a cigarette, preoccupied with business models and profit margins of her family's railway syndicate. In her unease, the train ride seems uncomfortable, her passion at odds with her state of mind. As she pauses for a moment, a sound begins to fill the air. A faint whistle by a mechanic in the corner begins to blossom into "a symphony of triumph...[embody]ing every human act and thought." The melody escapes its humble presentation, its "tension of purpose" resolving into a song of "deliverance...[from] ugliness and pain" for Dagny (1). Though she has never heard the music before, each sound is as instantly recognizable and compelling to Ms. Taggart as a childhood lullaby. With each passing phrase of the music, the din and hiss of the train settles into a comforting pattern in line with the concerto. Music brings order to life out of the mechanistic din, and Dagny connects with the contours, timbres, themes, and narrative of art for one fleeting moment.

The use of song for inspiration is nothing new, but in our modern approach toward music, we are more likely to treat the sound Dagny hears as merely the noise of a relentless train ride rather than an object for musical focus. iPods and earbuds, programmed to shuffle, provide soundtracks to our lives as we rush from one destination to another. Just as a locomotive spits off steam and blasts sound to its occupants, our music is a byproduct of the modern motion of our busy lives, often only heard in the background. When the way we approach music so drastically shifts, is the enveloping term "music" still adequate to describe all variations? The diminishing of fixed concentration and study of songs relieves music of its necessity to communicate ideas and emotions to its listeners, reducing it to a means of preserving the celebrity of the performers and to a subliminal static for the listeners. As the critical ear turns away from musical creation, compositions have no need to embrace their previous aesthetic function. Music is no longer subject to the judgment of what Immanuel Kant deems the "intellectual faculty" of aesthetics and to the heavy mantle of artistic aspiration.

The age of commercial music recording offers little in what one might concretely refer to as artistic creation. Production for the masses has often intuitively been paired with a simplicity of form and content. Current pop singles dominating all measures of commercial success are acknowledged as "low in communicative function...articulated with ordinary language," but quantifying exactly what such a phenomenon really means on a more academic level is a difficult task (Frith 270). Music that aims first toward a higher level of artistic fulfillment alters the way in which the audience approaches it and fundamentally changes the way in which we are affected by music and view its composers. In the modern age of commercial recording, it is tempting to dismiss complex, thematic works as financial suicide, but how then do we explain away the glaring exception of concept albums: a development in composition during the 1970s in which rock albums "were sculpted into complex, multi-movement works on a scale that was unprecedented in their stylistic tradition," while rewarded with "an intensely devoted fan base" and "lavishly remunerative deals" (Keister 433)?

During their brief existence, concept albums represented a period in which music products could both remain authentic to their defining artistic characteristics as well as viable as record-label productions. The first essential analytical step is identifying those artistic characteristics present—not just in concept albums, but in the broader scope of artistic musical productions. The three most prominent aspects in such an examination are technical virtuosity, cross-artistic collaboration, and thematic narrative. In this essay, I to use these perspectives to argue that concept albums constitute artistic creations, and that this elevation toward artistic character alters the way in which the listening public approaches both musicians and their craft. Listeners view rock artists involved in this process not simply as entertainers but as both heroes and allies, while their conceptual works take on a new ability to act as vehicles of progressive social change.

As is the case with most non-militaristic revolutions, the emergence of the concept album followed a Tocqueville description of social revolutions as slow transformations over the course of several generations (Boesche 86). Early attempts at crafting cohesive artistic products focused less on stories and more on conveying general sentiments or moods. Some of the first incarnations included Frank Sinatra's *In the Wee Small Hours* and The Ventures's *Colorful Ventures*, as albums linked not through any melodic or lyrical cohesion, but rather simply by presenting songs meant to centered around the topics of late-night isolation or the color wheel, respectively. This model was drastically altered, however, when The Who, led by principal songwriter and guitarist Pete Townshend, crafted the first "thematically based album," *Tommy* (Barnes 3). The tale of the messianic blind, deaf, and dumb pinball wizard was an instant success on all fronts when released in early 1969, and critics lauded the album as "the most important milestone in [popular music] since Beatlemania" while audiences helped the work fly to #2 on the UK Charts (Sanders).

A rather unique history followed, as the concept album as a medium produced a decade of great commercial success before suddenly disappearing into obscurity. Following Tommy's release in 1969, bands like Pink Floyd, Yes, Genesis, and David Bowie all produced mainstream concept albums, and each experienced their own distinct type of success. Pink Floyd's *The Wall* and *Dark Side of the Moon* were commercial smash hits, the latter setting a record for longest time spent on the Billboard 200 Charts, while Bowie's *The Rise and Fall of Ziggy Stardust and the Spiders from Mars* shot the singer-songwriter to stardom on the back of his following tours and stage persona (Werde 12). As quickly as the movement began, however, it seemed to come to a crashing halt in the early 1980's with the advent of punk rock—a stripped down reaction to what was deemed the bloated excesses of the concept album movement. Modern music is left only with fleeting glances of the movement in albums that either retain the original conceptual form but sacrifice commercial success, like Dream Theater's *Metropolis Pt. 2: Scenes from a Memory*, or commercial extravaganzas that had very little unifying concept, typified by Green Day's *21st Century Breakdown* (Jones). Over the past decade, critics have turned their eyes toward the 1970s and concept album movement, attempting to defend the merits and innovations that these works introduced to the public. In keeping with their contentions, it is necessary to not only discuss what makes concept albums good music, but also what makes music good art.

TECHNICAL VIRTUOSITY

> *There is no art without practice, and no practice without art.*
>
> —Protagoras

No artist stumbles onto success out of sheer fortune and circumstance. The architect commits himself to years of studying form and function, the painter to the creation of tones and perspective. The musician as artist is no different. Music theory classes and instrumental exercises of arpeggios and scales are taught not to stifle creativity and conform composition but rather to provide artists the capacity to capture their visions. Dedication to practice and study usually acts as a barrier to entry; listeners are quick to label classical musicians "virtuosos" and "artists" because they are assumed to have participated in both "rigorous[ly] practice[ing]" and "absorbing a long...tradition" (Pareles). This assumption, however, is not implicit in popular rock recordings; their deep entrenchment in the "anti-establishment" and counter-culture of the 1950s and 1960s put rock musicians in the trenches more than practice rooms (Pekacz 48). Still, the emerging concept albums of the 1970's bear more in relation to classical virtuosity than their more immediate predecessors. These works possess a deliberate ethos-driven argument made via allusions to classical works that lends both the musicians a virtuostic authority and the albums a more 'classical' feel that we traditionally associate with 'high art.'

In many circumstances, concept albums bind themselves to their classical and neo-classical predecessors quite explicitly. The influence of Stravinsky is central to Genesis's extended piece "Supper's Ready," where the "bassist and guitarist perform an extended instrumental ostinato...with displaced accents quite similar to [the] *Rite of Spring*," while vocalist Peter Gabriel lends lyrics of apocalyptical visions (Keister 442; Figure 1). The result, stresses Professor Jay Keister, is a musical product rendered artistic by borrowing "music of similar sophistication" (442). In fighting for their place as art, concept albums promote authenticity through association. Just as the traditionally artistic method of composition requires study of previous masterworks, a band like Genesis wish to include itself in that process as well.

Certainly more common, however, and perhaps more promising as a basis of analysis is a more general approach towards classical allusion. Rather than dissecting and transplanting notes and rhythmic passages, The Who's *Tommy* chooses to borrow the general form of earlier opera: overtures and entr'actes. The overture form, dating back to the 17th century, prefaces the work to follow by intertwining two or more melodic lines in a typically instrumental composition. In *Tommy*, original melodic lines from the album (quoted from "Pinball Wizard," "See Me, Feel Me," and "We're Not Gonna Take It") are dropped into the overture form, creating a track literally entitled "Overture," while a similar process is used in the entr'acte to open what is intended to be the second act of the rock opera. The use of these tracks is not purely aesthetic, for in placing the "Overture" first before any lyrical content the listener hears the musical product before they can settle back onto the reassuring comfort of a familiar vocalist. Even more important, in using an established classical form, The Who fulfills a more traditional approach to artistic creation. Aaron Copland notes that: "every well-trained composer has, as his stock in trade, certain normal structural molds on which to learn for the basic framework of his compositions. These formal molds...have all been gradually evolved over hundreds of years as the combined efforts of numberless composers seeking a way to ensure the coherence of their compositions" (24-25). Whether through direct allusion or adaptation of form, conceptual works utilize the framework standardized by classical works and provide their composers a layer of artistic authority. In doing so, the audience begin not only to appreciate these albums as art but begin to recognize and value the artists whose voice and music we hear.

CROSS-ARTISTIC COLLABORATION

I can look at a fine art photograph and sometimes I can hear music.
—Ansel Adams

Concept albums, in a nod toward the broader nature of art, do not exist as singular creations but rather expand beyond musical productions and utilize other forms of art to enhance the experience of the audience. Stravinsky's *Rite of Spring* was incomplete without Nijinsky's accompanying animalistic choreography. Michelangelo's "Last Judgment" loses some of its awe when removed from the confines of the architectural feats of the Vatican. And albums like *Dark Side of the Moon* and *The Wall* lose a portion of their iconic status without the art displayed proudly on their record jackets. In designing *Dark Side of the Moon*'s sleeve for Pink Floyd, Storm Thorgerson of Hipgnosis shied away displaying band members. "If the album is trying to say something," Thorgerson notes, "the cover should continue that experience, reinforce that idea" ("Seventies' Greatest Album Covers"). Hipgnosis's design called for the single prism over black background, and a single white light breaking into the color spectrum (see Figure 2). The inside gatefold continues with a linear representation of a heartbeat portrayed in various frequencies and colors. The album's primary concept of the madness, irrationality, and underlying static of everyday life is represented by the uneven heartbeats, the white light of our perception of life broken into its separate vibrant components ("Time," "Money," "Breathe") before resolving into the strains of "Any Colour You Like."

Pink Floyd's *The Wall* is even more explicit: a barren wall of white brick gives way to monstrous representations of the album's protagonist and those influences that seek to destroy him. Characters literally appear to us and heighten the sense of drama, extending the music into the art and the art into the music. The art is the Louvre to the music's "Mona Lisa." The listener enters into the experience only by first seeing the casing and being swept into a sense of drama before approaching the actual subject. Each piece can stand adequately on its own as a work of art, but together they create a sense of aura that intrigues the audience. We do not see the faces of the musicians plastered on the cover, but instead we are allowed to take in the product first—to appreciate art as art, not tied to the name or face of its creator.

THEMATIC NARRATIVE

Every picture tells a story don't it.
—Rod Stewart

A constant debate surrounds whether art imitates life or whether life falls in step with the force of art. What both positions in the debate concede, however, is that art has the ability to communicate with life and to speak within the context that society provides. Music is highly divided in following this premise, as most have "no capacity for discourse or consequence" (Nicholls 300). Concept albums, however, possess a unique quality: a sense of narrative focus that, according to Professor David Nicholls, can acquire a "leitmotivic function" (301). Music without narrative cannot be considered art, as critic Arthur Dano points out, because it fails to project "some point of view...while engaging audience participation" ("The Definition of Art"). A narrative structure is therefore essential, because it promotes essential discourse that cannot be achieved in static, account-driven works.

While a lack of narrative discounts artistry, however, we must be careful to also consider that a narrative by itself does not guarantee the classification of art. As Nicholls reminds us, we require a "narrative discourse"—a story that not only presents, but engages and argues as well (301). Both *Tommy* and The Beatles's "Norwegian Wood" tell stories, but only the former engages in broader implications. While presenting the narrative of Tommy Walker is important to The Who's *Tommy*, more important is the commentary that the band provides on the rise and fall of their protagonist. We are treated to the story of a categorically autistic boy who finally finds the ability to express himself through his gift at playing pinball. His success, however, becomes commercialized, as his messianic attempts are reduced to the creation of a seedy holiday camp. It is not simply a story but a mantra and a lesson as well, acting as an "introverted journey that helps us question everything about our lives" (Townshend). Certain songs throughout give us clues as to possible thematic focuses; "Sally Simpson" paints Tommy as a rock star, his music bastardized and the truly devoted fans knocked away from the stage. "See Me, Feel Me" implores us to free ourselves from false icons of religious ascension and instead experience enlightenment for ourselves. While these songs seem "paradoxically irrelevant" as devices of furthering the album's narrative plot, they take on a new role as opportunities for the band to argue for the broader implications of their plot (Nicholls 312). Picasso's *Guernica* used one image of horror, frozen in time, to argue against the atrocities of war. Tommy Walker is our *Guernica*, a musical construction that subtly maligns the commercialism that undermines music, artists, and religious experience.

ELEVATION AND INFLUENCE
THE EFFECTS OF ARTISTIC ACHIEVEMENT

The designation of concept albums as works of art does not simply function to extol the values of these works, nor are the previous categories simply an argument over definition. Rather, these classifications represent layers of expansion; in exhibiting some sense of technical virtuosity, musicians must call upon foundations laid down by previous artists, a sense of movement *beyond genre*. Cross-artistic collaboration allows cooperation between various disciplines of artistic achievement, a shift *beyond medium*, while a passage *beyond art* itself occurs with the final contribution of a thematic narrative structure. As a result, art takes on a life of its own when it reaches the public, resulting in a celebration of the musician as hero and his work as a vehicle for social change.

Artists of the conceptual movement achieved a type of fame not usually reserved for musicians, as Townshend, Entwistle, Wakeman, and Emerson became definitive heroes and idols for their eager audience. This may come as counterintuitive. Many rock artists forgo representing themselves on concept albums and hide behind elaborate costuming while on stage. However, this deliberate masking of bands helped to create a sense of mystique and fervor that perhaps even heightened the reputation of the musicians. As the studies of Paul Willis concluded in 1978, these progressive rock artists were seen by 70s counterculture audiences in dual roles: "heroes" who pushed the boundaries of music and ideas, and "distinct members of [the counterculture's] own group" (78). The incredible talent and grandiose stage shows made "creative leaders" out of these musicians, creating a radical fan base who acknowledged the prowess of their idols (Willis 79). This was never a detached connection between an audience and the band it placed upon a pedestal— "musicians served as a face for the fans, a creative outlet for the stories and struggles of the audience" (Keister 447). It is no mere coincidence that the hero role requires of musicians the dedication to virtuosity and collaborative artistry, while the intimate connection comes from message-driven storytelling. Just as concept albums accepted the conditions of artistic achievement, so do these aspects provide a symbiotic relation, allowing artistic creation to push audience-artist interaction. The result is a Beethoven, a T.S. Eliot, a Van Gogh—deified figures of the artistic pantheon who continue to inspire audiences not through a cult of personality, but through their accomplishments. Judging from the accounts of Willis and his anthropological contemporaries, it was a phenomenon that reemerged in the works of Genesis, The Who, and Yes as well.

The creation of heroes out of artists and accreditation of their craft allows them to use their newfound authority to push their works as vehicles of social change. In the weeks leading up to the Paris premiere of *The Rite of Spring* in 1913, audiences "were filled with rumors of the great artistic delight" that the mighty Stravinsky would put forth before the patrons (Eksteins 201). The maestro instead presented a controversial work, generating what critic Jean Cocteau described as a "feverish and seismic response;" a violent depiction of human sacrifice played out on an audience tense in the early years of the First World War (Eksteins 202). Art is not a restless entity; it pushes back upon the society that helped make it popular, along with its subtle, underlying tensions. The newfound ethos ascribed to concept albums by their artistic foundations allowed for these works and their creators to push back on society vehicles of social change. *Progressive Rock Reconsidered* notes that above all else, "concept rock was an attempt to create and express a socio-cultural movement," its revolutionary aspirations focused both on the working class who accepted its heritage and the upper-class who admired its classical form (Weinstein, 142). The artistic product has the capacity to argue to two disparate audiences and speak to both with the same level of sophistication and articulation.

The most notable target of concept albums revolutionary spirit was the American engagement in Vietnam. The Who's *Tommy* wrapped up production within months of the Tet Offensive, with the remainder of the war coinciding with the growth and maturation of the concept album movement. King Crimson's *In the Court of the Crimson King*, ELP's *Tarkus*, and Genesis's *The Lamb Lies Down on Broadway* all present blistering accounts of violence and struggle in the Far East as well as "viciously lashing at the U.S." and its arrogant approach to the conflict (Keister 443). As author David James writes, while the more commercialized and simplistic rock of the era kept those in the trenches satisfied, it was these concept albums "that were functional both within rituals of practiced anti-war movements, as well as to a previously apathetic middle and upper-class who needed to be shaken from slumber" (127). What, then, was the quality of the aforementioned albums that gave them such widespread influence?

We return to our earlier categorizations of artistic creation to derive possible answers for this phenomenon. First, the requirement of art to study its predecessors created in concept artists the ability to draw from previous revolutionary materials. Genesis's lead vocalist Peter Gabriel was an avid fan of Eliot's *The Waste Land*, often pulling from the work to paint pictures of war and collapse. Robert Fripp of King Crimson also drew from Eliot, going so far as to study his original manuscripts at Oxford University, as well as pursuing musical study of Stravinsky, Charles Ives, and their contemporaries (Weinstein 144). The study of these composers led to a repetition of revolutionary functions—dissonance, satire, elegiac tone—that proved effective in furthering their cause. Secondly, the use of thematic narrative creates a sense of stake in their anti-war arguments; working class audiences being shipped off to Vietnam felt their stories finally being sung, while more elite listeners could respect the complexity and engagement brought into the narratives. When Greg Lake of King Crimson sings the verses, "Blood rack barbed wire / Politicians' funeral pyre / Innocents raped by napalm fire / Twenty first century schizoid man," it is both horrific enough to provide a rallying point for the audience members and so obscure and violently poetic as to engage more academic audiences. Such mature and successful approach to revolutionary ideas could not have been born without a deep entrenchment in artistic standard.

SONGS FOR A NEW ERA

Perhaps, we are entering a period in which we simply demand less from our forms of entertainment. With the dawn of the digital age, 99-cent singles on iTunes, and easier access to music creation capabilities, modern songs and albums are meant to express a new type of revolution—one where the audience storms the stage and picks up the instruments for itself. The classical forms of music, drama, and art, at least viewed with mild interest by past generations, have begun to collapse in popularity as "our culture reaches a grand disparity with the classical art world" (Sandow). In the place of classic art, drama, and even the more modern conventions of concept albums come new genres of rap, alternative rock, and user-generated internet productions. It would not be fair to these new forms to dismiss them as shallow or inconsequential: they are products of their environment and certainly fulfill a distinct taste in music.

This transition, however, is one that does inevitably shift creation away from art, for better or worse. In losing the qualities that define art itself, our music ceases to function in the capacity that was once so essential—as a locomotive force of change, exchange, and interaction. Songs become written by celebrities, who now serve as the removed mediator between audience and craft instead of the converse, previous relationship. Paradoxically, even as technology and progress allows access and metaphorically brings us closer together, our society has little place for the intimate relationship between artist and audience that once existed. In tearing down the concepts of "hero" and "idol," we are left only with celebrities, who need not be virtuosos or artists to command our attention. Concept albums teach us that the recording industry does indeed have a place for artistic aspiration and creation, but it will once again require a monumental shift in music, and the acknowledgement that instant access does not mean instant gratification.

Appendix A

Figure 1.

Source: Stravinsky, Igor. *The Rite of Spring (Dover Miniature Scores)*. Minneapolis: Dover Publications, 2000. Print.

Figure 2. *The Dark Side of the Moon* Album Cover

Source: "Chronolog: Austin Chronicle Blogs - AustinChronicle.com." *Austin News, Events, Restaurants, Music - AustinChronicle.com.* Web. 03 Nov. 2009.

Works Cited

Barnes, Richard. *Story of "Tommy"* Eel Pie, 1977. Print.

Boesche, Roger. *Tocqueville's Road Map Methodology, Liberalism, Revolution, and Despotism*. New York: Lexington Books, 2006. Print.

"Chronolog: Austin Chronicle Blogs - AustinChronicle.com." *Austin News, Events, Restaurants, Music - AustinChronicle.com*. Web. 03 Nov. 2009. <http://www.austinchronicle.com/gyrobase//Blogs/index.html/tagID604118/>.

Copland, Aaron. *What to Listen for in Music*. Signet, 1999. Print.

"The Definition of Art." *Stanford Encyclopedia of Philosophy*. Web. 03 Nov. 2009. <http://plato.stanford.edu/entries/art-definition/>.

Eksteins, Modris. *Rites of Spring The Great War and the Birth of the Modern Age*. New York: Mariner Books, 2000. Print.

Famous Quotes and Quotations at BrainyQuote. Web. 05 Dec. 2009. <http://www.brainyquote.com/>.

Frith, Simon. *Performing Rites On the Value of Popular Music*. New York: Harvard UP, 1998. Print.

James, David. "The Vietnam War and American Music." *Social Text* 23 (1989): 122-43. Print.

Jones, Chris. "21st Century Breakdown." *BBC.com*. 8 May 2009. Web. 28 Oct. 2009.

"Kant: Aesthetics; [The Internet Encyclopedia of Philosophy]." *The Internet Encyclopedia of Philosophy*. Web. 05 Dec. 2009. <http://www.iep.utm.edu/kantaest/#SH2a>.

Keister, Jay, and Jeremy L. Smith. "Musical ambition, cultural accreditation and the nasty side of progressive rock." *Popular Music* 27.3 (2008): 433-55. Print.

Murray, Warwick E. *Geographies of globalization*. Routledge, 2006. Print.

Nicholls, David. "Narrative Theory as an Analytical Tool in the Study of Popular Music Texts." *David Nicholls* 88.2 (2007): 297-315. Print.

Pareles, Jon. "Don't Call Jazz America's Classical Music." *New York Times* 28 Feb. 1999, Arts sec. Print.

Pekacz, Jolanta. "Did Rock Smash the Wall? The Role of Rock in Political Transition." *Popular Music* 13.1 (1994): 41-49. Print.

"Practice quotes." *Dictionary and Thesaurus - Free Online at Your Dictionary*. Web. 29 Oct. 2009. <http://www.yourdictionary.com/quotes/practice>.

Rand, Ayn. *Atlas Shrugged*. New York: Plume, 1999. Print.

Sanders, Rick, and David Dalton. "Pete and Tommy, Among Others." *Rolling Stone* 12 June 1969. Print.

Sandow, Greg. "The Future of Classical Music?: Greg Sandow performs a book-in-progress..." *ArtsJournal: Daily Arts News*. Web. 03 Nov. 2009. <http://www.artsjournal.com/greg/2006/03/episode_3bigger_problems.html>.

"Seventies' Greatest Album Covers: Dark Side of the Moon." *Super Seventies RockSite!* Web. 03 Nov. 2009. <http://www.superseventies.com/ac19darksideofthemoon.html>.

Sheinbaum, John J. "Periods in Progressive Rock and the Problem of Authenticity." *Current Musicology* 85 (2008). Print.

Stravinsky, Igor. *The Rite of Spring (Dover Miniature Scores)*. Minneapolis: Dover Publications, 2000. Print.

Townshend, Pete. "Rolling Stone Interview (1968)." *The Hypertext Who*. Web. 03 Nov. 2009. <http://www.thewho.net/articles/townshen/rs68.htm>.

Weinstein, D. *Progressive Rock Reconsidered*. New York: Routledge, 2002. Print.

Werde, Bill. "Floydian Theory." *Billboard* 13 May 2006: 12. Print.

Willis, Paul. *Profane Culture*. Taylor & Francis, 1978. Print.

Works Consulted

Anderson, Jon, Steve Howe, Rick Wakeman, Chris Squire, and Alan White, perfs. *Tales from Topographic Oceans*. Yes. Rec. Oct. 1973. Eddie Offord, 1974. CD.

Bowie, David, Mick Ronson, Trevor Bolder, and Mick Woodmansey, perfs. *The Rise and Fall of Ziggy Stardust and the Spiders from Mars*. David Bowie. Rec. Jan. 1972. Ken Scott, 1972. CD.

Fripp, Robert, Greg Lake, Ian McDonald, Michael Giles, and Barry Sinfield, perfs. *In the Court of the Crimson King*. King Crimson. Rec. Aug. 1969. 1969. CD.

Gabriel, Peter, Tony Banks, Steve Hackett, Michael Rutherford, and Phil Collins, perfs. *Foxtrot*. Genesis. Rec. Aug. 1972. David Hitchcock, 1972. CD.

Gabriel, Peter, Tony Banks, Steve Hackett, Michael Rutherford, and Phil Collins, perfs. *The Lamb Lies Down on Broadway*. Genesis. Rec. Oct. 1974. John Burnes, 1974. CD.

Gilmour, David, Nick Mason, Roger Waters, and Richard Wright, perfs. *The Dark Side of the Moon*. Pink Floyd. Rec. Jan. 1973. 1973. CD.

Gilmour, David, Nick Mason, Roger Waters, and Richard Wright, perfs. *The Wall*. Pink Floyd. Rec. Nov. 1979. Bob Ezrin, 1979. CD.

Townshend, Pete, Roger Daltrey, John Entwistle, and Keith Moon, perfs. *Quadrophenia*. The Who. Rec. June 1973. Kit Lambert, 1973. CD.

Townshend, Pete, Roger Daltrey, John Entwistle, and Keith Moon, perfs. *Tommy*. The Who. Rec. Sept. 1969. Kit Lambert, 1969. CD.

Invent

What are the specific qualities of a concept album? In other words, what aspects must be present to make it a "concept album"? What are the challenges in today's .99¢ per song world that make such an album difficult to create? The concept album is often viewed as more artistic than "normal" albums. Do you agree with that view? Why or why not?

Compose

The notion of what constitutes a concept album has historically been a bit slippery. Go to Wikipedia, and look at the extensive list of concept albums. Pick one listed there, familiarize yourself with it by listening via Spotify or another Internet radio station, and then write a short critique in which you defend or challenge its inclusion as a concept album.

Collaborate

In small groups, come up with a theme or idea that could frame a concept album and identify a list of current songs that would work together to create that theme. If you would like, create an album cover and CD to accompany it. Burn your CD and make a presentation to the class.

Explore

Pick a concept album and listen to it in its entirety, journaling your thoughts as you do. You might also choose to view a concept album movie, like Pink Floyd's *The Wall*. You can find plenty of clips on YouTube, of course, but the point of a concept album is to have the listener experience it as a collective work. Pay attention to how different the experience is from just listening to singles from various artists.

Chris Willman is a senior writer in Entertainment Weekly's *Los Angeles bureau, contributing cover stories on the* Dixie Chicks, Coldplay, U2, Alan Jackson, Gretchen Wilson, Outkast, Avril Lavigne *and many others. Previously, he wrote for* The Los Angeles Times *and* Musician. *He is also the author of* Rednecks & Bluenecks: The Politics of Country Music.

A VERY DYLAN CHRISTMAS

By Chris Willman

Bob Dylan has been making records for 48 years, and deeply disappointing people for the last 44 of them. "Judas!" some disenchantee legendarily screamed during a Manchester concert in 1966—a peanut-gallery pissant who dimly knew that Dylan had traded in Pete Seeger purism for rock voltage the year before but showed up to register his protest anyway. The heckling has hardly ceased since. The next eruption was when he stopped going electric, sort of, with 1967's *John Wesley Harding*. Then came 1970's *Self Portrait*, alleged by the faithful (or various factions thereof) to be an act of self-sabotage. And the full-on embrace of female backing vocals and guy-liner in the late seventies...the Evangelical era, replete with walkouts when he refused to play his secular oldies live...the subsequent years when he played all his hits live, but audiences didn't realize it because he'd rendered them unrecognizable . . . an acting career with choices as hard to comprehend as 1986's *Hard to Handle* . . . the ad-licensing years . . . the Will.I.Am "Forever Young" remix.

In a career measured in both greatness and WTF moments, only mysterious, magisterial Teflon Bob could come out of it all as revered as ever. History would advise, then, against presupposing that Dylan might finally meet his Waterloo at the North Pole. But you'll come across no shortage of "last straw" comments concerning his 34th studio album, *Christmas in the Heart*. When I suggested to one aggrieved friend that maybe Dylan had the right to a lark, it was as if I'd told a Baptist it was high time Billy Graham got to enjoy a threesome. "You don't understand," the pal shot back at me, plaintively. "When *Another Side of Bob Dylan* came out, it changed my life, for good." What to do when your personal Jesus turns out to be Iscariot in a cardigan, betraying you with a kiss under the mistletoe?

Well . . . laugh, maybe? Although the idea of a Dylan Christmas album never struck me as inherently ridiculous, when it was first announced, I joined in the fun. What songs might he record? "Positively 34th Street"? "Don't Check Your List Twice, It's All Right"? Would the album be called *Blitzen on Blitzen*? *Elf Portrait*? *'Nog on the Tracks*? The Photoshoppers of the world got busy grafting Santa hats onto old LP-jacket photos, as if they could take the piss out of Dylan any more than he could take it out of himself. But it struck me that Dylan really had the potential to make one of the cooler Christmas albums ever. On his satellite-radio show, "Theme Time Radio Hour," he'd done a two-hour Christmas special, trotting out obscure sides by Lead Belly, Johnny Paycheck, and Celia Cruz. Surely his own album would follow that hepcat path.

Instead, it follows Mitch Miller's bouncing ball right down Santa Claus Lane. Filled largely with the most familiar carols, *Christmas in the Heart* is a full-on embrace of the old, not-so-weird America, a tribute to the kind of mass-market holiday records that his own Jewish family might have picked up in suburban Minnesota in the fifties, as a near freebie at the gas station.

Cue up the first track, "Here Comes Santa Claus," and the first thing you'll notice, other than a certain faithfulness to Gene Autry's mild version of Western swing, is that Dylan's trading off lines with a slick male chorus right off a Ray Conniff LP. For pure distaff sweetness, he also enlists the L.A. retro duo the Ditty Bops, whose prominent parts on several tracks manage to recall the Christmas recordings of both the Andrews Sisters and the Roches.

Roughly half the album finds Dylan in his vocal comfort range, including a surprisingly smooth "Little Drummer Boy," a wonderful reprise of the World War II soldiers' ditty "Christmas Island," and the excellent polka "Must Be Santa," with a heart-stoppingly frantic arrangement openly borrowed from the group Brave Combo. It's when he gets to the hymns that things get . . . interesting. His recordings of "Hark! The Herald Angels Sing" and a half-Latin "O Come, All Ye Faithful" are sung in a voice so ravaged, they could double as antismoking PSAs.

The hymnody here raises certain questions. Wasn't Dylan supposed to have converted back to Judaism? Maybe, but he has also continued to sing folk spirituals like "I Am the Man, Thomas" on tour; on the evidence of his last few albums, he's most likely just your garden-variety ecumenical Bible-as-literature liberal Christian-Jewish agnostic-mystic with a comically morbid streak. Anyway, perhaps we shouldn't look for spiritual clues in lyrics like Autry's "Let's give thanks to the Lord above/'Cause Santa Claus comes tonight," a conflation of sacred and spiritual magic that has warped kids' religious sensibilities for decades. In *Christmas in the Heart*, Dylan's being Bing again, not born-again.

A source in Dylan's camp has said this album was not a throwaway; it's a charity project (benefiting Feeding America, in the U.S.), and he wanted to actually bring in some dough.

You hear that in the arrangements, where he's done a terrific job of melding his live combo with the fifties easy-listening sound, even if the David Hidalgo–assisted "Must Be Santa" is the only time anyone rocks out. And he's clearly aware of the incongruity between the rawness of his instrument and the effectiveness of everyone else's. He milks it—not for kitschy juxtaposition but because the old-man's-prerogative, take-'em-or-leave-'em vocals and the eager-to-please slickness of the backing tracks aren't about ironic juxtaposition. Both represent honest impulses.

I get the betrayal some friends feel. With rock integrity ever waning, we want some bard to believe in, and moves like this are as if Yeats had indulged an inexplicable desire to write for *The Saturday Evening Post*. But what if the "integrity" old-school Dylan fans long for was just another phase—albeit a brilliant, culture-changing, and occasionally recurring one? As his "never-ending tour" of the past twenty years proves, Dylan really sees himself, first and foremost, as a roadhouse musician—one who happens to let collections of poetry slip through the cracks every few years.

The weirdest thing of all? The album feels . . . deeply felt. Dylan's vocals, for all their constant playfulness, have never betrayed much emotion. But to assume he's not feeling it makes an ass out of you and me. I recall an interview with Bill Flanagan in April in which Dylan claimed that when he visited cities, he liked to go stand in vacant lots. I thought, "Mmm-hmmm," and tried to picture Bob telling his driver to pull over by that batch of weeds. You know the upshot of this story: Dylan was picked up by Long Branch, New Jersey, police in July for being a suspicious person roaming the neighborhood. So should any of us doubt that he might actually have his tour bus stop alongside a meadow so that he can build a snowman and pretend it's Parson Brown? Stranger things have happened. Like, you know, that Victoria's Secret commercial.

Invent

Willman states that Dylan's musical career involves disappointing his fans for 44 years. From the beginning of the essay, Willman touches on the role fan expectations play in the perceived success or failure of an artist. In this album review, Willman takes Dylan to task for disregarding his fans, essentially doing what he wants rather than what they want. Via Internet radio, listen to this album and then imagine someone just starting in the music business released an album, like Dylan's Christmas album. Do you think it would lead to a successful career? Why or why not? What role do fans play in an artist's ability to adapt or experiment? Given current forms of social media, there is also an expectation by fans to be able to communicate with their favorite artists directly (via Facebook post, Twitter, etc.). How does that reality change the game?

Fans tend to identify with their favorite artists in some fashion (similar background, talents, experiences, world views, politics, etc.) Take a moment and think about the artists you like and jot down how many things you have in common with them. Write about a time you met an artist you admired. What was your first impression when you met him or her? How did (or didn't) he or she live up to your expectations?

In small groups, share your experience as it concerns your history of approving or disapproving of an artist or celebrity you admire. After everyone has shared, create a list of the top five reasons why fans might get upset with someone they admire. Share what you discover with the rest of the class.

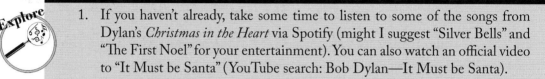

1. If you haven't already, take some time to listen to some of the songs from Dylan's *Christmas in the Heart* via Spotify (might I suggest "Silver Bells" and "The First Noel" for your entertainment). You can also watch an official video to "It Must be Santa" (YouTube search: Bob Dylan—It Must be Santa).

2. Using Google, explore the varied history of Dylan and controversy, especially as it concerns Dylan going electric. Listen to Dylan's "Maggie's Farm," released in 1965 and played live at the Newport Festival where he was booed for "going electric." Examine the lyrics, which have typically been viewed as a protest against folk protest. Explore the many bands who have covered the song via YouTube.

Walter Benjamin (1892-1940) was a Jewish literary critic, philosopher, social critic, and essayist. He is most often associated with the Frankfurt School, a highly influential group of scholars concerned with social theory. Benjamin's contributions to aesthetic theory and Western Marxism has long been celebrated, and "The Work of Art in the Age of Mechanical Reproduction" is arguably the most influential of Benjamin's essays.

excerpt from
THE WORK OF ART IN THE AGE OF MECHANICAL REPRODUCTION

BY WALTER BENJAMIN

I

In principle a work of art has always been reproducible. Man-made artifacts could always be imitated by men. Replicas were made by pupils in practice of their craft, by masters for diffusing their works, and, finally, by third parties in the pursuit of gain. Mechanical reproduction of a work of art, however, represents something new. Historically, it advanced intermittently and in leaps at long intervals, but with accelerated intensity. The Greeks knew only two procedures of technically reproducing works of art: founding and stamping. Bronzes, terra cottas, and coins were the only art works which they could produce in quantity. All others were unique and could not be mechanically reproduced. With the woodcut graphic art became mechanically reproducible for the first time, long before script became reproducible by print. The enormous changes which printing, the mechanical reproduction of writing, has brought about in literature are a familiar story. However, within the phenomenon which we are here examining from the perspective of world history, print is merely a special, though particularly important, case. During the Middle Ages engraving and etching were added to the woodcut; at the beginning of the nineteenth century lithography made its appearance. With lithography the technique of reproduction reached an essentially new stage. This much more direct process was distinguished by the tracing of the design on a stone rather than its incision on a block of wood or its etching on a copperplate and permitted graphic art for the first time to put its products on the market, not only in large numbers as hitherto, but also in daily changing forms. Lithography enabled graphic art to illustrate everyday life, and it began to keep pace with printing. But only a few decades after its invention, lithography was surpassed by photography. For the first time in the process of pictorial reproduction, photography freed the hand of the most important artistic functions which henceforth devolved only upon the eye looking into a lens. Since the eye perceives more swiftly than the hand can draw, the process of pictorial reproduction was accelerated so enormously that it could keep pace with speech. A film operator shooting a scene in the studio captures the images at the speed of an actor's speech. Just as lithography virtually implied the illustrated newspaper, so did photography foreshadow the sound film. The technical reproduction of sound was tackled at the end of the last century. These convergent endeavors made predictable a situation which Paul Valery pointed up in this sentence:

> "Just as water, gas, and electricity are brought into our houses from far off to satisfy our needs in response to a minimal effort, so we shall be supplied with visual or auditory images, which will appear and disappear at a simple movement of the hand, hardly more than a sign."

Around 1900 technical reproduction had reached a standard that not only permitted it to reproduce all transmitted works of art and thus to cause the most profound change in their impact upon the public; it also had captured a place of its own among the artistic processes. For the study of this standard nothing is more revealing than the nature of the repercussions that these two different manifestations—the reproduction of works of art and the art of the film—have had on art in its traditional form.

II

Even the most perfect reproduction of a work of art is lacking in one element: its presence in time and space, its unique existence at the place where it happens to be. This unique existence of the work of art determined the history to which it was subject throughout the time of its existence. This includes the changes which it may have suffered in physical condition over the years as well as the various changes in its ownership. The traces of the first can be revealed only by chemical or physical analyses which it is impossible to perform on a reproduction; changes of ownership are subject to a tradition which must be traced from the situation of the original.

The presence of the original is the prerequisite to the concept of authenticity. Chemical analyses of the patina of a bronze can help to establish this, as does the proof that a given manuscript of the Middle Ages stems from an archive of the fifteenth century. The whole sphere of authenticity is outside technical—and, of course, not only technical—reproducibility. Confronted with its manual reproduction, which was usually branded as a forgery, the original preserved all its authority; not so vis-à-vis technical reproduction. The reason is twofold. First, process reproduction is more independent of the original than manual reproduction. For example, in photography, process reproduction can bring out those aspects of the original that are unattainable to the naked eye yet accessible to the lens, which is adjustable and chooses its angle at will. And photographic reproduction, with the aid of certain processes, such as enlargement or slow motion, can capture images which escape natural vision. Secondly, technical reproduction can put the copy of the original into situations which would be out of reach for the original itself. Above all, it enables the original to meet the beholder halfway, be it in the form of a photograph or a phonograph record. The cathedral leaves its locale to be received in the studio of a lover of art; the choral production, performed in an auditorium or in the open air, resounds in the drawing room.

The situations into which the product of mechanical reproduction can be brought may not touch the actual work of art, yet the quality of its presence is always depreciated. This holds not only for the art work but also, for instance, for a landscape which passes in review before the spectator in a movie. In the case of the art object, a most sensitive nucleus— namely, its authenticity—is interfered with whereas no natural object is vulnerable on that score. The authenticity of a thing is the essence of all that is transmissible from its beginning, ranging from its substantive duration to its testimony to the history which it has experienced. Since the historical testimony rests on the authenticity, the former, too, is jeopardized by reproduction when substantive duration ceases to matter. And what is really jeopardized when the historical testimony is affected is the authority of the object.

One might subsume the eliminated element in the term "aura" and go on to say: that which withers in the age of mechanical reproduction is the aura of the work of art. This is a symptomatic process whose significance points beyond the realm of art. One might generalize by saying: the technique of reproduction detaches the reproduced object from the domain of tradition. By making many reproductions it substitutes a plurality of copies for a unique existence. And in permitting the reproduction to meet the beholder or listener in his own particular situation, it reactivates the object reproduced. These two processes lead to a tremendous shattering of tradition which is the obverse of the contemporary crisis and renewal of mankind. Both processes are intimately connected with the contemporary mass movements. Their most powerful agent is the film. Its social significance, particularly in its most positive form, is inconceivable without its destructive, cathartic aspect, that is, the liquidation of the traditional value of the cultural heritage. This phenomenon is most palpable in the great historical films. It extends to ever new positions. In 1927 Abel Gance exclaimed enthusiastically:

> "Shakespeare, Rembrandt, Beethoven will make films... all legends, all mythologies and all myths, all founders of religion, and the very religions... await their exposed resurrection, and the heroes crowd each other at the gate."

Presumably without intending it, he issued an invitation to a far-reaching liquidation.

III

During long periods of history, the mode of human sense perception changes with humanity's entire mode of existence. The manner in which human sense perception is organized, the medium in which it is accomplished, is determined not only by nature but by historical circumstances as well. The fifth century, with its great shifts of population, saw the birth of the late Roman art industry and the Vienna Genesis, and there developed not only an art different from that of antiquity but also a new kind of perception. The scholars of the Viennese school, Riegl and Wickhoff, who resisted the weight of classical tradition under which these later art forms had been buried, were the first to draw conclusions from them concerning the organization of perception at the time. However far-reaching their insight, these scholars limited themselves to showing the significant, formal hallmark which characterized perception in late Roman times. They did not attempt—and, perhaps, saw no way—to show the social transformations expressed by these changes of perception. The conditions for an analogous insight are more favorable in the present. And if changes in the medium of contemporary perception can be comprehended as decay of the aura, it is possible to show its social causes.

The concept of aura which was proposed above with reference to historical objects may usefully be illustrated with reference to the aura of natural ones. We define the aura of the latter as the unique phenomenon of a distance, however close it may be. If, while resting on a summer afternoon, you follow with your eyes a mountain range on the horizon or a branch which casts its shadow over you, you experience the aura of those mountains, of that branch. This image makes it easy to comprehend the social bases of the contemporary decay of the aura. It rests on two circumstances, both of which are related to the increasing significance of the masses in contemporary life. Namely, the desire of contemporary masses to bring things "closer" spatially and humanly, which is just as ardent as their bent toward overcoming the uniqueness of every reality by accepting its reproduction. Every day the urge grows stronger to get hold of an object at very close range by way of its likeness, its reproduction. Unmistakably, reproduction as offered by picture magazines and newsreels differs from the image seen by the unarmed eye. Uniqueness and permanence are as closely linked in the latter as are transitoriness and reproducibility in the former. To pry an object from its shell, to destroy its aura, is the mark of a perception whose "sense of the universal equality of things" has increased to such a degree that it extracts it even from a unique object by means of reproduction. Thus is manifested in the field of perception what in the theoretical sphere is noticeable in the increasing importance of statistics. The adjustment of reality to the masses and of the masses to reality is a process of unlimited scope, as much for thinking as for perception.

IV

The uniqueness of a work of art is inseparable from its being imbedded in the fabric of tradition. This tradition itself is thoroughly alive and extremely changeable. An ancient statue of Venus, for example, stood in a different traditional context with the Greeks, who made it an object of veneration, than with the clerics of the Middle Ages, who viewed it as an ominous idol. Both of them, however, were equally confronted with its uniqueness, that is, its aura. Originally the contextual integration of art in tradition found its expression in the cult. We know that the earliest art works originated in the service of a ritual—first the magical, then the religious kind. It is significant that the existence of the work of art with reference to its aura is never entirely separated from its ritual function. In other words, the unique value of the "authentic" work of art has its basis in ritual, the location of its original use value. This ritualistic basis, however remote, is still recognizable as secularized ritual even in the most profane forms of the cult of beauty. The secular cult of beauty, developed during the Renaissance and prevailing for three centuries, clearly showed that ritualistic basis in its decline and the first deep crisis which befell it. With the advent of the first truly revolutionary means of reproduction, photography, simultaneously with the rise of socialism, art sensed the approaching crisis which has become evident a century later. At the time, art reacted with the doctrine of *l'art pour l'art*, that is, with a theology of art. This gave rise to what might be called a negative theology in the form of the idea of "pure" art, which not only denied any social function of art but also any categorizing by subject matter. (In poetry, Mallarme was the first to take this position.)

An analysis of art in the age of mechanical reproduction must do justice to these relationships, for they lead us to an all-important insight: for the first time in world history, mechanical reproduction emancipates the work of art from its parasitical dependence on ritual. To an ever greater degree the work of art reproduced becomes the work of art designed for reproducibility. From a photographic negative, for example, one can make any number of prints; to ask for the "authentic" print makes no sense. But the instant the criterion of authenticity ceases to be applicable to artistic production, the total function of art is reversed. Instead of being based on ritual, it begins to be based on another practice—politics.

V

Works of art are received and valued on different planes. Two polar types stand out; with one, the accent is on the cult value; with the other, on the exhibition value of the work. Artistic production begins with ceremonial objects destined to serve in a cult. One may assume that what mattered was their existence, not their being on view. The elk portrayed by the man of the Stone Age on the walls of his cave was an instrument of magic. He did expose it to his fellow men, but in the main it was meant for the spirits. Today the cult value would seem to demand that the work of art remain hidden. Certain statues of gods are accessible only to the priest in the cella; certain Madonnas remain covered nearly all year round; certain sculptures on medieval cathedrals are invisible to the spectator on ground level. With the emancipation of the various art practices from ritual go increasing opportunities for the exhibition of their products. It is easier to exhibit a portrait bust that can be sent here and there than to exhibit the statue of a divinity that has its fixed place in the interior of a temple. The same holds for the painting as against the mosaic or fresco that preceded it. And even though the public presentability of a mass originally may have been just as great as that of a symphony, the latter originated at the moment when its public presentability promised to surpass that of the mass.

With the different methods of technical reproduction of a work of art, its fitness for exhibition increased to such an extent that the quantitative shift between its two poles turned into a qualitative transformation of its nature. This is comparable to the situation of the work of art in prehistoric times when, by the absolute emphasis on its cult value, it was, first and foremost, an instrument of magic. Only later did it come to be recognized as a work of art. In the same way today, by the absolute emphasis on its exhibition value the work of art becomes a creation with entirely new functions, among which the one we are conscious of, the artistic function, later may be recognized as incidental. This much is certain: today photography and the film are the most serviceable exemplifications of this new function.

Invent

Written in 1936, Benjamin's essay concerns mechanical reproduction, a process that was expanding rapidly at the turn of the century. Certain works of art (specifically photography and film) could now be reproduced fairly easily via various mechanical techniques. Now, more than 70 years later, much of our art is reproduced even more quickly and easily—not mechanically but digitally. In fact, much of our art now exists as zeroes and ones on the Internet. How might replacing "mechanical" with "digital" reproduction in this essay affect our understanding of Benjamin's insight on how our perception of art changes with new technology?

Compose

Take a moment and write down your ideas on the value of originality and authenticity in regards to works of art (music, painting, sculpture, etc.) Write about your history with art of any kind and the reasons you think you value the kind of art you enjoy.

Collaborate

In small groups, discuss the key concepts from Benjamin's essay: "Reproduction, Authenticity, Aura, and Originality". Make sure you come to terms with his definitions of these concepts and how they operate in affecting our views of art. Now, as a group, discuss how these ideas apply to the digital age of music. Discuss each of these concepts in regards to digital music, digital videos, the sale of digital music products and the devices on which we play them, and any other aspects that you think apply.

Explore

Many people think digital technology is very recent, but it has a longer history than most realize. Explore the history of digital technology, how it was invented, and how it was first utilized. Investigate the art forms with which it was first associated, look at the key people who aided in its development, and study the watershed moments in its progress.

MAJOR ASSIGNMENTS

MAJOR ASSIGNMENT #1
RHETORICAL ANALYSIS OF A MUSICAL ARGUMENT

BACKGROUND

In the simplest terms, rhetoric can be described as the art of persuasion. Aristotle defined rhetoric as "the faculty of observing in any given case the available means of persuasion." He divided those "available means" into three areas: ethos, pathos, and logos. In making an argument, a person might attempt to convince her audience that she is right by appealing to her own credibility or to her trustworthiness (ethos), or perhaps by making an appeal to her audience's emotions in some fashion (pathos). She also could attempt to convince them through sound reasoning and rational thinking (logos). Of course, often speakers and writers use a variety of these appeals, moving from one to another at different moments. Understanding how and why these appeals work aids in our understanding of how to make our own arguments more effective.

There is no shortage in opinions when it comes to music and therefore no shortage of arguments surrounding any given topic in music. People's views on music are often fueled by emotion first and foremost, but that is not always the case, as you've seen in some of the essays from this book. It makes sense, then, to reflect on how various arguments on the topic of music work rhetorically, especially those that get a lot of traction in the public sphere.

ASSIGNMENT

For this assignment, you will choose a text that presents an argument on a specific topic pertaining to music and the digital age ("text" here does not just mean a written work—it can be written, audio, or video). You will then write an essay in which you identify the major rhetorical strategies at work within it, assessing their effectiveness. The key to this assignment is to ask and answer the following questions: 1) What is the argument of the text? 2) What rhetorical appeals does the argument rely most upon and why? 3) Given the context of the text, how effective is the author of the argument in his or her use of rhetoric? Your answers will need to come from within the text (no research is required), so make sure you can defend your answers.

LEARNING GOALS

The goal here is for you to produce an argument about an argument (not about a topic). Be careful not to fall into the trap of simply describing the rhetorical moves, or the other trap of merely using the text as a springboard to "preach" on the topic. Keep your thesis in the front of your mind as you write.

CHOOSING A TEXT

There are a large number of articles, videos, and recordings in which someone makes an argument about some aspect of the digital age of music, and such texts provide ample material for rhetorical analysis. You might choose an article in a music magazine (*Rolling Stone*, *Vibe*, *Classic Rock*, *Billboard*, *The Source*, etc.) where the writer makes an argument concerning a particular musician, genre, or musical phenomenon associated with the digital age. You might also choose to evaluate a speech given by a musician (Dave Grohl's rant at the 2012 Grammys, for example), or a blog by a music critic. The text need not be very long, but be careful to choose a text that offers ample material to evaluate. You may also choose to use just a portion of a text, but be careful not to pull it out of context. You want to be able to appropriately manage your selection, so don't bite off more than you can chew here. Also, feel free to choose a text from *(E)Tunes*, even one you may have worked with in class; just be sure to take your analysis in a different direction or significantly extend the work produced in class (i.e., do not simply repeat what has been covered in class).

ROLE OF EVIDENCE

Your analysis here must include an evidence-driven thesis. As such, you will want to include a good amount of detail from the text you choose, while also providing significant analysis of that text.

ROLE OF CONTEXT

It would be hard to evaluate a rhetorical situation without including some details regarding the context of your text (the author, the audience, the occasion for its delivery). To that end, you can include some of this information in your essay, but don't let it become the focus. You should not have to do much research for this information.

MAJOR ASSIGNMENT #2
ALBUM REVIEW

BACKGROUND

In the past, album reviews served to advise music lovers on whether or not they should purchase an album, and readers often depended strongly on reviews in making their purchases. Much has changed in music, and the Internet has provided a variety of ways to listen to music before we buy it. Still, these short evaluative essays remain quite popular, and listeners still rely upon the advice of the music experts to guide their purchases and downloads. Although it looks simple, writing an album review is not easy, as it requires its author to pay careful attention to audience, tone, and purpose.

ASSIGNMENT

Using the classroom models as guides, you will write a professional review of a current album of your choosing. Your goal is to make a credible (i.e., defendable) case for your perspective on the album, providing concrete evidence for your claims throughout. You will also want to make it entertaining and easy to understand. It will help to have a specific magazine, webzine, blog, etc. as a potential target for the submission of your review. In fact, why not plan on submitting the review once you're done?

CHOOSING AN ALBUM

There are, of course, many possible albums from which to choose. Your primary goal is to demonstrate that your album is worthy, not worthy, or partially worthy of being purchased by your readers. No outside sources need to be used, and you should in no way look at other reviews of the same album, as that can lead to problems associated with making your own, independent case. In the end, you need only be familiar enough with the album to construct and support your own claims.

SOME ASPECTS TO KEEP IN MIND

- Your primary purpose is to *evaluate* the album, and you should share your *personal* response to the album.

- Not everyone shares the same *criteria* for judgment, and not everyone applies the criteria in the same way. For example, reviewers might agree that the vocal effects are important in hip-hop, but not all agree that T-Pain's use of them on *Revolve* (2011) is convincing or revolutionary in any way (especially compared to his previous three albums).

- Be fair: although your primary purpose is to share your opinion, the underlying purpose is to help the reader make a good decision about whether or not she/he should "consume" the album.

THE MAJOR MOVES OF THE ASSIGNMENT

- Take a stand about the album (good, bad, or a bit of both).

- Identify your criteria for evaluating the album.

- Using your established criteria, defend your stand by showing examples from the album being reviewed.

- You should include an attention-getting introduction.

- Your essay should include a summary of the album for those not familiar with it (no longer than one paragraph).

- You should assume that your audience is skeptical (i.e., they have some degree of initial resistance to your evaluation).

- You should anticipate what in your argument your audience might object to, and you should address these objections in your essay as well.

MAJOR ASSIGNMENT #3
MUSIC BLOG

BACKGROUND

Music blogs are common these days, and their topics range from serious music criticism to fan-obsessed updates. Some offer weekly updates on concerts and album releases in a specific genre, while some track the happenings of one specific artist. Regardless of their focus, music blogs must work hard to earn and keep their audiences. Pictures, videos, and music samples are common on the best of this genre.

On one hand, the ubiquitous nature of music blogs is exciting, but the sheer volume of potential information on any one topic can be overwhelming. And, since anyone can create a blog for free, there is plenty of bad writing to go around. As indicated above, these realities force authors of blogs to work particularly hard to get their voices heard. Thus, the creation of a blog provides a wonderful opportunity to grow as a writer.

ASSIGNMENT

For this assignment, you will create your own music blog. Blogs are easy and free to create. I would suggest using Tumblr or Google Blogger. This task requires you to take a number of steps in a particular order. Each requires you to make various moves common among good writers and good thinkers, regardless of their field of study. Take time to examine each step below carefully, and allow enough time in the process to approach each with the appropriate level of seriousness.

THE STEPS

1. **Research:** Your first task is to take a look at blogs, familiarizing yourself with the good, the bad, and the ugly in the blogosphere. I would encourage you to limit your exploration to a specific type of blog. For example, first focus on blogs related either to CD reviews or live concert reviews. Next, in the case of music reviews, choose a specific genre (i.e., hip-hop, country, etc.) or, if your interest is in live concerts, a music scene specific to a region (i.e, Chicago, Nashville, L.A., etc.). To do that, use Google. For instance, try Googling "hip-hop blogs" or "Chicago music blogs." Keep in mind that you can also focus on a specific artist too (i.e., "Adam Levine blog"), but that can often lead to fewer examples.

2. **Find a Model:** From the examples you discover, choose one that you believe to be credible and fairly active.

3. **Rhetorical Analysis:** Perform a rhetorical analysis of the blog you have chosen (see Assignment #1 for directions on this process).

4. **Sign up:** Set up your blog using Tumblr or Google Blogger. It's free and quite simple.

5. **Create a Blog.** Really. It's not as hard as it sounds. Templates will guide you through the process, and your model will help with your content choices.

6. **Launch It:** Launch your blog and see what happens next. Don't forget to invite your friends and family to read it.

7. **Reflect:** Write a reflection on the process of creating a blog, from conception to execution. What did you learn about the writing through this process? What did you learn about multi-media and its relationship to persuasion?

8. **Enjoy:** Work to keep your blog up even as your class ends. See how you can change and adapt to keep your existing readers interested while attracting new ones.

MAJOR ASSIGNMENT #4
MUSIC EXPERT ESSAY

BACKGROUND

If you turn on any news station (and there are many from which to choose), you are liable to find a number of "experts" providing their views on a variety of topics, from politics to pop culture. You may also notice that the label of "expert" is a bit haphazardly thrown around. Becoming a true expert is no easy task. It requires an investment of time and research. In academics, calling yourself an expert on any given topic requires that you become familiar with the history, controversies, key figures, key moments, and current scholarship. Familiarity with current scholarship helps as you work to find your own voice on your topic; once you're familiar with a conversation, you are better able to contribute your own ideas to it.

ANALYSIS OF AN EXPERT

This book is filled with writings from experts in music. Some are more academic than others, but all consider themselves to be experts in one fashion or another. To get you primed for this assignment, pick a couple of the essays and read them carefully. Mark up the essays where you see signs of the authors' expertise, noting the specific quality that convinces you to trust the author as an expert. If you find areas where you become more skeptical, note the reasons why. Keep in mind, some essays are written for more academic audiences and others for a wider public audience. As such, the degree to which they reveal their sources or demonstrate their depth of research may vary.

DESCRIPTION

This assignment is designed to help you familiarize yourself with the current public and scholarly conversation surrounding a music topic of your choice. Over the course of this assignment, you will be doing a fair amount of research in order to educate yourself on your topic, after which you will make a selection from those sources for the purpose of framing the conversation for your readers or live audience. You will analyze at least six sources that embody the various critical debates surrounding your specific topic with the goal of placing them in dialogue with one another. Finally, you will explain how these sources relate not only to each other but to your future research as well.

LEARNING GOALS

This assignment requires you to make four intellectual moves, all of which will prove valuable for your development as a writer and researcher. 1) You must research your specific topic, becoming familiar with the current and past conversations on it. 2) You must make appropriate choices regarding your sources. What makes one source better than another? What are the best sources on your topic and why? 3) You need to put your sources into a type of "conversation" with each other. In other words, you do not want to simply produce a list of article summaries. 4) You must make choices as to how to organize the information in this essay so that your reader can easily follow.

CHOOSING YOUR TEXT

Your choice of sources should be based upon the credibility of an author and his or her contribution to the topic you have chosen. To make that kind of decision, you must research a wide variety of sources on your particular topic. Only then can you select the best sources with any kind of confidence. With music, those sources may come from popular as well as academic sources. In many cases, your sources may be writing for a webpage or blog. The key here is that you are able to demonstrate that any given source you choose is credible. You need to be able to point to very specific reasons why each source can be trusted.

ORGANIZING YOUR PAPER

1) Begin your essay with an extended introduction where you establish the context and demonstrate the merit of the conversation on the topic. You might also point to a trend in the research on the topic. In short, you want to show that you are knowledgeable on the topic. 2) The body of the paper will contain summaries, paraphrasing, and quotations from your sources, framed in the context that you established in your introduction (i.e., don't *merely* summarize). 3) In your conclusion, pull the sources together, synthesizing them into a meaningful conclusion that gestures to the value of having explored this topic.

MAJOR ASSIGNMENT #5
MUSIC RESEARCH ESSAY PROPOSAL

DESCRIPTION

A proposal is not an abstract (a summary of a completed essay) or an introduction to an essay, but rather an attempt to describe what is planned before it has actually been done. It is not a huge document, but it is an important one. It should be roughly 500–750 words.

LEARNING GOALS

The proposal should provide a preliminary description of the proposed research essay. It should delineate what topic and area the presentation will explore, discuss why this topic and area merit such exploration, and include a provisional essay outline. The outline, which can be narrative in form, should be as precise as possible, even if it is likely to be modified in the course of composing the essay.

KEY COMPONENTS

These three elements should be clearly presented in the proposal.

1. What is the central problem that your presentation will address? This problem can be theoretical, critical, or historical, but it should, in most cases, be presented as a question or related set of questions to which the paper will attempt to find answers. It is important that the problem and hypothetical answers be stated from the outset so that your research will not risk becoming random or your exposition lapse into mere description. The sense that an argument is being made should be constantly kept in mind.

2. To persuade your reader that you are not just reinventing the wheel or restating what has already been said, you should include a brief review of the present "conversation" with respect to your topic. Has this topic been treated before? How does your approach differ from earlier ones? Has new evidence appeared (for example, a new primary source) since previous treatments?

3. Outlining a sequence of potential major points will help you clarify the argument of your thesis and check the balance of its parts in relation to one another. You will find that developing an outline helps your thinking to move forward substantially so that the actual composition of the presentation is more clearly focused.

MAJOR ASSIGNMENT #6
MUSIC RESEARCH ESSAY

BACKGROUND

Research-based essays provide an academic mechanism through which students explore their topics and interests and find a way to present their own ideas on those same topics. Proper research takes time and requires students to use various strategies of searching for information and deciding which information is valuable. It also involves narrowing your topic down and making it manageable for the required length of your essay. When choosing a topic, feel free to do some exploratory writing, brainstorming, and conversing with friends about your interest and the direction your research might take.

Also, notice the essays from this book that meet this academic criteria and can provide helpful models. For example, the essays written by Alex Kasner, Daniel Levitin, Greg Kot, Matthew Thibeault, and Rossen Ventizislavov provide just a few good examples of research-based essays on music. As you can see, these kinds of essays aren't always written for a specific academic audience, but they all still fulfill the requirements of this kind of assignment in some way.

CHOOSING A TOPIC

You need to choose a specific contemporary music phenomenon related to the digital age and outline a manageable research question and investigative plan on this topic. For example, you might choose to research the effects of digital recording on a specific musical genre, or you might look at the way technology has changed how we create, consume, and disseminate music in our culture. You might also investigate the way a genre has been changed in modern times (hip-hop, country, dubstep, etc.). Other topics might include: the digital recording process, music marketing, music consumption, music and social media, creativity and composition, authenticity and the artists, music videos (post MTV), music in TV, movies, and video games, digital music copyright laws, modern instrument design.

DESCRIPTION

For this assignment, you will draft an essay using a variety of scholarly sources and carefully chosen rhetorical strategies to make a compelling argument built upon research. You might choose to build upon the research you presented in your expert essay. In the end, your research direction should be fueled by a specific research question concerning the topic of music and the digital age.

LEARNING GOALS

The goal here is to produce an argument-driven research essay that integrates a variety of complex sources to develop a compelling argument about a topic of significance. Primary and secondary support may include essays, books, live performances, videos, music, scholarly articles, scientific data, government documents, images, interviews, and anecdotes.

ORGANIZING YOUR PAPER

Different kinds of materials suggest different kinds of claims, so there are a number of ways to organize your argument effectively. The strategies that work best depend on the kind of argument you are making. In general, however, your thesis should be clear and upfront, followed by a logical progression of your argument and meaningful conclusion that does more than restate the thesis. Be sure to address the "So What?" factor. In other words, why does it matter?

MAJOR ASSIGNMENT #7
MUSIC RESEARCH PRESENTATION
(MULTI-MEDIA OPTION)

BACKGROUND

This assignment is very similar in content to that of the music research essay (Assignment #5). The main difference here is in how you are being asked to present your argument. Whereas a written essay affords you just one way of communicating your ideas, a multi-media option allows you to present your argument in a written, oral, and visual fashion. For this assignment, you might choose to take your research essay and translate it into a multi-media presentation, or you might choose to focus only on the multi-media option as your research project. Such a task inevitably affects the content of our arguments as we are forced to focus on the differences between a written presentation and an oral/visual one, adapting our style, tone, and content to the different advantages and limitations of each. This assignment encourages you to introduce both audio and visual components into your presentation, which is quite appropriate when making an argument about music.

CHOOSING A TOPIC

You need to choose a specific contemporary music phenomenon related to the digital age and outline a manageable research question and investigative plan on this topic. For example, you might choose to research the effects of digital recording on a specific musical genre, or you might look at the way technology has changed the way we create, consume, and disseminate music in our culture. You might also investigate the way a genre has been changed in modern times (hip-hop, country, dubstep, etc.). Other topics might include; the digital recording process, music marketing, music consumption, music and social media, creativity and composition, authenticity and the artists, music videos—post MTV, music in TV, movies, and video games, digital music copyright laws, modern instrument design. Once you have your topic narrowed down, begin thinking of interesting way to incorporate audio or vision components into your argument presentation.

DESCRIPTION

Using a variety of sources, both academic and popular press, you will create and compose an argument on a topic related to music in the modern era. With careful attention to your rhetorical strategies, you will utilize a presentation software (Keynote, Prezi, or PowerPoint) to deliver your argument in a 10-minute conference-style setting. This argument will build upon your earlier work in the class and should develop from a research question informed by your inquiries into various aspects of the class topic.

LEARNING GOALS

As with a written essay, an argument-driven research essay's goal is to integrate a variety of complex sources to develop a compelling argument about a topic of significance. Primary and secondary support may include essays, books, live performances, music, scholarly articles, scientific data, government documents, images, interviews, and anecdotes.

The presentation should restrict itself to making a small, well-defended claim that, if true, has significant implications. Your time is limited, so make sure you can show a depth of research in a short amount of time.

ORGANIZING YOUR ARGUMENT AND PRESENTATION

As with the written essay, there are a number of ways to organize your presentation effectively. The strategies that work best depend on the kind of argument you are making and the kinds of sound, images, and videos you are using. Ask yourself what framing strategies would help your audience follow your particular argument. You will also need to think critically about your slide design. PowerPoint can be a very helpful software, but it can also work to distract or even bore your audience. It is a tool and must be used properly. There are many helpful tips on using presentation software effectively that can be found on the Internet. For a humorous one, check out Don McMillan's "Life After Death by Powerpoint" on YouTube (YouTube search: Life After Death by Powerpoint and Don McMillan).

FILMOGRAPHY

DOCUMENTARIES

24 Hour Party People (2002)
American Hardcore (2006)
Anvil! The Story of Anvil (2008)
Buena Vista Social Club (1999)
The Devil and Daniel Johnston (2005)
Don't Look Back (1967)
Downloaded (2013)
Gimme Shelter (1970)
I Am Trying to Break Your Heart: A Film About Wilco (2002)
The Last Waltz (1978)
Radiohead: Meeting People Is Easy (1998)
Searching for Sugar Man (2012)
Shut Up and Play the Hits (2012)
Standing in the Shadows of Motown (2002)
Stop Making Sense (1984)
This is It! (2009)
This Is Spinal Tap (1984)
Tom Dowd and the Language of Music (2003)
Who is Harry Nilsson (And Why Is Everybody Talkin' About Him)? (2010)
Woodstock (1970)

FEATURE FILMS

8 Mile (2002)
Almost Famous (2000)
Cadillac Records (2008)
Coal Miner's Daughter (1980)
Crazy Heart (2009)
The Doors (1991)
High Fidelity (2000)
A Hard Day's Night (1964)
Hair (1979)
Hedwig and the Angry Inch (2001)

Help! (1965)
Hustle & Flow (2005)
Inside Llewyn Davis (2013)
La Bamba (1987)
Last Days (2005)
I'm Not There (2007)
A Mighty Wind (2003)
Mutual Appreciation (2005)
O Brother, Where Art Thou? (2000)
Performance (1970)
Pink Floyd: The Wall (1982)
Ray (2004)
'Round Midnight (1986)
Saturday Night Fever (1977)
Sid and Nancy (1986)
That Thing You Do! (1996)
Tommy (1975)
Wattstax (1973)
Walk the Line (2005)
Yellow Submarine (1968)

TV SHOWS

American Bandstand
America's Got Talent
American Idol
Austin City Limits
Glee
Flight of the Conchords
The Monkees
MTV Unplugged
Nashville
Once
Soul Train
The Partridge Family
That Metal Show
The Voice
The X Factor

VIDEO GAMES

Battle of the Bands
DJ Hero
Guitar Hero
Rock Band

WORKS CITED

Adams, Jacob. "A Field Guide to the Indie Marketplace." *(E)Tunes*. Ed. Rod C. Taylor. Southlake: Fountainhead Press, 2014. Print.

Auden, W.H. "Musee Des Beaux Arts." *Another Time*. London: Faber and Faber, 1940. Print.

Benjamin, Walter. "The Work of Art in the Age of Mechanical Reproduction." *Illuminations*. Ed. Hannah Arendt. New York: Schocken Books, 1986. Print.

Bruegel, Pieter. *Landscape with the Fall of Icarus*. 1558. Oil on canvas. Musees royaux des Beaux-Arts de Belgique, Brussels.

Buff, Luiz Augusto. "Mash-Ups & Fair Use: Girl Talk." *Music Business Journal* 6.3 (2010): 4–5. Print.

Christgau, Robert. "Paisley's Progress." *Barnes and Nobles Review*. 18 Nov. 2009. Web.

Cosner, Anthony Wing. "Gotye's YouTube Orchestra Remix: The Sweetness of the Open Source Pop Star." *Forbes* 26 Aug. 2012. Web.

Davidson, Justin. "Beethoven's Kapow." *New York Magazine* 21 Mar. 2010. Web.

Detor, Krista. *Icarus*. Tightrope Records, 2008. CD.

Ewing, Tom. "Shiny Shiny: A Future History of the CD Revival." *Pitchfork* 5 Mar. 2010. Web.

Flippo, Chet. "Nashville Skyline: Searching for the Heart of Country." *CMT* 4 Nov. 2010. Web.

Frucci, Adam. "Record Labels: Change or Die." *Gizmodo* 11 Mar. 2010. Web.

Grigoriadis, Vanessa. "Growing Up Gaga." *New York Magazine* 28 Mar. 2010. Web.

Harvey, Eric. "Paper Trail: Mp3: The Meaning of Format." *Pitchfork* 9 Aug. 2009. Web.

Kasner, Alex. "Aspiring to Art: The Concept Album, Artistry in Music, and Audience Artist Interplay." *Etunes*. Ed. Rod C. Taylor. Dallas: Fountainhead Press, 2014. Print.

Kot, Greg. "Steve Jobs and the iPod 'Burglary Kit.'" *Ripped: How the Wired Generation Revolutionized Music*. New York: Scribner, 2010. Print.

Lawson, Steve. "Music Is Worthless." *Steve's Blog: Solo Bass & Beyond* 15 Oct. 2010. Web.

Levitin, Daniel J. "My Favorite Things: Why Do We Like the Music We Like." *This Is Your Brain on Music: The Science of a Human Obsession*. New York: Dutton, 2006. Print.

Lowder, J. Bryan. "Does Pop Music Sound Louder, Dumber, and More the Same? One Study Says So." *Slate* 27 July 2012. Web.

Marcus, Gary. "Learning to Crawl." *Guitar Zero: The Science of Becoming Musical at Any Age*. New York: Penguin, 2012.

Petchers, Brian. "The Branding Power of Today's Music Video." *Forbes* 25 Sept. 2012. Web.

Radiohead. *Hail to the Thief.* Parlophone, 2003. CD.

Roberts, James. "St. James." *How the Fender Bass Changed the World.* Backbeat Books, 2001. 68–77. Print.

Sisario, Ben. "The New Rise of a Summer Hit: Tweet It Maybe." *New York Times* 21 Aug. 2012. Web.

Taylor, Rod C. Taylor. "Winners and Losers in Digital Recording." *Etunes.* Ed. Rod C. Taylor. Southlake: Fountainhead Press, 2014. Print.

Thibeault, Matthew D. "Hip-Hop, Digital Media, and the Changing Face of Music Education." *General Music Today* 24 (2010): 46–49. Print.

Valéry, Paul. "The Conquest of Ubiquity." *The Collected Works of Paul Valéry.* Ed. Jackson Mathews. [. T. X, Xii-Xiii.]. New York: Patheon Books, 1956. Print.

Ventzislavov, Robert. "The Time Is Now: Acceptance and Conquest in Pop Music." *Journal of Popular Music Studies* 24 (2012): 57–70. Print.

Walker, Jesse. "2010: The Year John Cage Broke—Amateur Producers and Unexpected Music." 30 Dec. 2010. Web.

Williams, William Carlos. "Landscape With The Fall of Icarus." *Collected Poems: 1939–1962, Volume II.* New York: New Directions Publishing Corp., 1962. Print.

Willman, Chris. "A Very Dylan Christmas." *New York Magazine* 29 Nov. 2009. Web.

Wooten, Victor L. "Groove." *The Music Lesson: A Spiritual Search for Growth Through Music.* New York: Berkley Books, 2006. Print.

XTC. *Go 2.* Virgin, 1978. LP.